Camp Chase and the Evolution of Union Prison Policy

Camp Chase and the Evolution of Union Prison Policy

ROGER PICKENPAUGH

THE UNIVERSITY OF ALABAMA PRESS
Tuscaloosa

Copyright © 2007
The University of Alabama Press
Tuscaloosa, Alabama 35487–0380
All rights reserved
Manufactured in the United States of America

Typeface: ACaslon

∞

The paper on which this book is printed meets the minimum requirements of American
National Standard for Information Sciences-Permanence of Paper for Printed Library
Materials, ANSI Z39.48-1984.

Library of Congress Cataloging-in-Publication Data

Pickenpaugh, Roger.
    Camp Chase and the evolution of Union prison policy / Roger Pickenpaugh.
        p.   cm.
    Includes bibliographical references and index.
    ISBN-13: 978-0-8173-1582-5 (cloth : alk. paper)
    ISBN-10: 0-8173-1582-9 (alk. paper)
    1. Camp Chase (Ohio)—History. 2. Camp Chase (Ohio)—Administration—History.
3. Ohio—History—Civil War, 1861–1865—Prisoners and prisons. 4. United States—
History—Civil War, 1861–1865—Prisoners and prisons. 5. Prisoners of war—Ohio—
History—19th century. I. Title.
    E616.C4P53 2007
    973.7′72—dc22

                                                                2007007449

For Marion

Contents

Illustrations

Acknowledgments

It may be a tired cliché, but it is also an accurate one: nobody produces a book like this by himself, and in writing this one I have incurred numerous debts. Among those to whom I owe thanks are the staff members at the institutions where research for this work was conducted. They were uniformly polite, professional, and most of all, patient.

Among those who were particularly helpful are Stuart Butler (now retired from the National Archives); Jeff Flannery (Library of Congress); David Simmons (Ohio Historical Society); Nan Card (Rutherford B. Hayes Presidential Center); Gregory Stoner (Virginia Historical Society); Rebecca Rice and Jim Holmberg (Filson Historical Society); Naomi Nelson (Emory University); Carlos Torres (Western Reserve Historical Society); Janie Morris (Duke University); Merilyn Hughes (Tennessee State Library and Archives); and Ed Frank (University of Memphis). At other institutions I dealt with individuals too numerous to list, but to them also I offer gratitude.

The memory of Camp Chase remains strong in the Columbus area thanks to a number of local historians. Two of them, Lois Neff and Paul Clay, provided valuable assistance and encouragement. Another Columbus resident, Dr. Rick Nelson of the Ohio State University Hospitals, answered medical questions I encountered.

Mary Lou Podlasiak, Gary S. Williams, and Ken Williams, all of the Noble County, Ohio Authors' Guild, each read the entire manuscript. All made significant contributions to the final product. Equally important, all understood what I was going through, having been there themselves.

I am very fortunate to work in the Noble County School District, and I am particularly blessed to work at Shenandoah Elementary School. Every day at work I remember how thankful I am to have landed in the elementary building, where I am surrounded by professional and supportive colleagues. Deserving special mention is English teacher David Arbenz. Dave has proofread virtually everything I have ever submitted for publication, and his assistance with this project was especially helpful. Although now retired from teaching, he remains an active, albeit unpaid, freelance proofreader. My thanks also go to principals Mike Romick and Sandy Goff for their tremendous support.

Finally, I am grateful to my family. My sister and brother-in-law, Jill and Gene Stuckey, always offer moral support. On a more practical level, their residence in the heart of the Confederacy was an appreciated base of operations. Similarly, work in the Washington, DC area was made more enjoyable by the opportunity to visit stepdaughters Anya Crum and Jocelyn Brooks and son-in-law Patrick Brooks. I must confess, however, that the birth of Parker Diane Brooks has made it a lot tougher to leave for a day's work at the National Archives.

My mother, Fern Pickenpaugh, also served as a keen proofreader and eager supporter. Having a mother with a darkroom is also a tremendous asset for any writer who includes photos in his work.

And then there is Marion. She was with me on virtually every research trip. My wife likens research to a treasure hunt, and she dives in with tireless enthusiasm. Her patience and persistence have led her to many sources I would have missed. Beyond that, she is a proofreader, an indexer, and a patient listener as I spout out incoherent ideas about every book. Above all else, she is my friend.

Camp Chase and the Evolution
of Union Prison Policy

Introduction

In 1861, with the guns of Fort Sumter still resounding in their imaginations, most citizens in what remained of the United States had one thought—"On to Richmond!" Initially not wanting to believe that the war would come, most now chose to believe that it would be a quick, easy, and relatively bloodless affair. Even President Abraham Lincoln, who would soon become a grim military realist, seemed caught up in this idealistic vision. In his first call for volunteers, he asked that the eager recruits sign up for only a three-month term of service.

Among the few realists was Gen. Montgomery Meigs. As quartermaster general of the Union army, it was his job to address the mundane details and logistical challenges necessary to keep the Northern war machine functioning smoothly. On July 12 Meigs turned his attention to the question of military prisoners. Writing to Secretary of War Simon Cameron, he predicted that in "the conflict now commenced it is likely to be expected that the United States will have to take care of large numbers of prisoners of war. . . . Arrangements should be at once made for their accomodation."[1]

On October 3 the arrangements Meigs called for began to fall into place. The quartermaster general named Lt. Col. William Hoffman, an 1829 West Point graduate and career officer, to the post of commissary general of prisoners. Four days later Meigs dispatched Hoffman to Lake Erie with orders to locate an island that would be a suitable site for a Union prison. The commissary general recommended Johnson's Island, near the city of Sandusky, Ohio. For the next five months Hoffman oversaw the construction of the depot to the exclusion of virtually all other duties. The few prisoners that the Union took during 1861 ended up in Atlantic coastal fortifications. Commanders of those facilities were largely on their own in fashioning regulations concerning their captives.

On February 26, 1862 Hoffman proudly informed Meigs that his Lake Erie depot would soon be ready to house six hundred prisoners. He apparently did not realize that events in Tennessee had already rendered Johnson's Island woefully inadequate. On February 16 Gen. Ulysses S. Grant had captured Fort Donelson. His famous demand for unconditional surrender left Grant with fifteen thousand prisoners. "It is a much less job to take them than to keep them," Grant informed his superiors, and they soon learned that the Union's emerging hero was correct.[2] Unprepared for this deluge of Confederate captives, Henry Halleck, Grant's commanding general, scrambled to find places to put them. Some ended up in an abandoned medical school in St. Louis. Others were placed in a former state prison in Alton, Illinois. Most made their way to a variety of military camps in Illinois, Indiana, and Ohio. These facilities had served as training camps, and many still housed recruits when the Fort Donelson prisoners arrived.

For most of these early captives, their stay in a Union prison would not be lengthy. From the start of the war informal prisoner exchanges had gone on between commanders on either side. Even Grant, who would soon become a determined foe of the practice, had agreed to limited exchanges in 1861. As the war grew in scope and intensity in 1862, and thousands of Union soldiers fell into the hands of the Confederates, citizens began to demand that their government negotiate an agreement to exchange prisoners. Their elected representatives soon joined the clamor. Both Lincoln and Edwin Stanton, who had succeeded Cameron as secretary of war, opposed any formal agreement, fearing that it would imply a recognition of the Confederacy. The pressure was great, however, and the two men finally relented. On July 22, 1862 Gen. John Dix, representing the Union, and Confederate general Daniel Harvey Hill signed an exchange cartel. Based on a similar agreement reached by the Americans and the British during the War of 1812, the cartel established a sliding scale of prisoner value determined by rank.

Thanks to the cartel, thousands of captives on each side returned home. A large percentage likely owed their lives to the agreement. Despite this, the cartel was doomed to failure. The reasons were part practical and part moral. Under the terms of the cartel, captured soldiers were generally paroled and sent home to wait until they were formally exchanged for equivalent forces from the other side. Only then could they return to the field. Union soldiers quickly realized that capture would result in an immediate furlough. At the same time, Northern leaders realized that their superior population meant the Union could more easily afford to have both sides retain prisoners rather than exchange them. This gave them a reason to hope—and work—for the collapse of the cartel. The South provided the means when it refused to recognize and exchange black soldiers. Charges of cheating on both sides also entered into the mix, as did 1863 Union victories, which gave the North an advantage in the number of prisoners held. No conclusive evidence proves the motivation of Northern leaders, but by the late summer of 1863, exchange was a dead letter.

While the cartel remained in effect, the populations of most Northern prisons dwindled to a few hundred. A few, however, became home to unruly Union soldiers who had been captured and paroled. Stanton, upset by the propensity of some soldiers to surrender on purpose, demanded that parolees not be allowed to return home. Instead they were confined at various parole camps, where they encountered conditions no better than those endured by the departing Confederates. Some protested quietly, some snuck home, and some rioted, burning buildings and otherwise destroying camp property. The spectacle provided another reason for Union authorities to welcome the collapse of the cartel.

The end of prisoner exchanges opened a new and much harsher chapter in the story of Civil War prisons. For one thing, despite frequent camp rumors of new exchange agreements, most prisoners realized that their stays were likely to be lengthy. Escape attempts became more common and often more desperate. At many camps prisoners formed into battle units, charging the fences while pelting the guards with rocks and other weapons. At the same time, victories at places such as Gettysburg and Chattanooga placed thousand of additional prisoners in the hands of the Union. Despite the opening of such new depots as Point Lookout, Maryland, and Elmira, New York, Northern prisons became more crowded. As they did, captives quickly learned that nervous sentinels were suddenly more prone to open fire at the slightest provocation.

In 1864 retaliation became Union policy, adding extreme hunger to the other hardships of prison life. The policy was a response to reports of the alleged Confederate abuse of Union captives. The emaciated condition of many prisoners returning while the cartel was in operation confirmed much of what had been reported. Any extenuating factors, such as the Confederacy's lack of resources, were not taken into account as Stanton and other Union officials considered how to respond. By the summer of

1864 they had cut rations at Union prisons by 20 percent. Prisoners were also no longer allowed to receive packages of food from friends or relatives, nor could those with money purchase food from camp sutlers.

So things remained until the waning days of the war. In late 1864 Confederate officials were allowed to send a shipment of cotton to New York, with the proceeds to go for the purchase of clothing for the captives in gray. In February 1865, with Union victory in sight, exchange resumed. The ever-practical Grant and Stanton insisted, however, that it begin with prisoners who were wounded or too ill to be of use to the Confederacy. It was only after Robert E. Lee's surrender at Appomattox that the prisons began to empty for good. By the summer of 1865 they were virtually unoccupied, bringing to a close one of the ugliest aspects of the war.

Although neither the largest nor the worst of Union prison camps, perhaps none was more representative of evolving Northern prison policies than Camp Chase. Located four miles west of Columbus, Ohio, Camp Chase started, as did so many other prisons, as a training camp for eager Union recruits. By late 1861 it was also housing Confederate prisoners. Many were "political prisoners," citizens who were suspected of disloyalty. The evidence against some was substantial. In many other cases it consisted merely of alleged "disloyal utterances." Many came from western Virginia. They ended up at Camp Chase simply because it was the closest large Union post to which they could be sent.

With the fall of Fort Donelson, the number of prisoners at Camp Chase increased dramatically. Along with Camp Morton in Indianapolis, Chicago's Camp Douglas, the Alton, Illinois Prison, and Camp Butler near Springfield, Illinois, it became a major Union prison. Battles at Island No. 10 and Shiloh increased the prison population even more. As at those other facilities, officials at Camp Chase scrambled to accommodate the large influx of Confederate captives.

With the signing of the exchange cartel, Camp Chase's role once again changed. As Confederate prisoners departed, Union parolees arrived to take their place. Most were sent to Camp Lew Wallace, a new facility established nearby to house them, but many remained at Camp Chase. Disappointed at not being allowed to go home, they arrived in an uncooperative frame of mind. Many also arrived without officers, creating discipline problems that had not existed even with Confederate prisoners. Some deserted. Others simply headed for home without leave, intending to return after they were exchanged. Those who remained at the camps took out their frustrations on camp buildings, officers, and each other.

When the cartel collapsed, Camp Chase resumed its role as a military prison. Union officials had hoped to abandon the facility, but the renewed wave of prisoners made that hope impossible. For the next two years the camp's officers faced all the challenges experienced by officers at the Union's other major prisons; and its prisoners faced all the hardships that plagued prisoners throughout the North. Escape attempts were made. Some were successful, but most failed. Disease, especially smallpox, was an almost constant challenge. So, too, was hunger, especially after the Union instituted its policy of retaliation. Guards shot prisoners—sometimes with cause, sometimes without. Boredom was the prisoners' constant companion, although they devised a number of activities to battle it.

When the war finally ended, Camp Chase had one more role to fulfill. As the captives who had survived departed for Dixie, this time for good, Union soldiers arrived in Columbus to be mustered out of service. Many had been held in Confederate prisons. For a camp that had started out as a training facility populated by enthusiastic recruits, the arrival of these war-weary veterans marked a sobering close to its career. In the four years between, Camp Chase had evolved as a prison camp, reflecting the efforts of civilian and military officials to fashion a coherent prison policy.

I

Training Camp

April 12, 1861 fell on a Friday. The Ohio Senate was in session, "trying to go on in the ordinary routine of business," Senator Jacob Cox later recalled, "but with a sense of anxiety and strain which was caused by the troubled condition of national affairs." The previous fall, Abraham Lincoln had been elected the sixteenth president of the United States. In the months that followed seven Southern states had left the Union, formed a provisional government, and chosen Jefferson Davis as their president. Now the attention of all Americans, Union and Confederate, was focused on a military installation that rested in the harbor of Charleston, South Carolina. As the senators met in Columbus, their thoughts drifted to that suddenly important fort, "hoping almost against hope," Cox wrote, "that blood would not be shed."[1]

Suddenly a senator dashed in from the lobby and shouted to the presiding officer, "Mr. President, the telegraph announces that the secessionists are bombarding Fort Sumter!" The chamber fell into "a solemn and painful hush," quickly broken by the voice of a woman in the gallery. "Glory to God!" she shouted. It was Abby Kelly Foster, a veteran abolitionist, present that day to urge passage of a women's rights bill.[2]

Miss Foster's exuberance was not shared by the senators. "With most of us," Cox recalled, "the gloomy thought that Civil War had begun in our own land overshadowed everything, and seemed too great a price to pay for any good." Despite this gloom and any doubts its citizens may have harbored, Ohio responded quickly and decisively to the crisis. When President Lincoln asked for seventy-five thousand recruits from the states remaining in the Union to put down the rebellion, Governor William Dennison put out the call for thirteen thousand men to fill the thirteen regiments that would make up Ohio's quota. The general assembly appropriated $1 million "to provide for the defense of the state, and for the support of the federal government against the rebellion." Around the state a similar sense of patriotic resolution led to the formation of twenty companies by April 18.[3]

It was a scene familiar throughout the North as the states competed with each other to demonstrate their devotion to the cause. In major cities and rural villages mass meetings produced a flood of enthusiastic volunteers. So serious was the movement that it would result in 640,000 men by December. The rush to get these new military units to Washington was intense. In Massachusetts the first two regiments to be raised listened to a rousing farewell address from Governor John Andrew as a tailor sewed buttons on their overcoats. Thousands of men, imbued with an ardent spirit of patriotism, were soon descending on Columbus, so many that Governor Dennison could soon boast of fifty Ohio regiments. "The boys were perfectly crazy with joy all the way from home," a Hancock County soldier wrote of the train ride to the state capital. "Cigars, &c., were passed liberally, and joy and good feeling seemed to be the order of the day." A member of the Fourth Ohio Volunteer Infantry raised in the north-central part of the state later recalled the departure of the boys from his hometown. The recruits were "greeted on all sides by waving handkerchiefs and flags," he wrote, "the ready hat high in the air, and words of cheer of the gathered thousands." As they departed, "Never was there a gayer set of men."[4]

The enthusiasm of these early recruits was matched by the residents of the communities they passed en route to the capital. A Cincinnati enlistee wrote, "Every city, town, and village along the line of the [rail]road was resounding with cheers for the Union, the Constitution and the young *militaire*." Writing to the *Stark County Republican*, "VOLUNTEER," a member of the Canton Zouaves, wrote that "loud cheers" followed his outfit to Columbus. "We acceptably returned all compliments," he explained, "with 'three times three and a Zouave Tiger,' in consequence of which we are all pretty hoarse." Fayette County recruit G. W. Ross reported, "At all the principal stations along the [Cincinnati, Wilmington, & Zanesville Railroad] we received most tremendous cheerings." At the village of Morrow, Ross continued, the crowd remained large "although several companies had passed through previously." They met the same response at Cedarville and London, "and some of our company received cards and bouquets."[5]

Following this triumphal journey the eager soldiers-to-be reached a capital city that was not quite sure what to do with them all. The response to Dennison's call for volunteers had exceeded his expectations, and the state government did not have the capacity to house the hoards of recruits that arrived. "Last evening," reported the *Ohio State Journal* on April 26, "all the public halls and armories, the two Legislative Chambers, Supreme Court room, the large apartments in the Asylums &c., were called into requisition, and still there was a demand for more sleeping accommodations." A company from Highland County found quarters in the state library, but only after a state senator gave assurances to library officials that "no injury would be done to the room or books." The state penitentiary and Starling Medical College were also pressed into service. Companies of what would become the Fourth Ohio Volunteer Infantry were scattered in a wide variety of public buildings. One company was first quartered in the Capitol, sleeping on the building's marble floors. Later the soldiers moved to the Asylum for the Blind, where, noted one recruit, they had "excellent sleeping apartments." Thomas Thomson Taylor found himself in the basement of the Capitol, quarters he described as "a perfect livery stable." Still he managed to wax philosophical about the situation. He and a comrade had taken "a stroll around and through the building. It presented a very lively appearance," he informed his wife, "all filled with troops from the dome to the basement, the gas burners shedding a mellow soft light on all."[6]

The state quickly made arrangements to use Goodale Park to train and house the recruits. Located about a mile north of the Capitol, the forty-acre park had been a gift to the city from Dr. Lincoln Goodale. As barracks and other buildings hastily went up, the park was rechristened Camp Jackson, in honor of an earlier defender of the Union. A Cleveland reporter who visited on April 21 expressed mild surprise that carpenters had worked through the Sabbath to erect quarters for the troops who had arrived the previous night. Three days later a Lima soldier described the results of the carpenters' efforts. "On the left as you enter," he wrote, "there is erected a large dining hall about two hundred feet in length, with three tables extending the entire length of the building." A second hall was on its way up. Five large plank buildings, ranging from fifty to seventy feet in length, served as barracks. All contained five tiers of bunks. In addition, there were about a hundred tents, each sleeping six men, within the camp. Nevertheless, the recruit noted, the Capitol and other buildings remained filled with the overflow. In addition to being too small to accommodate the throng of men descending on Columbus, the site was not designed to serve as a military camp. Covered with large maple, oak, walnut, and elm trees, it was not well suited for drilling and training men. As one soldier complained, "A company could not march twenty paces in any direction, without coming in contact with trees. It would be a good place," he added wryly, "to teach [the men] Indian warfare."[7]

Trees were but a minor nuisance to the young innocents suddenly introduced to the realities of military life. For many eager recruits these realities set in upon their arrival in Columbus, dampening somewhat their military ardor. A Cincinnati soldier who had enjoyed stirring ovations during the ride to the capital complained, "After our arrival in Columbus (and about a mile from the camp) we were called into line, and had the extreme pleasure of being marched through the hot sun, *double quick,* to our camp." Once in camp, many of the volunteers were somewhat surprised to learn that they were expected to remain. After the war a veteran of the Fourth Ohio recalled his attempt to go for a walk shortly after his arrival at the camp. Suddenly he felt a rifle barrel in his side as the sentry shrieked, "Corporal of the guard!" The corporal arrived and informed the man that he had crossed his beat without the permission of an officer. "Crossed your beat?" the recruit replied. "Didn't know you had a beat. Didn't know I had to ask an officer." A trip to the guardhouse quickly provided an early lesson in military procedure. "It was my first forced march," the man recalled, "my first and last arrest." He was not alone. A less than tolerant reporter who traveled with a company from nearby Union County described the busy scene at the guard tent. "Many were the hearty laughs," he wrote, "at the expense of the muttering Dutchman and blathering Irishman, or explaining and apologizing Yankee as they were severely thrust by the expert police into the tent surrounded by armed guards."[8]

It is likely that all soldiers in all wars have complained about army food, and the recruits at Camp Jackson were no exception. One man wrote that his first meal consisted of "a piece of one of the hams belonging to a mastodon, of the period antediluvian." A lack of quality was not as serious a problem as the lack of quantity. As the troops descended upon Columbus, Governor Dennison and his staff had to make hasty arrangements to feed them. Too often these arrangements fell short. "The complaint appears to be," reported the *Ohio State Journal* on April 24, "that volunteers arriving, for instance in the morning, and having not tasted anything since the evening before, are suffered to remain on the ground until 2 o'clock P.M., before they can get a mouthful to eat." These reports came "from persons with whom we are well acquainted and on whose veracity we can implicitly rely. If this is the case," concluded the *Journal,* a Republican paper friendly toward Dennison, "it is very wrong." At least one soldier, while confirming that the problem existed, did not consider it nearly so serious. "They quickly have to muster out of camp to the number of five or six hundred," the man noted, "to get their meals at the hotels in the city." The men found this solution "quite satisfactory," since hotel fare was "much better than what they get in camp."[9]

Members of the state legislature did not agree with this cheerful assessment. The hungry soldiers were their constituents, as were the soldiers' family members and neighbors back home. When the men and their officers complained, the lawmakers listened. Further fueling the controversy was the arrival of thousands of tent poles in the name of the governor. Shortly after the shots rang out at Fort Sumter, Dennison had sent representatives to the East Coast to procure arms, tents, and other supplies. It had been a prudent decision, as the rifles that followed demonstrated. The poles arrived in advance of everything else, however, and the men could not eat tent poles, and Dennison looked silly, and the legislators and the press grew impatient. On May 1 the state House of Representatives passed a resolution urging Dennison to remove Quartermaster General Henry B. Carrington and Commissary General George W. Runyan. An attempt by Republicans to include an endorsement of the governor in the resolution failed.[10]

Even before the resolution was passed, the situation began to improve. Tents and rifles followed the poles. New contracts with businessmen to supply rations were signed. The governor relieved the strain on Columbus and Camp Jackson by establishing a new post on the Little Miami Railroad near Cincinnati. On April 29 fifteen companies were transferred from Columbus to Camp Dennison, as the facility was christened. That left 6,435 men at the capital, but complaints about the food had diminished. "For the first day or so after our arrival we had rather hard fare," a Mt. Vernon soldier wrote, but since then, "We have fared well, securing plenty of good, wholesome food." A Marysville soldier wrote, "Our meals are regular and good," and a reporter who ventured to the camp from Upper Sandusky added, "Their provisions are good and plenty of them. No lack of fine bread, butter, meat, beans, potatoes &c." On May 15 the men received their last prepared meals from hotels and private contractors and were issued their first rations to cook themselves. "Each mess had a trench dug in the earth, to contain the fire, about eighteen inches wide, eighteen inches deep, varying in length according to the number of camp kettles employed at one fire," reported the *Ohio State Journal.* The kettles were hung from "a piece of scantling," anchored by timbers driven into the ground. Pine boards served as tables. "We noticed that they had plenty of hot coffee, sugar, vinegar, &c.," the paper noted, "and they all appeared to enjoy their rural repast." Meanwhile, the officers continued to have their meals provided in one of the mess halls.[11]

Supplementing the men's rations were numerous edibles provided by women, both from Columbus and back home. "Again are we under obligations to those considerate ones of the 'fair sex,'" wrote a Fayette County soldier on May 18, "who sent some delicacies." He added, "Because we are at the present time doing our own cooking, those things were probably more highly appreciated." Union County soldiers received "several boxes of provisions" from both Marysville and Milford. Men from another outfit felt they had received more than they wanted. In a letter to a local newspaper they apologized to area women for having "inconsiderately uttered some complaints which were unintentionally borne to you." The men asked the women not to send any more packages, "believing you would still find opportunities to make charitable uses of them at home." In Columbus, Governor Dennison's wife helped organize the Soldiers' Aid Society to make clothing for the men. Sometimes the assistance was less formal. After services at the Bigelow Chapel Church on May 19, members each took from five to seven men from a Fayette County company home for Sunday dinner. "They have our best wishes and heartiest thanks," one of the men wrote, "as all were treated in the best manner possible."[12]

By that time Camp Jackson clearly resembled a military camp and had fallen into a regular routine. A visitor in late April offered this description of the scene.

> At all hours the camp presented a lively scene, companies were going and coming at all hours, some were drilling, others were disbanded and lounging around underneath the trees. Hundreds were occupied in writing letters. The greater number were setting with their backs against the trees with a small fragment of a board upon their knees as writing tables. Every kind of diversion was going on, summersaulting, jumping, wrestling, tower building by clambering

upon each other's shoulders even to the fourth person in height, fencing, boxing, &c.

As evening came on a new scene was presented, the camp-fires were lighted. As the light gleamed upon the boughs of the trees overhead and upon the gay uniforms of red and blue that gathered around, a charming scene for the artist's pencil glowed upon the sight.[13]

Diversions at the camp were numerous and varied. Military musicians enjoyed marching through Columbus, performing for local citizens. A company from Cincinnati included in its ranks a "circus fellow," who entertained his comrades with "numerous feats of twisting and tumbling peculiar to the ring, some of them really astounding, and wound up by swallowing a poker iron twenty-two inches long." Many of the men, facing an uncertain future, found comfort in faith. "As I was passing through the camp," one noted, "I came upon a group of several hundred soldiers holding a prayer meeting among themselves. It was to me a most solemn and impressive scene to witness those brave men kneeling under the great forest trees invoking the God of their forefathers and of battles to give victory to freedom and the right." According to one soldier the meetings were held every evening. Sunday services took place at the camp as well. "The pulpit was erected at the foot of a gentle declivity," wrote a reporter who was present at one of the services. "Around it were arranged the ranks of soldiers and back of these was an immense crowd of ladies and gentlemen from the city. All joined in the solemn exercises, and the soldiers seemed fully aware of the terrible nature of the work in which they were about to be engaged, and glad to receive, in the consolations of Christianity, encouragement and stimulus for bravery in the defence of their country and their homes."[14]

Although the Goodale Park site was meeting both the physical and spiritual needs of the men training there, state officials, realizing that it was too small and tree covered to be an adequate training camp, took action. On May 28 the *Ohio State Journal* reported, "Workmen were engaged yesterday in taking down the [Camp Jackson] barracks for the purpose of removing to a new camp to be organized four miles west of this city. It is to be a regular camp. It will contain 100 acres. It is plowed, harrowed and rolled smooth, and will make a good place for drilling purposes." The work proceeded quickly, and by June 12 the camp had "assumed the appearance of a liberally sized town with great uniformity of houses, about 160 in number."[15]

The men continued to pour into Columbus, each outfit, if local press accounts are to be believed, more impressive than the one before. "The 'Monroe and Noble County Rangers' passed through this city," the *Ohio State Journal* reported on July 22. "They number 83 men and are the finest company we have seen yet, hardy, stout, iron framed men of large uniform size, 25 of them we understand are over six feet in height." Commanding the camp and its "hardy, stout" recruits over the next several months was a succession of officers. Most were commanders of various regiments training at the site who, after a brief tenure, left to lead their men into the field. Among them was Col. William Starke Rosecrans of the Twenty-third Ohio Volunteer Infantry. Rosecrans assumed command of the relocated Camp Jackson on June 18. Showing an early recognition of the political realities of the war, he promptly rechristened it Camp Chase, "in honor of our distinguished fellow [Ohio] citizen the present Secretary of the Treasury [Salmon P. Chase]." The same day, "having noticed with regret among the troops the prevalence of profane swearing, a practice which even atheists must admit to be useless," Rosecrans issued an edict against "the pernicious and ungentlemanly habit." He explained, "Even were not abstaining from profanity, the dictate of reason, we are bound to it as soldiers by the rules and articles of war." It was his last order at Camp Chase. Two days later he was gone, headed toward western Virginia, a commission as brigadier general of U.S. Volunteers in hand.[16]

The coming and going of officers often led to a certain amount of confusion at the camp. Among those caught up in it were two officers and one enlisted man with bright futures. One of Rosecrans's junior officers in the Twenty-third was a young Rutherford B. Hayes. In a June 10 letter to his wife, Lucy, Hayes wrote, "Our quarters are not yet built; all things are new and disorganized." Four days later, with Rosecrans not yet present, Hayes and a fellow officer found themselves temporarily in charge of the camp. "What we don't know," Hayes confessed, "we guess at, and you may be sure we are kept pretty busy guessing." Still, he was happy to be away from "the crowd of visitors who interfere so with the drills at Camp Dennison." Hayes concluded, "I enjoy this thing very much. It is [an] open-air, active life, novel and romantic." Also serving in the Twenty-third was a youthful William McKinley, who enlisted as part of the Poland Guards from Poland, Ohio. Pvt. McKinley's routine at Camp Chase was far less glamorous than Hayes's. His June 20 diary entry read, "As usual was at roll call; no particular change or variety in the orders; on dress parade in the evening." It was a typical entry. Like many of his comrades, McKinley took refuge in his faith. Following a Sunday service he wrote, "All day I felt the love of God in my heart and notwithstanding the surroundings there was an inward calmness and tranquillity which belongs to the Christian alone."[17]

Completing Camp Chase's triumvirate of future presidents was James A. Garfield, who arrived as lieutenant colonel of the Forty-second Ohio Volunteer Infantry (OVI) and soon received promotion to colonel. Like Hayes, Garfield was learning as he went. On August 22 he confided to his wife, "It is a little odd for me to become a pupil again, but I come into it easily and have no fear of very disastrous failure in learning the duty." A week later Garfield wrote, "I am busy and cheerful in the work of tearing down the old fabric of my proposed life, and removing its rubbish for the erection of a new structure." Soon, however, Garfield was finding fault with the way the army did business. On August 31 he wrote, "It is very unfortunate for the service that regiments should be hurried into the field with so little preparation." One outfit, he noted, was "hurried off to Missouri before half of its companies had had two days' drill." Another had been quickly filled up with members of other partially formed regiments. "I should dread the responsibility of taking such a regiment into the field," Garfield concluded. Despite this desire for thorough training, by late October Garfield was "beginning to tire of the monotonous routine of camp duties. I hope we may soon be sent away to active service. The thought of remaining during the winter would be unendurable." He did not have to. Garfield and his unit departed in December.[18]

The confusion and difficulties that Hayes and Garfield experienced and McKinley likely witnessed were common during the early months of Camp Chase. A recruit from the Cleveland area who arrived shortly after the transfer from the Goodale Park site wrote: "The boys had been led to believe that they were to be encamped upon a large and beautiful meadow, and you can judge how well their hopes were realized when upon being brought to a halt they found themselves in the centre of a large cornfield, with a fair prospect ahead of having plenty of mud and some work before the ground would admit of actual daily drill." Even then the men were often led by officers whose civilian lives had not prepared them for the task at hand. "I never saw in my whole life a regimental drill till I took hold of the 67th [OVI] as its instructor," Lt. Col. Alvin Coe Voris admitted in a letter to his wife. "For a week, I have been instructing it in battalion exercises, the lessons for which I am compelled to learn the night before each day's exercises." He concluded, "The boys (simple fellows) think I am quite a military man, but I know better."[19]

Inadequate supplies also continued to plague the trainees. Writing to friends in Highland County, "Sergeant" of the Twenty-fourth OVI complained: "The soldiers have received nothing in the way of clothing, except shoes, socks, and drawers." After several days of drilling, he added, "Some of us begin to need pants very badly." A Marietta soldier wrote that companies had been in camp two or three weeks without blankets. His captain, the man added, had rejected the inferior-quality tents first sent to his company. In September an officer requested a "board of survey" to investigate the coffee sent to his company. The following month another captain requested a similar board concerning a shipment of blankets his outfit received. According to one observer, the shortages extended to the medical department. In February 1862 Dr. W. M. Kaull, an assistant regimental surgeon, complained that the supplies sent to him included "a very incomplete list of drugs. . . . I suppose," he concluded, "the medical purveyor must be either a man of limited Therapeutic knowledge or has little faith in the remedial virtue of drugs." The post surgeon Kaull termed "an old fussy dutchman who doesent know any too much [and] is very inattentive." The assistant post surgeon, he added, was "a young man whose attention seems to be more devoted to the ladies than his patients." Kaull had sent one man to the hospital only to later discover that he had received no treatment in two days. Other men, suffering from measles, had refused to go. "They dread the Hospital as they would the plague," Kaull wrote, "and I do not blame them much."[20]

Generally, the men endured shortages with a minimum of complaint. There was, however, one major exception to this tendency. When outfits were not supplied with weapons—or received what they considered improper weapons—officers had a problem on their hands. "Our company came very near disbanding at Columbus," wrote a member of the ironically named Geauga Rifles, "on account of some of our boys leaving because the State would not furnish them with rifles." Ten did depart before they were mustered in. The rest were assuaged with "muskets that bear the date of 1846" and the promise of more modern firearms to come.

Scioto County's Fullerton Rifles were upset when they received word that they were to be supplied "common muskets" rather than rifles. The men met and debated whether to remain, return home, or "go immediately to Washington City and offer ourselves to the general government." They finally agreed to "act not too hastily" but wait and see what happened. Andrew J. Duncan, William McKinley's brother-in-law, recorded in his journal on July 24 that his company and four others had agreed among themselves not to accept the 1855 model rifles they had been issued. A company that did accept the weapons was "greeted by groans" from the other outfits. By 11:00 a.m., Duncan recorded, "Every other camp but ours had been frightened into receiving those muskets." Duncan's company was won over by a lieutenant colonel who expressed regret that "a company which I had supposed formed of the best material in the country and the best in this camp is the first to mutiny against your superior officers." He proposed that the ten best shooters try out the weapons and report the results. When a favorable report came back, "the company universally accepted them but not without protesting the appearance of them."[21]

"The great difficulty with volunteer soldiers," wrote a volunteer soldier from Highland County, "is to restrain them—to convince them it is positively as necessary for them to go through the school of drill and discipline as for them to be armed with guns when they go into active service." Proceedings of an October 17 court-martial held at the camp reveal twenty cases demonstrating that point. Eighteen involved men who had been absent without leave. The one sergeant and two corporals found guilty were reduced in rank to private. The remainder, all privates, had to forfeit one-fourth or one-third of a month's pay. The other two men had broken guard "for the purpose of bringing intoxicating liquors into camp." One gave up one-third of a month's pay, the other one-half. More cases of absent men were heard in November. Monetary fines remained in force, but the men were also sentenced to hard labor for three to seven days. Wesley Hickman and Nelson Brooks of the Forty-second OVI each received fines of $1 for being intoxicated. Cavalryman John Ramsey was so drunk that he "neglected the proper care of his horse, whereby [the] horse became injured and was in danger of being lost." Cpl. Ramsey was reduced in rank to private and sentenced to seven days on bread and water.[22]

The men employed a variety of methods to get out of camp. According to Andrew Duncan, many cleared the gate by using an old pass with the date altered or by simply "shoving anything but a white blank piece of paper" in front of the sentries. Others were even less subtle, watching the sentinels and trying to run past them when they turned their backs. Such attempts were not always successful. During the Camp Jackson days, the *Ohio State Journal* reported that one man made a dash past the sentry "for the purpose of making his exit through a hole in the fence." He was halfway through when the alert guard "thrust the bayonet some two or three inches into the fleshy part of his hip." The wound healed, and a court of inquiry exonerated the sentry. Occasionally, groups of thirty or more men scaled the fence in an attempt either to desert or to reach the nearest liquor shop. When they did, pursuing parties were called out to retrieve them. Henry Otis Dwight was a member of one such party, which went out under the command of Col. Garfield. According to Dwight's memoirs, "Garfield told us to leave our blankets with him as they would encumber our movement." The men apprehended the missing soldiers, but sadly, Dwight recalled, "The last I saw of my blanket was when Garfield took it on his horse!" In another instance, two companies of infantry gave chase when about one hundred members of the First Ohio Volunteer Cavalry broke through brigade guard lines at about midnight. After a three-hour pursuit through woods and fields, the infantrymen returned with thirty-seven prisoners.[23]

Theft also became a problem in the vicinity of the camp. Some cases, involving farms in the area, were minor. Disgusted with peddlers who charged 4¢ for a pint of milk, recruit Jonathon F. Harrington admitted that he and his comrades "can get it cheaper by taking our canteens and going out for watter and then hunt[ing] up the cows and milk[ing them] into the canteen." In August the guard was increased to prevent the men from helping themselves to roasting ears in a cornfield south of the camp. Other cases were more serious. Members of the Cleveland Rifle Grenadiers were annoyed when they learned that rumors were circulating that they had become chicken thieves. "The fact is," one of them wrote home, "that someone does a heavy business in that line." In one night, he continued, one company had made off with "twenty chickens, three turkeys, six pigs, and two quite large calves." However, he added, "I don't think that innocent parties should suffer the stigma to be attached to them, which of right belongs to other parties." The company had passed a resolution that "the first man that steals even [one] chicken and brings it into camp shall have his head shaved and be drummed out of camp." According to a Fayette County infantryman, "a jolly set" of cavalrymen decided one night to supplement their diets with some poultry. Camp officers soon found out and sent two or three companies of infantry out on patrol. "Before very long," the Fayette County soldier wrote, "here come squads of three, five, eight and so on, until there were forty or fifty of them in the guard house." One man was caught climbing the fence back into camp, some eight or ten chickens, it was claimed, stuffed under his uniform.[24]

On August 9, 1861, Brig. Gen. Charles W. Hill assumed command of Camp Chase. Hill's orders, which came from the headquarters of the Ohio Militia, charged him with establishing "such rules and regulations as he shall deem expedient for the organization, and discipline of the troops there assembled, preparatory to going into the field." Hill remained in charge of the camp for seven months, bringing some needed stability. He also took his orders seriously, instilling a stronger sense of discipline in the recruits. When the general returned following a two-week absence, one of the men observed, "We may expect to work up to scratch again. The general must be considered a very good disciplinarian, and a man seemingly conscious of his duties as an instructor. There seems to be every facility in Camp Chase for schooling the soldiers."[25]

Six days after assuming command, Hill issued detailed orders regulating the men's behavior and establishing a schedule for drills. Officers commanding companies and regiments were responsible for informing their men "as often as may be necessary" that "excessive noise, yelling or disorder, will not be allowed within the camp." Guards were to be posted in silence. Firearms could be discharged only under orders. Public property was to be used only "in the public service." Except in necessary cases, passes could not be issued to visit any private place within four miles of camp. This applied especially to "the tavern opposite the camp." The orders also forbade marauding parties, drunkenness, and bringing in intoxicating liquor. Under Hill's orders, reveille sounded at 5:00 a.m. in August, 5:30 in September, and at 6:00 from October through March. Squad, company, and battalion drills made up most of the day, with inspections thrown in. Tattoo came at 9:00 p.m., "after which no soldier is to be out of his tent or quarters, except on duty or special leave." Taps followed thirty minutes later, "when all lights in soldiers' quarters are to be extinguished, and stillness prevail throughout the camp until *Reveille*." On Sundays, following an early morning drill, time was set aside for religious services. In place of afternoon drills, there was "a review of all uniformed and armed troops, followed by a thorough inspection of the troops and hospitals."[26]

Despite Hill's efforts, there were occasional lapses, although perhaps understandable ones, in Camp Chase's military discipline. "When I arrived in camp, on the morning before starting [for the field]," a member of the Fortieth Ohio wrote in December 1861, "I found everything in confusion and uproar." The camp was crowded with relatives and friends of the men who were about to depart. The following evening the outfit was formed into ranks as the band played patriotic music. Gen. Hill offered "a few touching and patriotic remarks," and the trainees began their four-mile march to Columbus. At the capital they endured "the most trying ordeal a soldier must pass through," as those same relatives and friends, "amid tears, were giving perhaps their last farewell to those who were near and dear to them." Well-wishers lined the streets so solidly that the departure of the recruits was delayed by an hour.[27]

It was a scene that would be played out many times over the next three years. Although its numbers would vary, Camp Chase would serve as a training camp for the remainder of the war. Yet even as the boys of the Fortieth departed, the camp's mission was changing. Its guardhouse was by then occupied not only by rowdy Ohio soldiers with a taste for their neighbors' chickens and strong drink but by prisoners who had been brought to Columbus on a variety of charges. At the time most were civilians and relatively harmless, but that, too, would soon change. After a modest start as a military jail of sorts, Camp Chase was about to begin its evolution into one of the North's largest prison camps.

2

Improvised Prison Camp

At the time of its occurrence, it is doubtful that the moment seemed particularly auspicious. On June 29, 1861, a single prisoner, the first brought there "for alleged participation in the rebellion," arrived in Columbus. According to the local press, he was lodged "in the Stationhouse." Six days later Lt. J. E. McGowan of the Twenty-first Ohio arrived with a contingent of twenty-three prisoners taken by his regiment in the Kanawha River Valley of western Virginia. It was not clear whether they had been captured in battle, but they likely were not. "The majority of them," reported the *Ohio State Journal,* "are wealthy and influential citizens of Virginia." They were first taken to a local hotel, and they reportedly spoke highly of the proprietor's hospitality. From there the group went to Camp Chase. They were released a few days later. During the next few months more prisoners arrived at irregular intervals. They came in groups ranging from eight to forty-three. Most came from western Virginia, but some were Kentuckians. Some were captured in battle, while others were simply described as "secessionists." By November 13 the number of prisoners at Camp Chase had grown to 278, with more on the way.[1]

For the men training at the camp, these arrivals marked their first sight of real flesh-and-blood Confederates. "Our camp was thrown into great excitement," one wrote of the news that the first contingent was on the way. "Every one," he explained, was "anxious to get a fair peep at a Secessionist." When they did get a look, many were less than impressed by the sight of their enemies. "The prisoners look pretty hard," Pvt. John A. Smith wrote in a letter home. "They keep holering hurrah for Jeff Davis if it was my say i should say shot them down the first time they said hurrah for Jeff Davis. They dont look like human to me." James Garfield, whose observations were a bit more polished, still considered the prisoners to be "a hard looking set of the species of the 'great unwashed.'" Recruit Mungo Murray wrote that many had lost limbs in battle and others were in "the decline of life. Some are 60, and many may be over 70 years old." One contingent of thirty-three prisoners, arriving in September, included four or five men in their sixties. At the other end of the spectrum was "a youth of probably 15. He seemed to be very weak and faint," Murray wrote. Eventually, the youngster was unable to walk: "He made a soldier feel [pity] all over," Murray noted.[2]

According to one recruit, the prisoners were, at least during the summer of 1861, confined to the same prison as "the unruly boys of our camp." A reporter who visited the prison in December described the quarters as comfortable. "Being mostly Western Virginia 'snake hunters,'" he wrote of those confined there, "aside from the loss of their liberty, they lose little by imprisonment." If the men who guarded them are to be believed, the prisoners tended to agree with that assessment. "Some of them are well Satisfide with their Situations," Jonathon Harrington wrote, "while others are down in the mouth." According to Mungo Murray, "They say they are better treated here than in the rebel army."[3]

Although the prisoners' treatment may have been good, their presence posed various problems for Governor Dennison. Unsure what to do with them, Dennison sought the advice of Simon Cameron, Lincoln's secretary of war. Some of the prisoners, the governor explained, were charged with such serious crimes as rape or murder. Should they be turned over to authorities of their home states, Dennison wondered, or tried in Columbus by courts-martial? Others were accused of "overt acts of treason against the Government." Dennison asked for guidance on whether to hand them over to the federal courts or detain them as prisoners of war. At the other extreme were men who were "only accused of an expression of opinion in favor of the rebels without [committing an] overt act of treason against the Government." Dennison sent a list of prisoners and allegations to the secretary, asking for advice in each individual case. If it ever came from Cameron, the record has been lost. When Dennison's successor, David Tod, assumed office in January 1862, he sent a request to Secretary of State William Henry Seward seeking similar answers. "Please define and point out my several duties," Tod requested, "and I will most cheerfully perform the trust."[4]

Failing to receive any instructions, Tod took matters into his own hands. On August 7 he proposed to Edwin M. Stanton, who had succeeded Cameron at the War Department, the appointment of "a good lawyer and sound man with authority to investigate and discharge political prisoners at Camp Chase." Tod included the names of three "safe men to appoint." The next day Stanton replied that one of the men Tod suggested, Judge Reuben Hitchcock, would be appointed special commissioner. Six days after that, Stanton informed Hitchcock of his appointment. The judge was to examine the captives personally and take any statements they offered. Ultimately, he was to determine in each case "whether the peace and safety of the government requires his detention or whether he may be discharged without danger to the public peace." Although Hitchcock's powers would "embrace the largest discretion," he was also to "confer freely with Governor Tod and avail yourself of his counsel and assistance." Writing to Tod, Stanton suggested the governor would make the final decision. "There will be no objection to the discharge of any person whose discharge you may recommend." Stanton then added a significant stipulation. "The President thinks that the State Governors [of the states in which the prisoners resided] should be consulted after the commissioner's report is made and their objections heard before final discharge."[5]

Hitchcock served only a few weeks before illness forced him to resign. His successor was Samuel Galloway, a former Ohio secretary of state and member of the U.S. House of Representatives. According to one press account, Galloway had "superior conversational powers and a fund of illustration and anecdote not unlike that of Mr. Lincoln." Regardless of whether those qualities were helpful in the task he faced, patience and persistence were essential. Between November 1862 and May 1865, Galloway considered the cases of 2,090 prisoners. At first virtually all involved civilians. As time went on and Camp Chase evolved into a military prison, more of the cases concerned captured Confederate soldiers who claimed they had been forced into the service and had deserted.[6]

The charges against the prisoners varied in their severity, and some were more specific than others. A few men were charged with "using treasonable language" or "uttering treasonable statements." Others were accused of being a "rebel mail carrier," a "rebel horse thief," or a "rebel spy." Many were simply charged with "being a rebel." A Jackson County, Virginia resident had been arrested for "being in company with men who had U.S. government property." Many faced no specific charges. Among them was George Donahoe, a British subject who had been a tailor in Abingdon, Virginia. He claimed he had left the Old Dominion with the intention of moving north. Along the way he reported himself to the provost marshal at Louisa, Kentucky, who forwarded him to Lexington. From there he was sent to Louisville and then on to Camp Chase. "His statement is consistent," Galloway concluded, "and I have no doubt of the truth."[7]

Some of the detainees seemed to have been residents of border regions who were caught, both politically and geographically, between rival armies. A man from western Virginia claimed that he had been suspected by the Confederates of aiding the Union. He was given the choice of going to a Richmond prison or moving within the Confederate lines. After relocating he had been pressed into service one day by a Southern postmaster, whose horse was sick, to carry some letters to a nearby community. On his way he was captured by Union soldiers and sent to Camp Chase. His claim was supported by a Union lieutenant colonel serving in Beverly County, Virginia, as well as a petition signed by twenty-five residents of Pocohontas County. Silas F. Taylor, a forty-six-year-old resident of Greenbriar County, Virginia, was arrested while helping his brother, Garrett Taylor, plant corn. The reason given for his arrest was that he had two sons serving in the Confederate army. Taylor insisted that the boys had been conscripted against both their will and his. He agreed to relocate to Ohio, where he had loyal relatives, if released. Galloway approved his release under that stipulation. His brother, who had been arrested with him, was also freed under the same terms.[8]

Often the commissioner received petitions from friends of the detainees. A Kentuckian informed Galloway that one of the Camp Chase political prisoners had been "a school mate of mine upwards of fifty years ago." He came from a family comprising "people of good repute" and was "a kind hearted and companionable man." The writer concluded, "I should have considered him amongst the last to hatch or practice treason—or risk anything in promoting it." Another man wrote to ask for mercy for his brother. He admitted that his sibling had enlisted in the Confederate army but insisted that he had done so "under the malign influence and persuasions of older persons." Occasionally the correspondents were prominent. During Hitchcock's brief tenure he reported to Tod that he had "examined the papers presented to me by Judge Pryor of Kentucky, in behalf of his nephew, W. L. Pryor." Among the papers was a letter from James Guthrie, a former U.S. secretary of the treasury who had gone on to serve as president of the Louisville & Nashville Railroad.[9]

Galloway recommended the release of a number of prisoners if they would agree to take an oath of allegiance to the Union. His reasons varied from case to case. Many charges were "not sustained by proof." In other cases petitions signed by loyal citizens influenced Galloway's decision. Sometimes simple observation carried the day. The commissioner concluded that a British subject being held was "an ignorant man and entirely unacquainted with the questions at issue." A teenager from Barbour County, Virginia, Galloway concluded to be "simple minded." Of a Mason County, Virginia man charged simply with "Disloyalty," Galloway noted, "He is manifestly an ignorant inoffensive man."[10]

The nature of Camp Chase as a prison camp changed on February 26, 1862. Ten days earlier, Gen. Ulysses S. Grant had captured Fort Donelson, and his demand for an unconditional surrender of the Tennessee fortification resulted in the capture of nearly fifteen thousand prisoners. Grant's success presented a tremendous logistical challenge for a government not yet prepared to deal with such a large number of captives. The Union was in the process of establishing a military prison on Johnson's Island in Lake Erie, but the facility was not yet ready to receive prisoners. As a result, Gen. Henry W. Halleck, commanding Union forces in the West, was soon sending out a flood of messages to officials in western states in an attempt to find facilities capable of holding the men Grant had captured. Among the sites pressed into service were a number of training camps, including Camp Butler in Springfield, Illinois; Chicago's Camp Douglas; and Camp Morton, near Indianapolis. The former state prison at Alton, Illinois was also converted into a military prison.

On February 19 Halleck telegraphed Governor Tod, asking how many prisoners he could accommodate in Columbus. Tod replied the next day that Camp Chase could be made ready for 1,000 in three days. On the 26th ninety-five prisoners, all officers, arrived in Columbus. Another 104 were delivered to the Ohio capital the next day. On March 1 came the largest contingent, 720 Confederate captives. Over the next two months, following fights at Island No. 10 and Shiloh, groups ranging from just twelve to "about two hundred" arrived at irregular intervals. Some were civilians, but most were military prisoners. By April 6 the latter category included 1,400 captives, 1,000 of whom were officers.[11]

The Columbus correspondent of the *East Liverpool Mercury* was on hand to witness the March 1 arrival. They marched four abreast through the city streets, he reported, "on their way to the traitor's prison at Camp

Chase." Six hundred guards, "with loaded Enfields and bayonets fixed," escorted them. Many still had their sidearms, but virtually none were in uniform. Rather, they wore "the peculiar and varied style of clothing common to the middle class of Southern chivalry." Offering no specifics, the *Mercury* reporter concluded, "They gave evident symptoms of feeling like fools, who were caught in their own folly, and about to suffer the consequences of their own guilt."[12]

The correspondent of the *Delaware Gazette* was also present for the arrival of the Confederates. The train bearing the prisoners, he noted, had been scheduled to arrive very early in the morning. It was delayed "till our good people had taken breakfast and were ready for a sensation." Like the *Mercury* man, he was unimpressed with the captives' uniforms. "Their clothing was without uniformity; some brown, some gray, some blue in color, of varying texture, and by no means to be coveted by the Union soldiers in guard over them." As to their countenances: "A few of the Rebels appeared downcast, but many made cheerful remarks to the persons that crowded near them, and all carried themselves with an independent air." Many still carried their swords. Others had them borne by slaves who accompanied them as they arrived in Columbus. "Indignant remarks," the *Gazette* reported, "were made by many prominent citizens against the mistaken generosity which treats rebels as if they were honored belligerents; and when 'contraband' were seen carrying their rebel masters' swords, indignation was expressed in phrases more vigorous than exemplary."[13]

As reports spread of slaves accompanying their masters to the Union prison camp, the "indignation" reported by the *Gazette* correspondent increased. It was expressed most vociferously by Republican newspapers, putting the Tod administration in an awkward position. The outrage was not limited to slavery reaching into the Buckeye State; there was a general feeling that "traitors" were being treated as guests rather than prisoners. On February 13 the *National Democrat*, published in the nearby community of London, reported that a state senator, while visiting the camp, had purchased a cane made by one of the prisoners. One month later the paper's Columbus correspondent wrote that a number of prisoners had been paroled to Columbus. Many could be seen at the American Hotel, which seemed to be "their principal rendezvous." They had "written the initials 'C.S.A.' opposite their names on the hotel register," the writer added, "which I consider decidedly cool." A Columbus newspaper reported that a number of parolees attended the theater, hissing when "allusion was made to standing by the good old flag in the play." On yet another occasion, Philip R. Forney, a Union officer, reportedly made one of the Confederate prisoners a guest of honor at a dinner he gave. The affair "resulted in considerable feeling owing to the fact that Forney's guest knocked down an intoxicated soldier from the Sixty-first Ohio who approached and annoyed him."[14]

In a letter to his wife, Charles Barrington Simrall, a paroled political prisoner from Covington, Kentucky, said he had "devoted much of my idle time in visiting the public institutions." The insane asylum particularly impressed him. "It is a large commodious building fitted up in a neat and elegant style." On another occasion he and some local residents went target shooting with pistols. "I was the most successful," he proudly reported, "and so sustained the honor of Dixie."[15]

In March the Ohio General Assembly became involved in the controversy. A committee of the state senate (perhaps including one member with a new cane) visited Camp Chase, discovering "seventy-four negroes in the prison, mostly taken at Fort Donelson." Of that number, about one-third were free blacks who had been hired as servants. As many as fifty were slaves, captured with their masters. "None of them were in arms," the committee reported, "all having been retained for menial service only." Officers and enlisted men, the report continued, had been separated, but masters and slaves had not. As a result, "The relation of master and slave [was] being as vigorously maintained by the master[s], and as fully recognized by the negroes and the other inmates of the prison, as ever it was in Tennessee."[16]

The slaves had not taken up arms against the government, the committee asserted; indeed, they had not even been at Fort Donelson voluntarily. "Why," the senators asked, "are they retained in prison? Is it to furnish the Rebel officers with servants?" If so, this did not, in the committee's opinion, justify the government's expense in transporting them to Columbus. It also made the provision in the Ohio constitution banning slavery "a nullity." The senators absolved officials at Camp Chase, as well as Governor Tod, of any wrongdoing. Instead they placed the blame on "federal authorities," whose control over the prisoners left state officials powerless to correct the problems. As a result, acting on the committee's recommendation, the general assembly passed a resolution of protest against "this outrage upon the feelings of the loyal people of Ohio."

It was sent to Secretary of War Stanton and to Ohio's congressional delegation.[17]

Meanwhile, Stanton was receiving complaints from other quarters. On March 30 Lazerus Noble, Indiana's adjutant general, wrote, "We are greatly annoyed by the laxiety prevailing at Columbus, Ohio, in guarding rebels." According to Noble, "Many are out on parole with side-arms, talking secesh on the streets and in bar-rooms to the great detriment of our cause." He concluded, "We ask that it be stopped." Stanton responded with two telegrams. One went to Halleck, who was told, "Frequent complaints are made to the President and this Department of the license permitted to the rebel officers who are prisoners at Camp Chase." Stanton continued, "The officer in command should be admonished and removed and some one else placed in command." To Governor Tod Stanton wrote, somewhat more diplomatically, "There is much complaint of the license permitted the rebel officers at Camp Chase." With his sharper message to Halleck in mind, Stanton added, "By general regulation the commander of the department has charge of prisoners."[18]

Tod responded to Stanton's telegram the next day. "There is no just cause for complaint of rebel prisoners at Camp Chase," he wrote. "The commander, Col. [Granville] Moody, is a strong anti-slavery Republican; does his duty faithfully and discreetly." Unconvinced, Stanton sent Maj. Roger Jones to Columbus to determine what the situation was. Jones arrived in early April and was informed by an upset governor that Stanton was "ignorant of the state of matters." The major submitted his report on April 6. It generally exonerated Tod and the officers at Camp Chase. Jones submitted to the War Department copies of orders issued by Tod disarming all prisoners and strictly limiting prison visitors. In addition, Jones noted, the only prisoners who had been paroled by the governor were those in ill health. All of them had subsequently "been remanded to the prison limits on their restoration to health." Those who had not returned to Camp Chase, the major continued, were prisoners who had been paroled by the commanders of the Department of the Mississippi and the Department of Western Virginia.[19]

Jones's report also noted that there were "nearly if not quite 100 negroes among the prisoners captured at [Fort] Donelson." All were considered prisoners of war and were treated accordingly. On April 21 Col. William Hoffman, the Union's commissary general of prisoners, instructed Tod to release all black prisoners. Hoffman urged that only a few be released

at a time. This, he said, would "give them the better opportunity of finding employment and . . . prevent excesses which might grow out of the
association of a number of destitute and ignorant persons whose numbers and necessities might lead them to serious crimes." The next day Tod
sent orders "to discharge all the colored persons now confined." In language more tactful than Hoffman's, the governor advised that only three
or four be set free per day, "that they may not be in each other's way in providing for themselves." Each was to be given three days' rations. Tod's orders called for no additional assistance.[20]

All of these events at Camp Chase were playing out in front of a continuing parade of commanders. By early 1862 there was more stability
than there had been the previous summer, when commanders changed
sometimes weekly as regiments headed continually to the front. Now
the changes occurred every few months. Still, the command situation led
Hoffman to complain in February, "Much embarrassment results from
the frequent changes of the officers in charge of the prisoners." He suggested to Tod that an officer be permanently assigned to the post. This
was not done, and in September the commissary general of prisoners was
still pointing out, "The frequent changes in the commander of the camp
leads to many irregularities." He once again added, "A proper responsibility can only be arrived at through a permanent commander and a permanent guard."[21]

On March 1, 1862 Col. Granville Moody assumed command of Camp
Chase, taking over from a Col. Campbell. The man whom Governor Tod
called a "strong anti-slavery Republican" prisoner Andrew Jackson Campbell termed a "Methodist preacher by profession, a black Republican of
the darkest hue by politics, a bigot and tyrant by nature." Moody himself painted a rather different picture. In his memoirs he cited a testimo-
nial that he claimed to have received from Confederate prisoners when he
gave up command of Camp Chase to take the Seventy-fourth Ohio into
the field. "Should Colonel Moody, at any time, become a prisoner of our
government," they wrote, "we hereby earnestly request for him the highest
consideration and treatment, as a proper acknowledgment of his kindness
and care of us, as prisoners of war, having given us every comfort, liberty,
and indulgence at all consistent with our position and with his obligations as commandant of this military post." Perhaps the most balanced
portrait of the colonel came from "Pete," a Morgan County, Ohio soldier, whose company of recruits arrived at the camp in late May. Moody

greeted the men, he wrote, "with a soul-stirring speech in a style pecu-
liarly his own. It stirred the patriotism of every person within the hearing
of his voice," Pete added, "except those hostile to their country." He was,
however, slightly less than thrilled by a sermon the colonel delivered the
next day on the parade ground. "The only objection to it from me was that
it was too long, as I never did like to stand very long in the hot sun without
the liberty of leaving when I got tired."[22]

On June 29 Moody departed for Nashville, where he joined his regiment. Col. Charles W. B. Allison of the Eighty-fifth Ohio, a three-month
regiment, succeeded him. Capt. Henry M. Lazelle, whom Hoffman sent
in July to inspect the camp, said of Allison, "He is utterly ignorant of the
most common requirements of the Army Regulations, but a 'good lawyer'
or he is said to be." The inspector further charged that "he has no knowledge of the importance of discipline and of the effect upon it of citizens
lounging in great numbers about the camp. It is pleasing to him to talk
and guide and explain to them all curious points of interest." He concluded that Allison was "not in any degree a soldier." He was, however,
the son-in-law of the lieutenant governor, and he remained in command
until his term of service expired. On September 26 Maj. Peter Zinn of
the Governor's Guards, a unit organized specifically for service at Camp
Chase, succeeded him.[23]

With Tod jockeying with federal officers for control of the camp and
a revolving door command structure in place, conditions at Camp Chase
were in a constant state of flux. It often appeared that inconsistency was
the only consistent policy at the post. This did not always bode well for the
prisoners, who were caught in the middle of the confusion. Despite the
many reports of "license" allowed Confederate officers, the vast majority
of prisoners was kept confined at the camp. As a parade of guards and
commanders passed through, trying to develop coherent policies for the
unprecedented number of prisoners arriving proved a daunting challenge.
Whatever the motives of the Union officials, the lack of a stable command structure virtually guaranteed that the conditions of the Confederate captives would fall far short of ideal.

Determining just how far short of ideal those conditions fell—and
why—is one of the most difficult challenges of Civil War historiography.
No aspect of the war, it seems, was more fraught with—and obfuscated
by—emotion. Published postwar accounts from both sides of the Mason-
Dixon Line were marred by exaggerations and dubious charges against

the sadistic barbarians who ran the enemy's prison pens. Not everyone, however, waited until the guns had ceased firing to launch accusations. Early on, soldiers and government officials on both sides of the conflict recognized the propaganda value of charging each other with acts of cruelty against defenseless prisoners. Divining where the facts end and the propaganda begins poses a serious challenge for anybody wishing to determine the truth about Civil War prisons.

In November 1861, A. J. Morey, editor of the *News*, a Cynthiana, Kentucky, paper, escaped from Camp Chase. An account of his stay in Ohio was printed in the *Nashville Avalanche* and presumably many other newspapers. In it Morey marshaled all his skills as a writer to paint a picture of shameless barbarity at the Union camp. Prisoners, he wrote, were "almost naked and were engaged in perpetual strife with the vermin with which the loathsome den literally swarmed." Except for the bread, Morey asserted, the food was "of the most inferior kind and in insufficient quantities for the sustenance of the famishing men." In addition, prison officials supplied only five small sticks of wood each day for cooking to a mess of twenty-five prisoners. The women of Columbus, he added, had asked permission to supply comfortable bedding for the captives but had been denied by prison officials. "When these kind-hearted ladies visited us in our vile prison and beheld our wretched condition," Morey wrote, "they involuntarily burst into tears."[24]

Morey's account contained a few minor factual errors. He placed Camp Chase four miles south of Columbus, when in reality it was west of the city. He also wrote that the prison took up half an acre of ground. It was actually much larger. Beyond that, his statement that the prisoners' "only offense was that we dissented from the measures of Lincoln" suggested that the writer had a political motive.[25]

It does not follow that Morey's claims were totally without foundation. Officers' reports during the late summer and fall of 1861 bear out much of what the editor wrote. On August 25 the officer of the day reported that the sick in the prison hospital were greatly in need of blankets. One patient had none of his own and had to depend upon a friend for the use of his. Four days later it was reported that the prisoners had inadequate facilities for washing their clothes. All had to rely upon the single pump available. "A tub should be furnished to them," the officer of the day suggested. "Our prisoners of war are not comfortable," the September 8 report stated. "Some lack blankets and other complain of filth and vermin on their persons." These poor conditions were not endured only by Confederate prisoners. "I would call the attention of the commandant of the camp to the miserable condition of the brigade prison," wrote the officer of the day on October 28. This and similar subsequent reports suggest that apathy and ineptitude had more to do with poor conditions than deliberate hostility.[26]

Camp Chase officials eventually made some attempts to address the problems of the military prison. One action placed much of the responsibility on the prisoners themselves. On October 10 they were given the authority to select three of their fellow prisoners, one to be superintendent and chief executive officer, the others to serve as assistant stewards. All appointments were to be approved by the camp commander. They were authorized to "make and enforce all such rules, regulations and orders as to the care, distribution and cooking of rations, the cleanliness and comfort of the quarters, the sanitary condition of the prison and the health, peace and order of the inmates." Later in October cavalry blankets reported to be unfit for service were forwarded to the prison. An October 30 order required that a different officer be appointed each week to "inquire daily into the sanitary condition and security of [the] prisoners" and make any change he deemed proper.[27]

The influx of prisoners following the fall of Fort Donelson necessitated more regulations. In February 1862, camp officials addressed a longstanding problem when they hired a local woman to wash the prisoners' clothing. Governor Tod, signing his correspondence as "Governor and Commander in Chief," continued to keep involved in the operations of the camp. On March 2 he issued what he termed "definite and specific instructions" to handle "the recent large addition of prisoners." All captives were to give up their arms, which would be "marked and carefully preserved so that each may at the proper time be restored." Detailed descriptive lists of the prisoners were to be made without delay. Tod further ordered that the prisoners be divided into "conveniently sized messes" and that officers and men be separated. The commander could permit family members to visit prisoners but only outside the prison area of the camp and under strict supervision. Prisoners could also receive money from outside to purchase items from the camp sutler. Perhaps most significant, Tod said prisoners were to receive "the same rations that are allowed to our private soldiers."[28]

Col. Moody added a lengthy list of regulations to the governor's orders.

Under Moody's instructions prisoners were responsible for their personal cleanliness and that of their quarters and yards. Any prisoner "committing a nuisance away from the sinks" was to be punished. None could approach closer than ten feet to the fence, bringing to Camp Chase the "dead line" that would become a fixture of Civil War prisons. Although Tod permitted visitors, Moody insisted that such visits be brief, "and if any language disrespectful to the government of the United States is used, the interview will be immediately terminated." Moody restricted letters to and from the prisoners to two pages and made all such letters subject to inspection. Prisoners were required to "be respectful in their language and deportment" toward Union soldiers. At the same time Union officers and men were "strictly forbidden to use any insulting or ungentlemanly language towards any prisoner."[29]

Among the many prisoners arriving at Camp Chase after the fall of Fort Donelson was Capt. Andrew Jackson Campbell of the Forty-eighth Tennessee Volunteers. On February 16 Campbell was placed aboard the riverboat *Neptune* along with a contingent of prisoners from the Third Tennessee. "Much suffering was caused among the prisoners," Campbell wrote in his diary the next day, "by the boat being so crowded and so many being sick from exposure and bad diet and water." Because of the crowding the men had to "pile up like hogs" at night to lie down on a deck that was covered "with mud, slop, and tobacco spittle, well tramped up through the day." Continuing down the Ohio and up the Mississippi, the boat dodged ice, and the captives endured the taunts of Union soldiers gathered along the shore. "Our boys, determined not to be outdone, cheered lustily for Jeff Davis," Campbell wrote on the 19th. The next day, Campbell noted in his diary, Union soldiers at two points responded to the prisoners' cheers by firing at the boat, wounding several captives.[30]

The *Neptune* reached St. Louis late on the 20th. The next day the enlisted men were sent to the Camp Douglas prison in Chicago. The officers were transferred to the *Hiawatha*, which was anchored offshore. They received rations of bread, raw pork, and "half-cooked beef." Southern sympathizers from the city approached on ferryboats and attempted to supplement the prisoners' rations by throwing apples to them. Federal officials arrested some of them and threatened others.

After remaining six days in the middle of the Mississippi aboard the *Hiawatha,* the men were taken to the Illinois shore and marched a mile. There they boarded railroad cars and started east. Their route took them through Terre Haute and Indianapolis and into Ohio. At Xenia, where the men arrived on the evening of February 28, abolitionists approached the train and tried to talk a captured slave into leaving his master. "Among them," Campbell wrote with disgust, "was a free negro."[31]

On the morning of March 1, the prisoners reached Columbus, where they received "bean coffee in tubs, crackers, and raw meat." From the city they marched the four miles to Camp Chase. The frozen ground had thawed, and the march was a muddy one. Campbell ended up in Prison 1, one of three adjoining prisons at the camp. It and Prison 2 were small, holding only a few hundred captives. Prison 3 was larger. It had recently housed Union trainees, and at the time of Campbell's arrival was not yet ready to house the Confederates. Tod had kept his promise to Halleck that Camp Chase would be ready to accommodate a thousand prisoners, but with the largest of the prisons not yet available, those accommodations were less than desirable. Campbell noted that there were shanties for only about one-third of the prisoners. "Tents were stretched in the mud for those to pile up in who could not get into the shanties." Campbell continued, "Our clothing was all left outside to be examined and we were tramping around like a herd of swine, so thick we could hardly turn around."[32]

The men lacked plates and cutlery, and they had "a very scant supply of wood" with which to cook. Rations were adequate, but Campbell complained of "bad soap" and no dishrags to clean the camp kettles they used for cooking. As a result, the Tennessee soldier recorded on March 3, "Everything was what we would call at home very filthy, not fit for a dog to eat." As time went on, the conditions improved somewhat. On March 8 several prisoners, including Campbell, were moved to Prison 3. With the largest of the three prisons now in use, all were now adequately housed. On March 21 each of the prisoners in Campbell's mess received a shirt and a pair of socks, the first clothing issued to them since their arrival.[33]

As his living situation improved, Campbell's main source of irritation was the prison commander's political outlook. "Col. Moody will not permit any paper to come in the prison," he wrote on March 25, "that does not advocate the mobbing of paroled prisoners, the hanging of all Rebels and the petting of the negro." A week later he noted that Moody had sent in sergeants to bring out all the black prisoners. Then, "he proceeded to speak soothing words to his favorite race, telling them that they had been wronged by the wicked men of the South and that they need not serve their masters any longer." Campbell was pleased to record that at least one beneficiary refused to be emancipated. "Dick, a boy belonging to Captain Clopton, told Moody that he did not want to be free, but that he wanted to go to Dixie." Campbell got away from Moody on May 1, when he and some two hundred other prisoners were transferred to Johnson's Island.[34]

For James Calvin Cook, another Tennessee soldier captured at Fort Donelson, the journey to Columbus had a number of parallels with Campbell's experience. Although nobody shot at his boat, Cook did record that someone threw rocks at the vessel. At St. Louis, he, too, was put aboard the *Hiawatha*. Like Campbell, he was heartened by the displays of sympathy shown the prisoners by civilians at St. Louis. The women, Cook noted, were not deterred by the threat of arrest. "That dont stop them," he wrote in his diary, adding, "When ever the ladies can by any means get the name of any officer on bord they are sure to send them some thing that they supose they kneed."[35]

Cook may have been aboard the same train as Campbell. In any event, he also reached Columbus on March 1. Arriving at 6:00 a.m., he recorded that the Ohio capital was a "thriving looking city." He wrote that it had a "magnificent State House tho not equal to that of Tennessee." He received coffee and some meat, his first meal since leaving St. Louis, then marched the four miles to Camp Chase. The accommodations were cloth tents and straw for bedding. Despite the conditions, Cook slept well his first night, catching up on the sleep he had lost while aboard the train. "Waking up the next morning," he wrote, "one could fully realize that we were prisoners of war." Provisions of bacon, beef, crackers, potatoes, beans, hominy, coffee, and sugar were plentiful. Wood was not. This not only made cooking difficult, but with the weather frigid and snow falling, the men were soon "suffering with violent colds." As the temperature warmed, water seeped into the tents. Cook noted, "The officers show every sign of having our welfare in view," furnishing planks for flooring. On March 6 Cook moved into "a cabin," which, he wrote, "renders us as comfortable as one could be under the circumstances."[36]

Beyond the physical discomforts, finding a way to pass the time was the most trying aspect of prison life. "I begin to feel greatly the want of mental stimulant," Capt. John Henry Guy of Virginia's Goochland Light Artillery wrote on April 15. Another Fort Donelson captive, Guy complained of being virtually alone in a sea of fellow prisoners. "No exercise, no regular employment, being in a crowd all the time, with little in common with most of those one meets, little advantage of books, & too much bustle for the mind to get heated in pursuit of any train of thought," he complained, "these are circumstances powerful in inducing bodily & mental lethargy." Guy found it hard to read "with the hum of conversation & the ring of laughter in my ear." He also expressed disgust with prisoners he clearly considered his inferiors. Frequently, he wrote, he had to "avoid the advances of some bore" or "dodge contact with some dirty looking wretch who looks as if he had some contagious disease."[37]

Yet another soldier taken at Fort Donelson, Timothy McNamara of the Fourth Mississippi, also tried to find solace in reading. "Myself and a few others read every thing that we can get," he wrote on March 23. The other men in his mess found what McNamara considered dichotomous methods of passing the time. Going to bed early one Sunday evening, he could hear the prayers of some men through the partitions "except when the poker players get into a squabble over their game." Despite such squabbles, McNamara was pleased to record that there was "not a great deal of profanity." Capt. Guy also noted that card playing was the "chief amusement" in his mess. He received a certain amount of entertainment observing "the fascination cards seem to have for those who are just learning to play." Many of the participants, he noted, had never played before arriving at Camp Chase. "The rage," he predicted, "will to some extent die away."[38]

Occasionally visiting speakers replaced the monotony of prison life with disgust. One such guest was William G. "Parson" Brownlow. A Tennessean who had remained loyal to the Union, he was viewed as a patriot by Col. Moody and as a traitor and abolitionist by the prisoners. Among the latter was Lt. Joseph Warren Westbrook of the Fourth Mississippi. In his memoirs Westbrook recalled that Brownlow tried to persuade his fellow Southerners to sign the oath of allegiance and, at least figuratively, lay down their arms. "If he got anyone," Westbrook noted, "I never found it out." All he could remember of Brownlow's speech was his assertion that "the Confederacy was about out of soap." An officer of the Forty-ninth Tennessee wrote that Brownlow was jeered from his platform soon after he started to speak. Another Tennessee Unionist, Andrew Johnson, arrived at Camp Chase on March 31. Referring to Johnson as "His Mightiness," McNamara wrote that the future president "kindly notified us that he will in *private* hear our application for *pardon.*" To that McNamara simply responded, "Bah."[39]

McNamara's defiant tone is definitely lacking in the letters sent from Camp Chase by the prisoners. Camp officials screened all outgoing correspondence. As a result, surviving letters are generally lacking in useful information about life in the prisons. One of the largest collections of letters from 1862 is contained in the Camp Chase Papers at the Virginia Historical Society. According to one account, they were written after Mrs. Charlotte Moon Clark, an Ohio resident of Virginia ancestry, offered to deliver the prisoners' mail to Virginia. Union officials became suspicious of her, and she fled to Niagara Falls, Ontario. As a result, the letters remained undelivered. They were discovered some forty years later at the State Library of Ohio.[40]

The positive tone of the letters and the similarities of many of the comments suggest that the prisoners were given instructions concerning what to write. There is, however, no direct evidence that this was the case. J. P. Jackson told his father, "We have good quarters & good rations & very kind treatment." Writing to his parents, Charles Ray remarked, "I assure you that we are well cared for here plenty to eat." In a letter to his family, W. A. H. Shackelford wrote, "The [prison] officers treat us kindly and give us aplenty to eat." Similarly, W. J. Rogers informed his mother, "The officers in charge are vary kind to us we have no wright to complain." Letters from M. S. Miller, Z. M. Hall, and M. B. Locke, all written on April 21, are very similar in their observations. "We have a plenty to eat and verry good quarters to stay in," Miller wrote to his family. In a letter to Mrs. S. S. Griffen, Hall wrote, "[We] get plenty to eat and have [a] good house to stay in." Locke wrote in the same vein, informing Mrs. John F. Allen, "[We] get plenty to eat and have very good quarters." Some of the letters are so positive as to test the reader's credulity. S. M. E. Russell claimed to be eating so well that he was "getting very fleshy, and too big for my clothes." Added J. W. Haywood, "This is the best prison I ever saw we live as well here as in any of our hotels in Dixie."[41]

Only a few negative observations crept into the prisoners' letters, and those tended to be innocuous. "Am treated very well although rather crowded," A. S. Levy wrote to his sister. After insisting that he, too, was well treated, Charles A. Ray still lamented to his brother that there was "nothing to do but cook eate sleepe [and] read." Perhaps the most extreme complaints to get past the censors were those of John B. Stuart. In a letter to his wife, Stuart said he had to sleep on "a hard plank." He added, "Our prison is very damp and the house we are in leaks very bad."[42]

Prisoner J. W. Rush, who was captured at Island No. 10, wrote in much the same vein. "The treatment we all receive is very courteous and kind," he informed his wife on April 19. "Indeed so clever are they," he continued, "that I am very much astonished." The food, Rush wrote, was wholesome and, contrary to the diary entries of others, he said that the prisoners' supply of wood was sufficient. "When you hear of barbarity, cruelty, and the like," he informed his wife, "just say it is *all false.*" Rush insisted, "I have not seen the *least bit of it.*"[43]

If Rush's claims were true, it was despite a system that allowed for very little consistency in the guarding of the prisoners. The regiments of Camp Chase's early commanders served as prison guards. The frequent changes in command, therefore, resulted in an equally frequent turnover in the guard force. During Col. Moody's tenure, it was reported that four companies of his regiment were constantly required to guard the prisoners after the Fort Donelson captives began to arrive.[44]

As for the quality of guards, such evidence that survives suggests that it was mixed at best. In August 1861 a sentinel was charged with sleeping at his post. Upon closer examination, the officer of the day reported, "The guard was found to have swallowed tobacco juice (accidentally), which caused him to vomit until he slept from exhaustion." The unfortunate sentry was released from confinement. More serious was the November 15 report that several German-born guards could not understand English well enough to be certain of their duties. Those who could be certain often found ways to avoid performing them. Writing to his wife in March 1862, Thomas M. Covert of the Sixth Ohio Volunteer Cavalry reported, "There is so damd many that makes sick to be relieved of gard that it makes gard duty come round pretty often." On January 13, 1862, the officer commanding the guard reported that members of the Sixty-seventh Ohio "became very disorderly" when they learned that not enough men had shown up to relieve them at the 9:00 p.m. changing of the guard. "One contended that he had as good a rite to be relieved as another," the officer reported, "so they nearly all went to there quarters." Several noncommissioned officers and privates of the relief detail could not be found. The officer of the guard wrote down the names of those who failed to appear. But, he went on to explain, "It being night the list got lost." Three nights later the same officer reported, "There is a great indifference manifested in the non commissioned officers in regard to gard duty." A sergeant from the Fifty-eighth Ohio, he wrote, had reported for duty half an hour late and was then not seen the rest of the night.[45]

If the men were less than dedicated, their equipment was often less than desirable. On October 14, 1861, the officer of the guard reported, "The arms for use of the guards are in very bad condition, many of them being partially filed with mud and trash." On January 3, 1862, the officer of the guard requested a lantern for the use of the sentinels. The request was repeated on March 22. Guardhouses were reported to be in "such a condition that it is almost inhuman to compel *soldiers* to remain there." The situation was so bad that the men often went to their own barracks after being relieved, rather than remaining in the nearby guardhouses as they were supposed to when they were off duty for only a short time. As a result, reinforcements were frequently not available when needed.[46]

Despite the shortcomings of both the guards and their equipment, escapes from Camp Chase were rare. Indeed, there are few official accounts of escape attempts during the facility's first year as a prison. It must be kept in mind, however, that record keeping at the camp was sporadic. For example, on Christmas Day, 1861, federal recruit John A. Smith informed his family that one of the prisoners tried to cut a hole through the prison wall. "The guard shot him down," Smith wrote, although he did not make clear how serious the wound was. On May 9, 1862, Thomas M. Covert wrote in a letter to his wife, "There was another Secesh escaped from the Hospital last night." How many had gotten away before this incident Covert did not say. Surviving camp records mention neither incident.[47]

A potential mass escape was averted on May 28, 1862, when Col. Henry B. Carrington, the quartermaster general who had drawn the ire of the Ohio General Assembly, led a detachment of 104 men from the Eighteenth United States Infantry to Camp Chase. Carrington's force came from Camp Thomas, which was located about four miles north of Columbus. The colonel reported that he acted "upon the pressing requisition of Governor Tod and [former] Governor Dennison." The guard at Camp Chase had diminished, and Col. Moody advised Carrington that "only immediate support in force would prevent open outbreak."[48]

Carrington was skeptical of Moody's plea, but upon arrival he found the situation as serious as described. "Occupants of the different barracks would pelt the sentries with chunks of bread," he later reported, "jeer at them on the sentry platforms, step across the clearly indicated 'dead line,' sing aloud and go from building to building during sleep with undisguised contempt." This outward defiance came from the enlisted men. Among the officers there was "a spirit of insubordination that indicated a proposed outbreak, when sufficiently organized for the purpose." Carrington immediately replaced the camp guard with his men. They were clad in full dress uniforms, complete with white gloves, polished shoes, and felt hats with ostrich plumes. Occupying the sentry platforms, they followed "the most rigid rules as to sentry duty." After giving the prisoners time to observe the regulars in action, Carrington and Moody met with the Confederate officers, informing them that "open mutiny would be fatal to all concerned." The result, according to Carrington: "There prevailed a marked decorum throughout the Prison Camp."[49]

In early July 1862, a group of prisoners in Prison 3 attempted to dig their way out of camp. Camp officials discovered the plot, and on July 8 the prisoners in the rooms where the tunnels were located were placed on half rations and denied mail privileges and candles. The rations were restored two days later. Writing home about the incident, members of the Eighty-fifth Ohio said fifty guards were sent to investigate rumors concerning the tunnels. "The investigation confirmed the rumor," they wrote. "Some four subterranean channels were discovered leading from [the prisoners'] quarters to the fence, some of them ten or twelve feet in length and large enough to admit a man." The soldiers continued, "How they succeeded in secreting shovels and picks to execute their plans is yet a mystery." Three months later the investigation of an escape attempt from Prison 1 pointed toward the camp sutler as the source of "tools used for such purpose." Camp officials immediately ordered that the sutler's "stand be closed from any further dealing or intercourse with prisoners."[50]

One of the largest escapes from Camp Chase occurred on September 17, 1862. Twenty-two prisoners got away, although all but seven were later recaptured, most in neighboring Madison County. Col. Allison offered a reward of $600 for their apprehension. This drew a sharp rebuke from Hoffman. The commissary general of prisoners wrote, "You were not authorized to pay rewards for the apprehension of prisoners . . . nor do I deem it proper to pay rewards at all. Such a course would be little short of an encouragement to the guard to neglect their duty for the purpose of gaining a reward for the apprehension of prisoners who had escaped through their neglect or perhaps connivance."[51]

Hoffman's letter was an indication that the federal government was finally wresting control of Camp Chase from Governor Tod and other state officials. A lieutenant colonel of the Eighth United States Infantry, Hoffman had been named commissary general of prisoners on October 23, 1861. He brought to the job a certain measure of experience as a military prisoner. His regiment had been surrendered to Texas officials in February 1861 by Gen. David Twiggs, although he and his fellows were almost immediately paroled. Except for a period of a few months in 1864 and 1865, Hoffman would remain in the post for the duration of the war. He brought to the job a genuine concern for the welfare of Confederate prisoners—though it was a concern tempered by Hoffman's almost obsessive penchant for cost cutting.[52]

Even before Hoffman's appointment was made official, Quartermaster General Montgomery Meigs ordered him to locate a site for a new Union prison. Meigs knew the war would result in significant numbers of prisoners, and he wanted to be ready. He instructed Hoffman to examine a group of islands on Lake Erie near Sandusky, Ohio for their suitability. After a thorough round of island hopping, Hoffman recommended Johnson's Island. Meigs approved the choice, and Hoffman secured a lease and set to work establishing the camp. On February 24, 1862, he informed the quartermaster general that the camp was "ready to receive a limited number of prisoners." By then Fort Donelson had fallen. Although the facility was not yet ready for the large number of captives that had suddenly fallen into Union hands, Meigs's concerns had been proven prescient.[53]

The establishment of Johnson's Island had monopolized Hoffman's time and forced him to neglect the situation at the other Union prisons. Once the Lake Erie depot was established, he immediately turned his attention to Camp Chase. Hoffman headed to Columbus, and on February 28 he sent Tod a message that was both forceful and diplomatic. "In virtue of my office of commissary-general of prisoners, I am invested with the supervision of all prisoners of war," Hoffman wrote. He immediately added, "In the performance of these duties it will afford me much pleasure to consult with you in relation to those at Camp Chase." Hoffman then went on to explain several decisions regarding the camp that he had made without consulting Tod. The most significant was to fence the area occupied by trainees, converting it into Prison 3. The commissary general had also made arrangements with the assistant quartermaster to provide clothing, bedding, and "cooking utensils as may be absolutely requisite."[54]

Hoffman strengthened his control over operations at Camp Chase in July when he sent Capt. Lazelle on his inspection trip. This was the visit that left Lazelle unimpressed with Col. Allison. His opinion of conditions at the camp were equally low. Lazelle reported thoroughly on each of the three prisons. Number 3, the largest, contained about eleven hundred prisoners. They were housed in buildings that were twenty by fourteen feet. Eighteen men, Lazelle wrote, "could be made comfortable in each." The huts were arranged in clusters of six, separated by narrow streets. "Had the materials of each cluster been appropriated in erecting a single building," Lazelle observed, "more room, better accommodations and an infinitely better arrangement of the camp as regards health and comfort would have been secured." Instead, "The spaces between the clusters of the quarters are heaped with the vilest accumulations of filth which has remained there for months, breeding sickness and pestilence." Streets, drains, and gutters were in the same condition. The sinks were "open excavations with a single rail placed over them lengthwise." Drainage was not sufficient, Lazelle added, to carry away the waste. As a result of all this, "The air of the camp, and more particularly of the prison, is polluted and the stench is horrible." The inspector noted that the prisoners, federal soldiers, doctors, and even the camp commander and Governor Tod had complained of the situation. Despite that, "Not a step has been taken to remedy this terrible abomination."[55]

Prison 2, Lazelle reported, had three buildings, each about a hundred by fifteen feet. Two were well constructed. The third was somewhat smaller and much more poorly built. It sat on low ground, making it damp, and the roof leaked. There were two buildings in Prison 1, roughly the same size as those in Prison 2. Both were raised from the ground, with vertical boards extending around them below the floor. Lazelle's only recommendations for the enclosure were to remove the lower boards, which would improve ventilation, and to clean up "the accumulations of earth and rubbish from their sides and vicinity." The inspector reported that there were about 250 prisoners in Prison 2 and 150 in Prison 1.[56]

The provisions supplied to the prisoners Lazelle considered "very inferior." Beef issues were necks and shanks, and the salt pork was of poor quality. The bread he described as "sour, dark, and heavy," the beans and peas "as bad as they can be." The rice, sugar, molasses, potatoes, and coffee were no better, Lazelle reported. Even the salt he described as being "coarsely ground." Lazelle did, however, note that the bacon and cornmeal were good. The soap issued the prisoners was "seldom resinous and never as good as the worst commonly issued in the Army."[57]

Lazelle traced much of the problem to Allison, who signed requisitions for rations "without inquiry generally." The result, Lazelle asserted, was, "The most extensive frauds have been constantly committed in the issues." Nobody connected with the camp inspected the rations upon their arrival. Rather, they were "dealt out by the contractors alone, pitched into a cart in the coarsest roughest manner." When Lazelle questioned the agents making the deliveries, they were "insolent at my interference. . . . They even attempted to inform me that necks were always issued in the Regular Army." As for Allison, "The commanding officer is ignorant of any method of remedying this, but resignedly informed me that he thought it wrong."[58]

Before departing, Lazelle left a lengthy and detailed list of instructions for Allison and other camp officials. To address the poor sanitary conditions, the quartermaster was to dig vaults at least ten feet deep in each of the three prisons. New privies were to be built, and drainage facilities were to be constructed to assure that all filth was carried outside the camp. Lazelle ordered that the main sewer be thoroughly cleaned and planked over. Leaky roofs were to be repaired in the barracks and floors raised. To increase room for cooking, Lazelle called for outside shanties that would house "Farmer's Boilers," forty-gallon cooking boilers that Hoffman was soon recommending for all prisons. The quartermaster would be responsible for seeing to it that sufficient rations of wood were issued. Lazelle expected prisoners to perform the labor on the various projects "so far as it is practicable."[59]

Addressing the problem of rations, Lazelle ordered Allison to appoint immediately "a high-toned and careful officer" to serve as assistant post commissary. This officer would deal directly with contractors. Specifically, he would make sure that "the precise amount called for" was received from them. In addition, Allison was to "see by a frequent personal inspection" that provisions be "of the first quality."[60]

Lazelle's inspection seemed to snap Allison out of his lethargy, and the commander quickly issued orders to put the inspector's demands into effect. Prison Order No. 4, issued on July 16, addressed many of Lazelle's concerns. First came the construction of the privies. They were to be built to Lazelle's exact specifications, from a capacity of fifteen men all the way down to such details as hinge covers to contain the stench. The order also called for an extensive program of trenching, whitewashing, and cleaning. Buildings were ordered raised, galleries for sentinels were to be erected, and roofs were to be repaired. Allison ordered that the prisoners be issued one hundred brooms and twenty-gallon tubs. He had the Farmer's Boilers placed outside the barracks and covered by shelters. All of these instructions matched Lazelle's orders to the letter.[61]

Prison Order No. 5, issued the next day, addressed more of the issues Lazelle had raised. The order required the prisons to be "thoroughly policed" at 6:30 a.m. and 4:30 p.m. each day. The prisoners were to perform the work under the supervision of two "Officers of Police." Those officers would also conduct the roll call every morning. They were required to "be present personally and satisfy [themselves] of the presence of the prisoners."[62]

Lazelle returned in late July and pronounced himself pleased with the progress being made. He informed Hoffman, "A marked change is observed in the health, cleanliness, police and comfort of the prisoners and decidedly for the better." The Farmer's Boilers were in operation, and fresh beef was being issued five times a week. The prisons received a thorough policing twice a day. On August 4 Lazelle reported that all the drainage projects were completed. In addition, the huts had been raised, and the new privies were all in operation. The previously overpowering stench was "almost removed."[63]

There was one exception to Lazelle's glowing report. The inspector charged that Capt. Benjamin P. Walker, the post commissary, was neglecting his duties. Allison informed Lazelle that Walker had been at camp only three days during the previous two weeks. During his absence a civilian clerk carried out the commissary duties. Lazelle further charged that Walker was "either willfully neglectful of the quality of the provisions furnished under the contract or grossly ignorant of what should be required." Lazelle included a number of statements supporting his charges. Hoffman was persuaded, and he informed Stanton of the situation. Stanton concurred, and Walker was dismissed from the service. Things might have ended there had Walker not had a powerful friend, Congressman

Schuyler Colfax of Indiana. Colfax produced a wounded soldier who accused Lazelle of drunkenness and otherwise pulled strings, and on December 2, President Lincoln ordered Walker restored to his position.[64]

The problems Lazelle discovered at Camp Chase were not unique to the Ohio prison. Lazelle's visit followed an inspection trip Hoffman made to the major western prisons in March in which his findings were similar. His first stop was Camp Morton. Although he found the Confederates at the Indianapolis prison "as well cared for as could be expected under the circumstances," he ordered a number of improvements. Among them were to put windows in the barracks occupied by the prisoners and to lessen the crowding in those barracks. Camp Butler, he reported, was "in a very unfavorable condition." He found the quarters poorly policed and the health of the prisoners not good. "The hospitals are crowded and are in a deplorable condition," he informed Meigs, "and the sick could not well be more uncomfortable." The supply of water was insufficient, Hoffman continued. Finally, he reported, "The camp is not inclosed and the detention of the prisoners thus depends more on their willingness to remain than on any restraints upon them by the guard."[65]

Although Hoffman's initial inspection of Camp Douglas was positive, he changed his mind when he returned in late June. The commissary general of prisoners reported to Meigs that the barracks were crowded, the sinks were overflowing, and the entire camp was "in a very foul condition from want of drainage." Hoffman placed the blame on Col. James A. Mulligan, the recently departed camp commander. Reporting to Adj. Gen. Lorenzo Thomas on recent escapes from the camp, Hoffman charged, "There has been the greatest carelessness and willful neglect in the management of the affairs of the camp, and everything was left by Colonel Mulligan in a shameful state of confusion." Hoffman concluded that the situation was so poor that the camp should be abandoned. However, with no other site available, "there seems now no alternative but to make the best of what we have."[66]

As Hoffman left Chicago, Capt. Henry W. Freedley, a member of his staff, was making follow-up inspections of the other camps. Freedley visited Camp Butler on July 4 and found many problems remaining. He discovered that much of the guard force consisted of men who had been enlisted only a few days. "These regiments are perfectly inexperienced troops," Freedley reported. As at Camp Chase, there was a frequent turnover of regiments responsible for guarding the prisoners. "It appears that the guard have been changed so often," Freedley wrote, "that the instructions heretofore given [by Hoffman] have not been so strictly observed as might be desired." Lost in the confusion were the names and numbers of prisoners who had recently died or escaped.[67]

Continuing on to Alton Prison, Freedley discovered, "The commanding officer has not given as much of his personal attention to the prison as was required." There, too, the names of prisoners who had escaped were not to be obtained. Freedley found the prisoners to be lacking clothing, and he reported that the policing of the prison was unsatisfactory.[68]

For a time it appeared that the shortcomings of Camp Chase and the other prisons might not matter much longer. On July 22 Union general John A. Dix and Confederate general Daniel H. Hill agreed to a cartel for the exchange of prisoners. Patterned after a similar arrangement used during the War of 1812, it calculated a sliding scale for captives of different ranks. In the North the cartel represented a victory for public pressure over the Lincoln administration's desire to avoid any kind of formal recognition of the Confederacy. Among the first to be exchanged was the commissary general of prisoners, Hoffman still being under parole following the Texas surrender.[69]

Prisoners from Camp Chase and other western camps were taken to Vicksburg for exchange. Adj. Gen. Thomas, who was in overall command of the exchange process, ordered Capt. Lazelle to supervise those sent from western prisons. In addition to Camp Chase, these included Camp Morton, Camp Douglas, Johnson's Island, Camp Butler, and the military prison at Alton. On August 24 Hoffman ordered Col. Allison to prepare for the transfer. The prisoners were to be sent under guard and provided with two days' rations. Transportation would be by rail to Cairo, Illinois, then by river to Vicksburg. The commander of the guard was to be alert to prevent escapes and to ensure that the prisoners were not "interfered with in any way at stopping places along the route." Prisoners who did not wish to be exchanged and return to the South could take the oath of allegiance. On August 25 Hoffman ordered Capt. C. A. Young to take his company, plus ten additional men, as guards for the Vicksburg trip.[70]

Hoffman's August orders implied that all Camp Chase prisoners, some 1,200, would be exchanged at once, a fact seemingly confirmed by local press accounts. Camp records show that 1,096 were exchanged during the month. Yet, despite the exchanges, Confederates continued to arrive at the camp. On September 13 Hoffman reported this fact to Adj. Gen. Thomas.

The situation confused the commissary general since "provision is made in the cartel as I have seen it published in the papers for their immediate release on parole." Hoffman's concern proved unfounded, and soon the prisoners were again headed south. Camp records indicate that at least seven more groups were sent for exchange between October 27 and December 23. Their numbers ranged from the 29 sent out on the latter date to the 177 who departed for Cairo on November 19.[71]

With the cartel in effect, it appeared that Camp Chase's days as a prison camp were numbered. On August 10 Hoffman predicted, "Camp Chase will probably be abandoned as a military prison." However, as the Confederates departed, the cartel was responsible for a new class of men arriving at Camp Chase. They were paroled Union soldiers, men who were not quite prisoners but not exactly free, either. Their presence would present officials with an entirely new set of problems. It would also present Camp Chase with a new, albeit temporary, role in its evolution as a federal prison.[72]

3

Parole Camp

For thousands of families, Northern and Southern, whose relatives were being held as prisoners of war, the signing of the exchange cartel was a source of tremendous relief. For Union officials it quickly became a source of problems. Chief among them was the realization by Union soldiers that capture now meant a quick release and a furlough home until they were exchanged. This produced a strong incentive to straggle in the direction of an enemy camp to obtain what one referred to as a "little rest from soldiering." Generals in the field quickly realized this, but under the terms of the cartel they could do little to stop the practice.[1]

It was Governor Tod who offered a solution. Writing to Stanton on September 9, 1862, following a Union defeat at Richmond, Kentucky, Tod complained, "The freedom in giving paroles by our troops in Kentucky is very prejudicial to the service and should be stopped." Stanton agreed, noting, "There is reason to fear that many voluntarily surrender for the sake of getting home." The secretary admitted that it was "difficult to see what remedy can be applied." The governor had one in mind. Realizing the Sioux in Minnesota were on the warpath, he asked, "If the Indian troubles in Minnesota are serious and the paroled Union soldiers are not soon to be exchanged, would it not be well to send them to Minnesota?" Stanton pronounced the suggestion "excellent" and assured Tod that it would be "immediately acted upon."[2]

Tod's concern was pressing because Camp Chase had become the rendezvous for thousands of unruly parolees. On June 28, nearly a month before the cartel was formally signed, the War Department had issued a set of orders governing "sick men [and] paroled prisoners." The orders stated that no more furloughs would be granted to paroled prisoners. Those already granted were revoked. Parolees from eastern states were ordered to report to a camp of instruction near Annapolis, Maryland, soon to be rechristened Camp Parole. Soldiers from regiments raised in Virginia, Tennessee, Kentucky, Ohio, Indiana, and Michigan were sent to Camp Chase. Those from points farther west would head to Benton Barracks in Missouri. In his message to Stanton suggesting that the soldiers be sent to Minnesota, the governor explained, "It is with great difficulty we can preserve order among them [the paroled men] at Camp Chase."[3]

Although he promised to act upon Tod's suggestion, Stanton's reply to the governor may have been less than reassuring. He informed Tod that he was sending fifteen hundred more men to the camp. Stanton wanted them "kept in close quarters and drilled diligently every day, with no leave of absence." To carry out these instructions, Stanton sent Gen. Lew Wallace to Columbus with orders to organize the paroled men into regiments and brigades for service in Minnesota. Gen. Halleck informed Wallace of his orders on September 17 and ordered Brig. Gen. James Cooper, already in Columbus, to remain and assist him. Halleck gave Wallace a hint of the challenges ahead when he noted, "Officers will be sent to you as soon as possible."[4]

"That . . . order," Wallace wrote in his autobiography, "was intended deliberately and with malice aforethought to put me to shame." The future novelist considered declining the assignment and resigning his commission. Wallace wrestled all that night, he wrote, with his decision, finally deciding to pack his bags for Columbus. Upon arriving he was shocked by the quarters the paroled men were occupying. According to Wallace, "They were stained a rusty black; the windows were stuffed with old hats and caps; greasy blankets did duty for doors; the roofs were of plank, and in places planks were gone, leaving gaping crevices to skylight the dismal interior." As for the men, Wallace recalled, "Such a sight I had never seen or imagined." Their hair and whiskers had grown long, and most lacked coats, caps, or shoes. Many did not even have shirts, covering themselves instead with blankets. "I could see vermin crawling over their unwashed bodies," Wallace wrote, "while the smell with which the mass thickened the air was pungent and peculiar."[5]

On September 21 Wallace reported the situation to Adj. Gen. Thomas. He pronounced the men's quarters "uninhabitable" and "filthy beyond description. Why a plague has not visited the camp this summer will always be a mystery to me." Fewer than two thousand of the five thousand men who were supposed to be in the camp were present, "and if they have deserted," Wallace wrote, "they should not be blamed." All were owed at least some back pay, Wallace claimed, and some had not been paid in over a year. Scores had neither shoes nor socks, and many lacked breeches. "I assembled them on the parade ground and rode amongst them, and the smell from their ragged clothes was worse than that in an ill-conducted slaughterhouse." From what he had seen, the general concluded "that it would have been as well for them to be [prisoners] in a Richmond tobacco house closely confined as in Camp Chase treated as they are."[6]

Despite the bleak report, Wallace believed he could turn the men into an excellent outfit. He proposed to form them into a brigade of mounted rifles. If not sent to Minnesota for Indian duty, they could be used to suppress guerrillas after their exchange. "They are too valuable to be lost," Wallace wrote of the parolees. He deemed money to pay them, tents, and five thousand "arms of the best quality" to be "essential to the purpose."[7]

Tod joined Wallace in requesting that the men be paid. "It will be impossible for General Wallace to bring them to any kind of order or discipline," the governor wrote Stanton on September 22, "until they are paid, and I feel it my duty to so inform you." Tod's appeal apparently convinced Stanton. Despite protests from the paymaster general's office that thousands of men in the field were owed more back pay than the parolees, a special paymaster was dispatched to Columbus. Otherwise Stanton was less than sympathetic to Wallace's requests. "We have no tents," he brusquely informed the general. "You must cause temporary sheds to be erected." Arms would not be supplied until Wallace's forces were organized.[8]

Wallace did what he could with the resources he had available, but the results were mixed at best. His plan, as he explained it in a September 28 letter to Thomas, was to organize one regiment at a time. He informed the men that no one would receive pay or clothing until he was enrolled in a company. As the companies were formed, they were marched to the capitol building in Columbus for their pay. From there they continued on to Camp Lew Wallace, which was established just northwest of Camp Thomas. Cooper was in command of the camp, while Wallace maintained his headquarters in downtown Columbus. In establishing the new camp, Wallace hoped that "by separating the willing from the unwilling a better state of feeling might be brought about." He planned to use pay and new clothing as incentives to encourage the demoralized men to return to duty.[9]

Things did not work out as the general had planned. Wallace soon had one regiment organized and a second in progress. "But what will such regiments be worth?" he asked Thomas. Wallace answered his own question with excerpts from a morning report showing large numbers not present for duty. Rather than acting as an incentive to return to soldiering, the pay provided the financial means to desert. The officer of the guard had discovered during his morning rounds three muskets resting against trees and the sentinels "gone to parts unknown." One company, Wallace reported, had been marching to camp immediately after being paid when the soldiers suddenly dashed off down a cross street. The provost guard went after them, returning with about fifty. Wallace had the leaders sent to the penitentiary after they threatened the lives of their officers. In other cases men used false names to enroll in different companies and draw pay from all of them. Wallace virtually begged the War Department not to send any more parolees to the camp, explaining to Thomas, "Whoever gets into Camp Chase or comes in contact with its inmates is instantly seized with the mutinous spirit I have described." On September 29 he issued orders in an attempt to stop Camp Chase from being "turned into a loafing place." No more rations, Wallace announced, would be issued at the camp. The men remaining there could report for duty at Camp Lew Wallace "or lay at Camp Chase and starve, or desert and be dishonorably discharged and published accordingly."[10]

Twelve days later Wallace reported that the situation had improved. A force of men sent to assist with discipline had arrived at Camp Chase, and Wallace had placed the remaining unorganized parolees under guard. "In a day or two more," he informed Thomas, "I hope to be able to report the whole of them organized." On October 18 Wallace announced that he had done just that. "The order that sent me here is now fully complied with." Wallace left no doubt that he was ready to get away from Columbus and the paroled men. A brigade had been formed under the command of Gen. Cooper, he wrote, "and [Cooper] is amply able to manage his command." In case he had not made his intentions clear, Wallace concluded, "Having thus discharged all the duties required of me at this post I have no doubt of being permitted to take the field, with a command suitable to my rank."[11]

On November 4 Wallace departed for the Army of the Mississippi, and Cooper assumed command of all paroled prisoners in the vicinity of Columbus. Although Wallace insisted that he had fulfilled his mission, he left a number of problems in Cooper's lap. Before departing, Wallace instructed his successor to track down a number of absent man still at large. Even those officially present for duty often strayed from the camp. Many ventured to Columbus under the pretext of having papers that needed to be signed or to seek information about pending exchanges. An order issued December 4 admonished officers not to leave camp overnight. On at least one occasion an effort to get men to return to the camp resulted in even more absentees. On December 23 an order appeared in a Columbus newspaper requiring all absent men to report by January 5. Soldiers were soon departing, claiming that the order tacitly allowed them to go home if they returned by the specified date. Before the day was over, a second order was issued, clarifying the intent of the first.[12]

At times officials may have wished that all of the men had deserted. "Lewd women *have* been found dressed in soldiers' clothes in the quarters of the paroled forces," one report revealed, "and even whiskey has been sold by the dram out of canteens." Upon assuming command of Camp Lew Wallace, Gen. Cooper issued orders reminding the men that "all marauding and plundering is strictly prohibited." Despite these orders, complaints continued to come in from nearby farmers about their fence rails being burned and their hogs being killed. "Daily complaints [are] preferred to these Head Quarters," a November 4 order announced, "of insults and outrages perpetrated in this neighborhood and on the way between this camp and Columbus, on peacible citizens pursuing their ordinary avocations . . . by drunken and disorderly soldiers." The problems were not limited to civilians and their property. A January 21, 1863 circular complained of the "unnecessary destruction and damage to the public buildings at this camp." The men were informed, "It will be no excuse that soldiers have not received their allowance of wood."[13]

The most contentious question was whether the men's status as parolees excused them from basic military duties. Under the terms of their paroles they had agreed not to take up arms against the Confederacy or perform any duty that would free other men for such service. Many believed—or at least claimed to believe—that this excused them from drilling or policing the camp. Even some officers questioned whether they could be required to drill the men under their command. Although such basic duties would not have violated any parole terms, other orders the men received were more questionable. The brother of parolee Thomas Horner wrote to Stanton on September 4, complaining that Horner and his comrades had been placed on guard duty upon their arrival at Camp

Chase. "They refused to comply until exchanged," the man wrote, "and were reported to you as 'rebellious.'" Although he was lame, Horner was "willing to do what he can, but wishes first to be exchanged." His brother's only request was that the war secretary secure his exchange "at the earliest opportunity." On October 3 parolee Abner Royce of the Fifty-fifth Ohio informed his parents, "There is great dissatisfaction among the paroled men. General Wallace requires them to perform camp duty, when their parole *positively says they must not perform such duty until exchanged.*" Although Royce was still at Camp Chase, he had heard that the men at Camp Lew Wallace "were generally firm and stood up boldly for the rights of each other." The controversy was so intense that one man told Royce there was "a prospect of its terminating in a battle."[14]

One area of contention quickly proved moot. The men had objected strenuously, with much justification, to Governor Tod's plan to send them against the Sioux in Minnesota. Following his defeat at Second Manassas, John Pope had been sent west to suppress the Indian uprising. He found the Sioux to be a less troublesome foe than the Army of Northern Virginia. On October 9 Pope announced, "The Sioux war may be considered at an end," removing one source of controversy between the government and its paroled soldiers.[15]

Although government and military officials expressed shock at the men's behavior, the parolees brought a different perspective to the situation. "Let us see who these paroled men are," one of them wrote to the *Springfield Republic.* "They are men who have left comfortable homes and dear friends, and gone forth to battle for those rights so dear to every heart." After facing death and enduring capture and confinement, the soldier continued, they gave their parole and were allowed to return to the Union lines. "Then what?" he asked. "They were ordered to report at camps set apart for . . . the rebel prisoners." Their quarters "were very filthy and alive with vermin, no materials were furnished for cleaning said quarters, and no effort made by those in power to contribute to the comfort of the men."[16]

The soldier pointed out that the paroled men had been "content to serve their country and remain absent from their families" while in the field. However, since their arrival at the parole camps they were "doing no good for the service of their country" and felt entitled to a furlough. It was under these circumstances, he insisted, that many collected their pay and headed for home. "I do not say they did right in thus going without leave, but place yourself in their places, and then tell me what you would do if you had been absent from home as long as they had and then received such treatment here." Those who remained, he added, endured cold weather without being properly clad, while many had no blankets. Often, in an attempt to stay warm, they slept outdoors close to a fire. The soldier concluded, "Imagine all this and then tell me, have the paroled men nothing to complain of; and would it not have been better to have given them furloughs until exchanged?"[17]

Ohio soldier William L. Curry enjoyed a happier life as a paroled soldier. Arriving on August 13, Curry was among the early parolees to reach Columbus. After paying a brief visit to the camp the next morning—not even bothering to report at headquarters—he returned to Columbus to spend the night. Over the next four months he was away from camp at least as often as he was present. Trips to his home in neighboring Union County for "a fine buggy ride" or to thresh grain for his family occupied part of his time. He even ran a store for a friend one day. "Quite a comparison from hunting 'Butternuts' to measuring tape for the ladies," he recorded in his diary. When in the vicinity of Columbus, Curry was a frequent guest at parties. He also attended the theater and a minstrel show in Columbus.[18]

Curry did not record how he was able to get away from camp to enjoy such a festive social life; nor did he express any concern about possible arrest. On October 6 he received his commission as second lieutenant in the First Ohio Cavalry, and his status as an officer may have been a factor. He described Camp Chase as "dull and irksome" and was "well pleased with the change" when he and the other paroled men were moved to Camp Lew Wallace on October 16. By the end of the month, however, he noted, "We are becoming very much demoralized here with no duty to do." As a result, "Prize fights and black eyes are all 'the go' now." On November 6, Curry recorded, "Boys have been playing the *Devil* generally. Burn the guard house. Whip all the officers who show their heads."[19]

The commanders of Camp Lew Wallace and Camp Chase were not entirely to blame for the situation in the facilities. Twice during October Wallace requested permission from the War Department to erect winter quarters. Cooper repeated the request on November 8, suggesting that the men be sent to Camp Dennison if quarters could not be put up at Camp Lew Wallace. It was not until December 20 that the War Department responded, issuing orders to transfer the men back to Camp Chase.

Camp Lew Wallace was effectively out of business. At the same time orders for exchanges began to arrive. In an attempt to maintain order during the transition, one company from each regiment was detailed for provost guard duty. One of their assignments proved ironic. After so many men had slipped out of the parole camps, a January 8, 1863 order threatened with arrest those who remained in Columbus after being ordered to rejoin their regiments.[20]

The chain of events at the two camps illustrates the low position the paroled soldiers occupied on the War Department's list of priorities. Sent to the camps because it was believed that they had intentionally fallen into the hands of the enemy, the men arrived under a cloud of suspicion. Their high desertion rate and rowdy behavior did not help the situation, nor did their belief that their paroles released them from military duty until exchanged. Not serving in the field, the men came to the attention of government and military officials only when they left for home or otherwise caused trouble. They had no advocates in the War Department to speak on their behalf. Hoffman seemed more interested in the status of the few remaining Confederate prisoners. Officially the parolees were also his responsibility, but he tended to ignore them unless the situation was extreme. In a December 1863 report to the secretary of war, Hoffman willingly confessed his detachment from the issue of paroled prisoners. "Camp Chase is too remote from [Washington]," he informed Stanton, "for me to give the discipline of the paroled troops there my personal supervision." Hoffman blithely continued by claiming that the reports he received from Columbus left him with "no means of ascertaining whether a satisfactory state of discipline is kept up or not." As with Confederate prisoners, cost often trumped humanity when the commissary general did make a decision. When the commander of Camp Parole requested permission to replace parolees' clothing, "filled with vermin," Hoffman instead insisted that the clothing be cleaned. Confederate prisoners, with much justification, often complained of the conditions in Union prisons. Although it would have been little consolation, those conditions appear to have been no better when it was blue-clad soldiers occupying the camps. Further, the officials responsible for those camps appeared no more willing to do anything about the conditions their own men had to endure.[21]

Like his counterparts at Camp Chase, Lt. Col. George Sangster, the commander of Camp Parole, looked upon the parolees with disdain. "If the men of my camp were a sample of our Army," he wrote to Hoffman, "we would have nothing but a mob of stragglers and cowards." The overwhelming majority, he insisted, did not know to which corps they belonged. Regardless of their unit, many refused to build barracks at the camp, citing the terms of their parole. Hoffman ordered Sangster to report the names of the men who refused to perform the duty, promising to forward the list to Stanton. It seems unlikely, however, that such a list ever reached the busy war secretary. It is yet another example of problems at the parole camps being treated as local matters unworthy of Hoffman's personal attention.[22]

Hoffman did visit Camp Parole after two shocking reports of the conditions there reached Washington. A soldier of the Forty-fourth New York Infantry wrote Stanton on November 18, 1862, asserting, "Drunkenness, fighting, burglary, robbery, gambling, &c., are witnessed by us daily, and even murder is not of infrequent occurrence." Six days later, Governor Edward Salomon of Wisconsin forwarded to Hoffman a petition signed by forty-eight paroled soldiers from his state. "Men are being assaulted, robbed, and killed," they wrote. Hoffman responded by writing to Sangster, telling him that complaints had been received "of great disorders at your camp." The commissary general of prisoners requested an immediate report of "the state of discipline of your command." Sangster responded by sending transcripts of interviews with men from the complaining outfits. None had direct evidence of murders, but many had heard rumors. Virtually all had personally witnessed gambling and drinking. In March Hoffman finally made his way to Camp Parole. He concluded that the most extreme reports were, "except perhaps in some rare instances, wholly false or very much exaggerated." The situation, Hoffman wrote, was satisfactory, but he conceded that "much remains yet to be done before anything like perfection will be arrived at." In dismissing the men's concerns, Hoffman concluded, "The great obstacle in the way of a favorable state of things [at Camp Parole] is the anxiety of the men to go to their homes and their unwillingness to do anything to better their condition, which would deprive them of any reasonable ground of complaint and the claims which they base upon it for furloughs."[23]

If a desire to get home was the paroled men's main motivation, it also motivated the governors of their home states. In forwarding the men's complaints from Camp Parole, Governor Salomon requested the return of all Wisconsin parolees. Andrew Curtin, Pennsylvania's governor, also forwarded a petition to Stanton. "All they say of the treatment they receive [at Camp Parole] is true," the governor wrote, "and many of them would prefer to be returned to Richmond." Curtin concluded, "I earnestly ask that the people of this State now at Annapolis be brought within our borders." Michigan governor Austin Blair made a similar request on behalf of his constituents at Camp Chase. Governor Samuel J. Kirkwood applied to get the paroled men from Iowa sent from Benton Barracks to Davenport. Even President Lincoln got into the act. On December 26, 1862 he informed Stanton that two Ohio regiments and a regiment from Illinois had recently been sent to Columbus on parole. "This brings the Ohio regiments substantially to their homes," Lincoln reasoned, and he felt his home state outfit was deserving of the same treatment.[24]

No governor was more persistent in his demand that his constituents be sent home than Oliver P. Morton of Indiana. He first brought up the matter on September 26, 1862. "Our accommodations are at least as good as those at Camp Chase," he informed Stanton, "and the men would be better satisfied and render more service here than at any other rendezvous." Stanton replied brusquely that no parole camp would be established at Indianapolis. "Sending prisoners to their own State operates as an inducement for shameful surrender," he wrote. Undeterred, Morton repeated his request on October 21. "They have had continued trouble at Camp Chase which I am sure can be avoided here," the governor insisted. This time Stanton promised to look into the matter and see what he could do. Nothing happened, and Morton tried again on December 16 and yet again on February 21. He got a certain measure of satisfaction in May, when members of two depleted Indiana regiments were transferred from Camp Chase to Indianapolis to be brought up to strength with new recruits. Eventually more Hoosier regiments returned to their home state thanks to the efforts of their indefatigable governor.[25]

Meanwhile, exchanges were finally allowing other paroled soldiers to get away from Camp Chase. On January 13, 1863 Hoffman informed Cooper that all troops captured and paroled in Kentucky, Tennessee, Mississippi, Alabama, South Carolina, and Florida before December 10 were exchanged. "Those at Camp Chase," he ordered, "will be prepared for the field without delay." Over the next four months, forty-two special orders were issued to conduct exchanged prisoners to a number of points. Anywhere from seven to three hundred at a time departed.[26]

As the men departed, others arrived to take their place. A large detachment of the Kentucky Home Guard arrived from Camp Parole in late

December. Other members of the same outfit, "[n]ow scattered through Kentucky," were ordered to Camp Chase to be mustered into the service, a detail that had been overlooked before they were sent into the field and subsequently captured. In notifying Gen. Cooper of their imminent arrival, Hoffman suggested that a guard be stationed at Camp Lew Wallace to protect the buildings in case the parole camp had to be reoccupied. The need did not arise, but in early April another 1,045 paroled soldiers were transferred from Camp Parole to Camp Chase.[27]

By September 25, the number of paroled men at Camp Chase was 1,475 enlisted men, with only twelve officers. As the population again swelled, with the number of officers remaining low, problems with discipline continued to plague the camp. On April 24 Hoffman asked Maj. Gen. Ambrose Burnside, then commanding the Department of the Ohio, to investigate reports of "the great want of discipline among the paroled troops at Camp Chase." Hoffman offered few specifics other than to complain that parolees deserted "almost as fast as they can be brought back." He suggested that "an active and efficient commander with a reliable guard of at least five full companies" was needed to curb the problems. Statistics bear out Hoffman's complaints, at least in terms of desertions. Between April and October seven hundred deserters from the camp were retrieved, at a cost ranging from 48¢ to $23.90 per man.[28]

For those who remained, life as a paroled soldier at Camp Chase brought a variety of experiences and reflected a variety of attitudes. "T.H.W.," whose letters appeared in the *Morgan County Herald,* a McConnelsville, Ohio, newspaper, was simply grateful to be back in the North. Captured at Murfreesboro, Tennessee, in late December, he had been shipped first to Chattanooga, then on to Montgomery, Atlanta, and finally north to Richmond. T.H.W. and his comrades spent a week in the Libby Prison, which he described as "the most filthy house I think on earth. The smallpox was very prevalent there." Parole came as a much-appreciated deliverance, and on January 27 he started north. "Never did the Stars and Stripes look so bright as on that morning, as they floated from the mast head of the vessel that was to bear us back to the dominion of Uncle Sam," he wrote of his voyage to City Point. Along the way he observed the wreckage of the *Virginia* as well as the remains of some of the Union ships the Confederate ironclad had sunk.[29]

After about six weeks at Camp Parole, T.H.W. learned that he and other western soldiers were to be transferred to Camp Chase. "The Ohio boys are in high spirits," he wrote of the news. His enthusiasm was not dampened upon his arrival, although he described the camp as "a perfect lake of mud." He noted, "The quarters here are good, and the commissary is bountifully supplied with all the provisions necessary to satisfy the animal appetite." The shanties had been freshly whitewashed, and camp officials had graded the streets and walkways and dug "splendid ditches" to address the ever-present drainage problem. Loneliness was the only drawback, and the soldier admitted that many of the men desired a trip home. "There is not enough excitement here to keep the boys in good spirits." T.H.W. placed some of the onus on the home folks, noting, "If people at home would only write half as many letters to us as we do to them, we would be a great deal better satisfied." Instead, the men had to accept whatever diversions came their way. In May a Professor McCoy of Washington, DC, presented a lecture on the anniversary of George Washington's Farewell Address. About two thousand men attended, listening "in the broiling sun for two hours and thirty minutes," and considering the event a special treat.[30]

Another paroled soldier who was satisfied with the treatment he received at Camp Chase was Benjamin Franklin Heuston of the Second Wisconsin. A patient at the camp's general hospital, Heuston informed his wife that he was suffering from "'Endo-Cordidis with Chron Pneumonia,' which means Disease of the heart with permanent affection of the lungs." Even if he did not fully grasp the diagnosis, Heuston was pleased with conditions in the hospital, at least at first. Writing on March 15, he noted, "We are well used here—have plenty to eat, a library to get books from, and the medicine I take is not bad." He did not appear to appreciate the irony when he added, "There is not quite one funeral a day." By April 1 the number of patients in the hospital had grown to over 500, making it quite crowded. There were 154 in Heuston's ward, which had only forty-three beds, forcing most to sleep on the floor. The numbers were so great that meals were reduced to two a day, and those, Heuston pointed out, were "rather scant."[31]

Pvt. Fernando E. Pomeroy of the Eighteenth Michigan was captured on March 25, 1863 near Danville, Kentucky. Pomeroy had been on picket duty when the pickets from the Eighteenth and 104th were cut off from their regiments. As they headed down the Lexington Pike, trying to get back to their outfits, Pomeroy and his comrades encountered Confederate soldiers. They took to the woods, but the Confederates gave chase and overtook them. The Michigan men were taken to a courthouse in Lancaster. They spent four nights there before being marched to Lexington. Parole came quickly, and on March 30 the men were sent by train to Covington, Kentucky. From there they crossed the Ohio to Cincinnati and started for Camp Chase the next day.

"Well it is not a very pleasant place," Pomeroy confided to his diary upon reaching the camp. He and his messmates cleaned out their shanty and settled in as best they could. Over the next several days Pomeroy witnessed a number of fights, including one in which a participant got knocked down with a stone, and became involved in at least two. It was about the only diversion in what Pomeroy termed "a verry poor place for amusement." After losing 10¢ on dice, he noted that it was "the first of my betting and I guess it will be the last." On June 29 Pomeroy secured some civilian clothes. "I do conclude to go home if I can get there or go to the bullpen," he wrote two days later. He left camp on July 8. It is not clear if he secured a furlough or followed the example of the many men he saw take "French leave." Pomeroy returned to camp on July 22, and on August 6, after four tedious months as a parolee, left to rejoin his regiment in Nashville.[32]

Another Michigan soldier, Charles Holbrook Prentiss of the Ninth Michigan Infantry, began his journey to Camp Chase at Brentwood, Tennessee. Prentiss had been on picket duty and was eating breakfast on the morning of March 25, 1863, when "a negro slipped into our camp, informing us that the rebels were tearing up the railroad track south of our camp and preparing to attack us." The warning did no good. Before the men could react to the information, the Confederates had them surrounded with artillery well posted. After a brief skirmish the Union men, 210 strong, surrendered. The Confederates were kind to their captives, many shaking hands with the prisoners. The friendly disposition of the captors did little to ease the march that consumed the next forty-eight hours. Prentiss and his comrades were driven hard, getting little chance to rest as they trudged over hills and waded through cold streams.[33]

Early on the morning of March 27 they were ferried across the Duck River, where they found warm fires and the opportunity to rest. Following this respite the men marched another fifteen miles to Columbia. They were confined there in "an old filthy court house, hardly fit to put hogs into." Prentiss received little to eat but still found the Confederates to be "very kind and good-hearted boys." On March 29 he signed his parole.

Under its terms Prentiss agreed "not to bear arms against the Confederate States or to perform any military or garrison duty whatever until regularly exchanged." Difficult marches marked the next three days. The men went on through rain and snow, along rugged roads, through forests, and over "mountains and every other obstacle you can think of to tire a man out." On April 2 the paroled captives arrived at Chattanooga, where they had to give up their overcoats and blankets before being crowded into cattle cars. Their route carried them through Knoxville, Bristol, and Lynchburg, Virginia, en route to Richmond. They were searched at the Confederate capital, Prentiss losing his canteen and his watch. Rations were very skimpy, and a hard floor served as a bed, but the men's stay was brief. On April 11, two days after arriving, Prentiss and his fellow prisoners took the train for City Point. There, Prentiss noted, "the Stars and Stripes [were] waiting for us."[34]

Prentiss arrived at Camp Parole on April 15. "Each man," he recorded, "drawed an over coat, dress coat, pants, drawers, shoes, & socks, Charged $30." He remained at the camp for the rest of the month, often walking into Annapolis to take in the sights. On at least two occasions he visited the state capitol building, climbing the steeple and enjoying "a fine view of the city." Although he wrote in his diary that Annapolis was "quite pleasant," he informed his wife in a letter that it was "a small stinking place." Whatever his true views of the city might have been, Prentiss did not remain long, departing on May 1. After a boat ride to Baltimore, he took the train to Pittsburgh, drawing rations along the way at Altoona.[35]

Prentiss awoke on the morning of May 3, having traveled some sixty-seven miles from Pittsburgh. "Many of the boys are droping off and leaving for home," he noted. He reached Camp Chase about 7:00 that evening. Prentiss was pleased to discover about ten men from his company there, and he spent his first night in camp with them. They informed him that two of their comrades had ended up in the bullpen after trying to reach home. The men had been apprehended in civilian clothing and were expected to be court-martialed. Writing to his wife, Prentiss said the camp provided "first rait water and very good board for Uncle Sam." He supplemented an early meal with milk from a nearby farmer's cow. He tried to repeat the process a few days later "but found the cows gone."[36]

Prentiss could get by without milk. "I have enough to eat & a library to draw books to read," he wrote his wife on May 10. His main problem was loneliness, compounded by worry. "When I received your last [letter], you sayed that you was haveing a time with your throat. That makes me feel rather uneasy about you." The fact that he had sent her seven letters since receiving her last one added to his concern. Men were leaving camp at a high rate, fourteen departing the previous night, and Prentiss had made up his mind. "I shall see you in less than 4 weeks," he asserted, "if I dont get shut up in some bull pen." He had no money but was determined to begin the 298-mile trip on foot and "beg my way." Of one thing he was sure: "I never shall go into servis again untill I *see you*."[37]

On May 13, accompanied by a friend, Prentiss set out for home. The two got up at 5:00 a.m. and went to a nearby hotel, where they got a free breakfast. They reached their destination in just under three days. Along the way they got thrown off a passenger train and hopped a freight. Sympathetic farmers and a saloon proprietor fed them. Prentiss was grateful to his benefactors but arrived home to discover that much of the effort had been unnecessary—his wife had sent him $20 to make the trip. He remained at home until June 3. While there he visited a number of friends and helped his father plant his corn crop. Prentiss also saw his captain, who told him he needed to return to camp by June 4. Prentiss arrived one day late, but if he got in any trouble he did not mention it in his diary. Four days later he started for Nashville, where a new Enfield rifle and new duties awaited him.[38]

As parolees came and went, so, too, did commanders at Camp Chase. Sometimes the command structure seemed unnecessarily complicated. On December 25, 1862, acting under orders from Stanton, Cooper assumed command "of all troops at Camp Chase." Maj. Zinn, who had been in command since September 26, retained command of the prison and the guard. Col. August Kautz of the Second Ohio Cavalry was appointed commander of the post, which was a part of Cooper's command. Zinn may have regarded Kautz's appointment as a slight because he resigned his commission four days later. Capt. Edwin L. Webber of the Governor's Guard succeeded him.[39]

For Kautz command of Camp Chase was an unwanted honor. A captain in the Sixth United States Cavalry, he had been appointed colonel of the Second Ohio in September. He joined his new outfit at Fort Scott, Kansas. The regiment had served along the Missouri-Kansas border region, where it lost several men to "a peculiar brain fever." On December 2 Kautz and the dismounted portion of the regiment started east to remount and refit at Camp Chase. The mounted men, serving in Arkansas, soon followed. According to Kautz, command of the camp became his by default. "It was [Gen. Cooper's] duty to have personally commanded the camp," he wrote in his memoirs, "but in addition to his want of experience he was in very feeble health from the use of opium." Kautz dismissed Zinn as "ignorant of the duties" of command. As a result, Kautz wrote, "I found the camp in a bad state and many irregularities prevailing and some time was necessary to restore order." He resented the time he had to spend on such problems. "The duties of camp," the colonel wrote, "necessarily took up much of my time that I Would have preferred to devote to my own regiment." Despite this concern, Kautz managed to find time for socializing. At one event, a dinner at the governor's mansion, he met Miss Charlotte Tod, the governor's daughter and his future wife.[40]

Kautz set to work to improve the discipline of the camp. He detailed Lt. H. C. Pike, a member of his regiment, as provost marshal. Among his duties was providing a mounted detail to patrol the camp and surrounding area to protect camp property and track down any men who were absent without leave. Kautz also cracked down on soldiers guilty of destroying camp property. Few details escaped the vigilant cavalryman. He even issued orders directing officers to correct "the informal manner of writing their signatures" when filling out official papers.[41]

"The camp was composed of a great variety of troops," Kautz recorded in his memoirs. New regiments were still being organized, Confederate prisoners continued to arrive, and of course the paroled soldiers were there. "Of these," he remarked, "the paroled prisoners were the most troublesome." They came from many different regiments, and virtually none arrived with their regimental officers. "Consequently, the officers had little control over the men and the men had no respect for the officers." When a large number was exchanged on January 12, Kautz noted in his diary, "I am glad they are gone as they are a very perplexing kind of troops to deal with."[42]

Kautz soon found that his own men could be equally troublesome. On March 5, 1863 members of the Second Ohio Cavalry participated in one of the most serious incidents to involve soldiers stationed at Camp Chase. It grew out of the men's disdain for the *Columbus Crisis,* a newspaper owned and edited by Samuel Medary. A Democrat, Medary alternated between journalism and public office during the 1850s, serving as governor of both the Minnesota and Kansas territories. In 1861 he launched the *Crisis*. The paper quickly established a reputation as a staunch advocate of the Peace Democrat (or "Copperhead," depending upon one's point of view) position. Medary used his pen to condemn abolitionists and the Lincoln administration and to call for an immediate cessation of hostilities against the South. Negotiation and compromise, the editor believed, could then work to restore the Union.[43]

To the soldiers at Camp Chase, the *Crisis* was, as William J. Smith of Kautz's regiment termed it, "the hottest rebel sheet to be found in the Country, either North or South." According to Smith, a camp rule permitted church parties to go into town with a noncommissioned officer in command. Taking advantage of that proviso, about one hundred men from the regiment headed toward Columbus on a snowy Sunday evening. Oddly, nobody questioned why the men would need hatchets, axes, and clubs for divine services. At the *Crisis* office the sergeant in charge of the church party posted guards at nearby street corners to prevent any interference. "Then he took several men," Smith later wrote, "and posted them across the street, then a column of men poured up into the building, then the windows were SMASHED, and furniture, books, paper, maps &c came pouring out into the street."[44]

The men then headed for the offices of the *Ohio Statesman*, another Democratic sheet, where the *Crisis* was printed, but the presence of Columbus police and the provost guard discouraged them. Instead they returned to camp, where their actions did not meet with the approval of their commanding officer. "I was in the city the same night," Kautz recalled in his memoirs, "but was not aware of the affair until it was over and did not learn until the next day that my regiment was concerned in it." He called a meeting of the officers the next day and urged them to repudiate the actions of the men. He also issued an order calling for the perpetrators to be given up. "I fear," Kautz confided in his diary, "that there is too much sympathy with the act in the Regt. to enable one to get hold of the offenders." He did manage to recover some of Medary's property, which he ordered returned. By threatening to resign from the regiment, Kautz also persuaded the officers to sign a paper repudiating the attack. They went no further, however. "Their sympathies are in favor of the men," Kautz noted, "and their prejudices are strong against the paper, and they do not wish to see any of the men punished."[45]

Cooper supported Kautz's views. The morning after the incident he issued orders decrying "such outrageous violations of the law." He continued, "To the soldiers who participated in last night's outrages and violence, I have to say, your conduct is strangely inconsistent with your duty, and the holy purpose for which your country put arms in your hands." Cooper did not call for the guilty parties to be turned in. Instead he appealed to their soldierly pride, terming them "rioters and burglars." The general concluded by warning the men against committing any future offenses. "The persons and property of citizens are sacred in the eyes both of civil and military law, and any outrage or assault upon them will be visited by inflicting upon the perpetrators, the moment they are detected, the extremest penalty authorized by law."[46]

It proved to be one of Cooper's last orders. He died on March 31. On April 16 Brig. Gen. John S. Mason succeeded him. Hoffman used the change in command to push once again for a permanent commander and a permanent guard force at Camp Chase. Writing on April 20, he also informed Mason that he planned to ship all the Camp Chase prisoners to Johnson's Island. "In the meantime, I will be much indebted to you if you will have me informed of any irregularities occurring at the prison that may be brought to your notice," Hoffman added.[47]

Kautz and his regiment left Camp Chase on April 7, bound for service in Kentucky. His successor was Capt. Alexander E. Drake, who was relieved of command on May 14. Capt. Webber succeeded him, remaining in command of the camp until June 23, when Col. William Wallace replaced him. Webber then returned to his previous post as prison commander. Clearly, the consistency that Hoffman desired remained elusive.[48]

Also changing as 1863 progressed was Camp Chase's role as a parole camp. Almost from the start the cartel struggled as both sides used it to secure leverage against the other. It began with Gen. Pope. While still commanding the Army of Virginia, the future Indian fighter issued orders threatening to charge Virginia landowners as spies, subject to hanging. The South responded by threatening to treat men from the Army of Virginia as criminals rather than prisoners of war. The Union's plan to send the parolees after the Sioux in Minnesota also upset Southern officials, who understandably considered such duty to be a violation of the terms of the cartel. The main area of contention—at least in terms of public discourse—was the Union's decision to employ black soldiers. The

Davis government refused to regard black captives as prisoners. Instead it threatened to return them to the states—and eventually to their previous masters—and to try and execute their white officers for inciting servile insurrection. This announcement came in May 1863. At the same time Union officials were realizing that prisoner exchange disproportionately benefited the South because of the region's significantly smaller population. Ever since, historians have tried to determine which factor had a greater impact on Union policy toward prisoners. Unfortunately, no conclusive documentation has been uncovered to provide a definite answer. Whatever the motivation, Halleck reported to Stanton in his annual report for 1863 that all exchanges had ceased that spring.[49]

The last of the paroled Union prisoners left Camp Chase in April 1864. (Others would appear several months later when exchange was resumed during the waning weeks of the war.) Long before then, the last of the Confederates to benefit from the policy of exchange had departed Camp Chase and other Union prisons. At the least, exchange represented to these men salvation from months or years of tedious prison life. At the most, it meant they would not die in a lonely, unpleasant place far from home. With the collapse of the cartel, thousands of men were soon to face both of these harsh prospects.[50]

4

Exchange and Escape

While the cartel remained in effect, the number of Confederate prisoners at Camp Chase remained low. Between September 1862 and June 1863 it ranged from 756 to 1,367. During that time a total of 2,063 Confederate soldiers was exchanged. As the cartel collapsed in the summer of 1863, the prison population again began to rise, exceeding 2,000 for the remainder of the year. The numbers would have gone much higher had the government not maintained a policy of transferring Confederate officers to other posts. Nearly 3,000 left during July and August 1863. Johnson's Island was the most common destination, although they were occasionally sent to Fort Delaware, Camp Douglas, or Fort Warren in Boston Harbor. When Tod complained to Halleck that he wanted rid of "at least 200 . . . of the most dangerous prisoners" at Camp Chase, Halleck replied that the governor could ship "such prisoners of war as you may deem proper to Johnson's Island" if Tod could make arrangements for guarding them.[1]

Among the exchanged Confederates departing Camp Chase in 1863 was Lt. J. K. Ferguson of the Nineteenth Arkansas. He had been captured when Arkansas Post surrendered on January 12, 1863. "I shot away twenty rounds of cartridges at the enemy which was lying in the brush below the fort," Ferguson wrote in his diary. It was not enough. The white flag went up shortly thereafter, and he soon found himself a prisoner. A native of Virginia's upper panhandle, Ferguson had spent most of his boyhood in Madison, Indiana. His captors included members of the Sixty-seventh Indiana, and he was greeted by a number of boyhood friends. Three days later he found himself aboard one of three riverboats, each carrying one entire brigade of prisoners, proceeding slowly up the Mississippi. Progress became even slower when Ferguson's boat "broke a wheel" and had to be attached to another vessel.[2]

Temperatures were low, and rain added to the unpleasant conditions.

"It has caused us all to suffer more or less," Ferguson wrote on the 18th, adding, "Several came very near freasing to death." Two days later he wrote, "The distress on board excells anything that I have ever witnessed before. The sick is prostrated all over the cabin floor, and but very little aid can be rendered them." The men received some relief at Memphis when sympathetic citizens brought them clothing, "although it was strictly forbidden by the federal authorities." Those authorities at Memphis apparently were not very vigilant because, Ferguson recorded, "A great many of our men left the boat while we lay there in disguise of citizen dress."[3]

On January 25 the men reached St. Louis. "Boats and [railroad] cars can be seen coming in and going out at all times," Ferguson noted, "which is a great sight for some of the back pine woods boys of Arkansaw." The lieutenant's boat lay on an island just south of the city for two days. Union officials then removed the officers and took them to East St. Louis, Illinois. There Ferguson and his fellow officers were put aboard freight cars, although some of the sick were allowed to ride passenger cars. "For nearly 48 hours we remained on board the freight cars," Ferguson wrote, "the weather being intencly cold, having no fire and but very little food. Our sufferings were indescribable." Members of the Twelfth Iowa served as guards. Captured at Shiloh, the Hawkeye soldiers had just been released from a Confederate prison. As a result they were sympathetic to the Southerners' plight.[4]

The Ohio & Mississippi Railroad carried Ferguson and his comrades across Illinois and Indiana, passing within twenty-two miles of the lieutenant's hometown. On the morning of January 29 the train reached Cincinnati. From there to Columbus the prisoners were allowed to ride in passenger cars. At a stop in Xenia, "The citizens came and gazed upon us with as much wonder as if we had been a lot of wild beasts in a managery." Reaching Columbus, the captives were required to march the four miles to Camp Chase. Ferguson was ill and was allowed to ride in a wagon. Union soldiers searched the men when they arrived at the camp. "But boot legs," Ferguson noted, "answers a very good purpose in special occations."[5]

The next morning, Ferguson was pleased to record, his pocketbook was returned to him, its contents safely intact. He was in a mess in Prison 2 with nine other officers. "We have goten it arranged in a tolerable order and are doing very well," he wrote on January 31. "We have received much more provisions than we have been able to consume." On February 5 camp officials moved all prisoners in Prison 2, except those who were hospitalized, to Prison 3. Ferguson continued to be satisfied with his treatment. "We are all fairing much better than we were in the other pens," he wrote. Although Ferguson was a native of the North, his remarks were not those of a man with mixed loyalties. He described as "heart rending" the plight of the two hundred citizen prisoners still in the camp. They included women, old men, and children. Some, he noted, had been there for sixteen months. After writing to his mother, he recorded in his diary, "I . . . had to leave the envelope unsealed to undergo abolition inspecting." When his mother and sisters wrote back, Ferguson was "surprized to find them quite hostile towards me on account of my acting acording to my own opinion." His sister, he wrote, "ridicules me a great deal for being a reble." She wanted him to take the oath of allegiance to the Union, an idea he would not consider. On February 16, "I wrote a scorching letter to the folks at home yesterday eve—giving them a few ideas that they had probably not thought of." A former neighbor arrived a few days later, bearing letters that could have secured Ferguson's release upon taking the oath. "But I respectfully declined," he proudly noted, "giving as my reason that I could not take it without sacreficing my principles and sence of honor and also betraying a trust."[6]

Early in March Andrew Johnson returned to Camp Chase. "Several great nabobs of the same stripe" accompanied him, Ferguson observed. "But he received a cool reception from our officers," he added. One of the Confederates, Gen. Thomas J. Churchill, refused even to see him. Johnson departed in disgust. As he did, Ferguson happily recorded, "Cheers from evry side could be heard for Jeff Davis and the secesh."[7]

Ferguson's stay at Camp Chase was rather brief. Late in the afternoon of April 10 he and about five hundred comrades, all of whom had been exchanged, began the long journey home. "We was all ready and waiting long before the [departure] time," he noted. As they left, Union soldiers stripped them of their overcoats, blankets, gloves, and even toothbrushes before marching them to Columbus. The procedure left Ferguson, who generally did not complain of his treatment, bitter. "The higher the rank," the lieutenant wrote, "the less mercy they were shown." One man had nothing of value, so the Union soldiers took his haversack and provisions "for the sake of robing him. And while this shameful piece of business was going on," the disgusted Confederate wrote, "there was a large crowd of federal soldiers looking on—even women that had the appearance of ladies were sitting in cariges scoffing and laughing at us." Watching the entire procedure from the parapet was Capt. Webber.[8]

Although stripped of their possessions, the men had the satisfaction of knowing that freedom lay ahead. They boarded a train of the Columbus & Pittsburgh Railroad, filling eleven cars. On April 12 the men reached Philadelphia, where they produced something of a sensation. "Men women and children came flocking to see us as if we were a cargo of wild beasts," Ferguson wrote. The men endured a number of hisses and taunts as the train passed through the City of Brotherly Love. They were repeated at the wharf, where the Confederates were put aboard a steamer for Fort Delaware.[9]

For the next several weeks Ferguson was a military tourist of sorts. He remained at Fort Delaware for two weeks, examining the facility carefully and watching as an ironclad Union ship chugged by. Like most prisoners who spent time there, Ferguson was not impressed with Fort Delaware. "Our quarters is very unpleasant compared with those at Camp Chase." From there the steamer *State of Maine* took the exchanged prisoners to Fortress Monroe, where they remained a short time before boarding the *Express* for the voyage to City Point. Along the way Ferguson viewed the wreckage of the *Cumberland,* one of the victims of the ironclad *Virginia.* Continuing up the James River, he passed Jamestown and the remains of homes destroyed during the Seven Days Battles between McClellan and Lee. As they continued up the river, the men passed into Confederate lines.[10]

On May 4 Ferguson arrived at Richmond, taking a train almost immediately for Petersburg. "Evry thing is extraordinary costly here," he noted, adding, "Board at the Hotel is $8 per day." Ferguson purchased a saber for $60. On the 12th he began his rail journey to the western theater of the war. Along the way he recorded descriptions of Lynchburg, Bristol, Knoxville, and a number of smaller towns. In eastern Tennessee, he noted, "As well as I could judge from the sentiments of the people they are as they have the name of being some what tainted with abolition principles." If the people of the Volunteer State proved disappointing to Ferguson, the news that he was to remain there was a much greater disappointment. "From unknown reason to us, we have been sent to [Gen. Braxton Bragg's] army instead of Vicksburg," he wrote on May 19. "I am fearful that we will not be able to get on the other side of the [Mississippi River] to our original command." It marked a sudden and bitter end to what had been to that point a fascinating journey of liberation.[11]

Also disappointed with the exchange process, although for different reasons, was "E.H.M.," who recalled the events of his imprisonment in 1884. His account appears credible because, unlike so many other postwar writers, E.H.M. avoided hyperbole. Indeed, he referred to Camp Chase as "one of the best prisons in the North" and conceded, "Our fare was good enough." He arrived at Camp Chase after being captured during a scouting expedition in the fall of 1862 in the vicinity of Keyser, Virginia.[12]

Although he did not give the date of his exchange, it was likely during the winter or spring of 1863. Like so many others exchanged at that time, his destination was Vicksburg via Cairo. Traveling with E.H.M. were "several hundred" other exchanged soldiers. They reached Cairo in a pouring rain and were marched and halted for several hours before finally getting to their quarters. Those quarters were "wooden stables in the center of muddy yards." When E.H.M. complained about the conditions, the officer of the guard "ordered his men to load their guns, and [said] if those prisoners came within five feet of them, or gave them a word of impudence, to *shoot them down*." After he left, the guards, Michigan soldiers, said the officer belonged to the staff of the local post and "had never smelt gunpowder and probably never would." The guards were more sympathetic, building fires to keep the men comfortable.[13]

"Our rations," E.H.M. recalled, "consisted principally of 'slippery' bacon and mouldy crackers, the former we used as fuel mostly." The men remained at Cairo for several weeks before the steamboat *Minnehaha* arrived to carry them on to Vicksburg. Prisoners picked up at Louisville and St. Louis were already aboard, and the total number of passengers was about twelve hundred. Before the boat reached Cairo, many of the men from E.H.M.'s camp had become ill with smallpox. As the *Minnehaha* floated down the river, the outbreak became an epidemic, and daily stops to bury the dead became necessary. One case particularly stood out in the writer's mind. He was a West Virginian, a political prisoner, who had been "torn from his wife and large family of children the year before" because he was suspected of supplying information to the Confederates. "Every day we could see him gradually sinking," he recalled. Before dying the man had murmured, "If I could only feel the leaves of the trees under my feet and breathe the mountain air again, I would get well."[14]

Lt. W. H. Herbert of the Eighty-ninth Virginia may have been the only Confederate prisoner who enjoyed his trip to Camp Chase more than he did the journey home. At least, this was the case if his postwar account is accurate. Captured near Winchester, Virginia, in October 1862, Herbert and eleven other captives, some of whom were civilians, soon found themselves in a Wheeling prison. In early November, under a guard of seven, they started for Camp Chase. When their train stopped in Newark, Ohio, a man came aboard and took the seat in front of Herbert's. The two became engaged in conversation. When the man learned that his companion was a Confederate prisoner, he asked how many were being transported. Herbert told him, and the man replied, "When we get to Columbus I would like to do something for you boys. If we find a restaurant open, I'll set up supper for the party." When the commander of the guard learned that he and his men were to be included, he readily gave his consent.[15]

They reached Columbus at about 11:30 and found a restaurant opposite the capitol building. "Here we had a supper fit for the gods," Herbert remembered. Several paroled Union officers were also present. Owing perhaps to their recent status as captives, they were "exceedingly kind" to their enemies. According to Herbert's account, liquor flowed freely, and the subsequent march to Camp Chase was unique. "Most of the party were groggy," he wrote, "and wabbled along as best they could."[16]

Herbert's stay at Camp Chase was brief. Less than a month after arriving, he and about two hundred other exchanged prisoners began their return trip to their units. Although he was a member of Stonewall Jackson's corps of the Army of Northern Virginia, the lieutenant was sent to Vicksburg via Cairo. At the Illinois town, prisoners from Johnson's Island and Louisville joined them, swelling the contingent to some eleven hundred men. Herbert and the other forty-eight members of Jackson's command reached headquarters at Fredericksburg on December 26, "and got what was left of the Christmas turkey."[17]

A number of Confederate prisoners preferred not to be exchanged. Many claimed to have been conscripted, saying they deserted and came voluntarily into the Union lines. On August 1, 1862 Tod informed the War Department, "A large number of rebel prisoners beg of me to protect them against unconditional exchange." The soldiers remained liable to military duty in the Confederate service, which they were eager to avoid. Christopher P. Wolcott, an assistant secretary of war, informed Tod that no prisoners willing to take the oath and "abide by it in good faith" would be exchanged. On September 22 Hoffman reaffirmed the order, adding that Confederates thus discharged were on their own to secure transportation. Hoffman soon further refined the policy. On December 4 he informed Zinn that spies often claimed to be Confederate deserters. Others, he added, simply lied to secure their release. "You will refer to this office all cases where this claim is set up," Hoffman ordered, "with all the circumstances which are given to sustain them, in order that a decision may be made."[18]

The commissary general of prisoners reversed this order in May. Although he repeated the warning that many would claim to be deserters to escape confinement, he gave Mason authority to release those who took the oath of allegiance. "Let it be clearly understood," Hoffman ominously warned, "that death is the penalty for violation of the oath." The next contradiction came on August 8, this time from the Department of the Ohio. Brig. Gen. N. C. McClean, the provost marshal general of the department, was given the responsibility of examining the cases of Confederates desiring to take the oath of allegiance. Perhaps that order did not apply to deserters because their fate remained, at least in many documented cases, in the hands of Samuel Galloway. The special commissioner's role had evolved from investigating the cases of political prisoners to examining the claims of alleged Confederate deserters. In February 1864 Hoffman warned him to tread carefully. "There are probably many men among the prisoners at Camp Chase who may have been always loyal citizens, or would become so if they had the opportunity," the commissary general of prisoners wrote, "but it is impossible to single them out, and so many rebels have been released under false representations of various kinds that the Department will not now release any one unless the proof is very pointed, or the case is strongly recommended by the Governor of the State from which the applicant came."[19]

Despite Hoffman's warning, Galloway generally recommended the release of deserters upon their taking the oath. Surviving records indicate that his recommendations were usually followed. Most often Stanton made the final decision, although occasionally the case ended up on the president's desk. In many cases the men claimed that they had been forced to join the Confederate army and had deserted at the first opportunity to enter the Union lines. Among these was James R. Pitts of Lawrence County, Alabama. According to Pitts, he was "forcibly carried" from his home and forced into the Confederate cavalry. He was caught twice attempting to desert, but succeeded on his third try. Another Alabama resident, Thomas Pennington, claimed he had been taken from his father's home in Fayette County by a squad of thirty men. He was then kept in a guardhouse for eight days before agreeing to "volunteer." He deserted two nights later and returned home. Later, fearing recapture, he and seven others began an eleven-day hike to the Union lines. Azariah W. Riggle, a sixty-year-old resident of Frederick County, Virginia, insisted that both he and the team of horses he was driving had been "pressed into the rebel service." Henry H. Taylor offered the most compelling evidence, a wound still visible from being shot across the forehead as he deserted from the First Virginia Cavalry. He and the other three were released.[20]

Occasionally the cases involved Northerners who chose the wrong time to visit the South. One was Lemuel B. Jones of Muskingum County, Ohio, who claimed he had been forced into a Mississippi artillery battery while attempting to return home from Vicksburg. What he was doing that deep in Confederate territory Jones did not explain. He was released largely on the strength of the testimony of his mother, "whose loyalty and veracity is substantiated," Galloway noted. James Dooley, a resident of Chester County, Pennsylvania, testified that he and four others had left home in 1860 to find work in the South. He secured a job ditching near Montgomery, Alabama, but in the winter of 1862 decided to start for home. Dooley ran out of money at Knoxville. There a squad of Confederate horsemen captured him and forced him into the Second Tennessee Cavalry. He rode with the outfit to Kentucky, where he deserted and gave himself up to Union soldiers. Both Jones and Dooley secured their release from Camp Chase.[21]

Not every case involved conscripts. Some of the men Galloway examined had joined willingly and later deserted. Such was the case with Benjamin L. Ryan of Russell County, Alabama. Ryan had enlisted with the Fifteenth Alabama in June 1861 and served over two years before deserting with three others. "He expresses regret for his error in joining the rebel army and professes a sincere attachment to the Union," Galloway wrote. Harris Sitberry, whose place of residence was not listed, admitted that "he with others [enlisted] whilst under the influence of liquor." William Love of Wheeling, West Virginia, also claimed that he had joined while intoxicated. Contradicting the claim somewhat was his own statement that he had traveled to Harpers Ferry to enlist, making his a very lengthy binge. William D. Kelly of Roane County, Virginia, claimed to have been "misled by the false representations of designing men." While the other three were released, the disposition of Kelly's case was not recorded.[22]

Although most of the men Galloway interviewed secured their release without condition, there were some exceptions. One was Kentuckian Henry Clay Stimson. A Confederate lieutenant, Stimson resigned his commission "because of his opposition to the purposes of the rebellion." Although the evidence showed that he had since "demeaned himself loyally," Galloway still recommended that Stimson post a $500 bond before being released. Francis I. Baehr, a Maryland resident, told the commissioners that he had deserted "not from any conviction of the error of the rebellion, but from a dissatisfaction with their conduct." Galloway considered Baehr "an ignorant and reckless man and not a safe man in any community." He therefore suggested that he remain at Camp Chase "until his repentance and resolution to do better are clearer." William Robinson, arrested at Dayton, was suspected of being one of John Hunt Morgan's cavalry raiders. He claimed to have passed the lines of both armies in the process of deserting. "The narrative appears incredible and conflicting," Galloway wrote. He recommended retaining Robinson at Camp Chase until more substantial proof was offered.[23]

With large numbers of prisoners being released upon taking the oath of allegiance, the question of their responsibilities as repatriated citizens arose. On February 18, 1863 Hoffman gave a partial answer. He instructed Webber to explain to each prisoner released "that by taking the oath of allegiance he becomes liable to be called for military service as any other loyal citizen." Four months later Hoffman informed Burnside that enlisted prisoners who wished to join the Union service could do so "when it can be reliably shown that the applicant was impressed into the rebel service."[24]

As Hoffman's message to Burnside suggests, a cloud of doubt hung over the heads of the men suddenly converting from gray to blue uniforms. With Union officials admitting the difficulty of judging the sincerity of those taking the oath, sending them south to fight against their former comrades was a risky proposition. One option was to send the men in the opposite direction. On September 12, 1863 E. D. Townsend, assistant adjutant general, ordered the army's provost marshal general to send all Confederate deserters who had been drafted into the United States Army to report to Camp Chase. From there they would be "distributed among regiments serving in the Department of the Northwest." However, nothing in surviving camp records makes any further mention of the plan.[25]

One plan that was pursued at Camp Chase and other Union prisons was enlisting the men in the U.S. Navy. Here, too, records are sparse, but on at least one occasion a number of Camp Chase prisoners headed east for naval duty. On July 5, 1864 Hoffman received word from camp officials that 111 Confederates had volunteered. Three days later a guard at the camp repeated the news in a letter home. On July 15 Lt. John D. Hartz announced that he had been given the duty of recruiting prisoners from Camp Chase and other points for naval service. He was to take the volunteers to Philadelphia for assignment.[26]

For prisoners whose commitment to the Confederacy precluded them from taking the oath of allegiance, options for leaving Camp Chase were few. Once the cartel collapsed, they faced the prospect of confinement for the duration of the war. At that point escape became virtually the only remedy consistent with their sense of honor. Camp records indicate that it was also a difficult remedy to achieve. Between July 1862, when Union prisons began submitting monthly reports to the War Department, and January 1865, when Camp Chase's last reported escape occurred, 37 men managed to get safely beyond the walls of the camp. Compared to other prisons, Camp Chase appears to have been very secure. Among facilities in operation during the same span, there were 114 escapes from Alton, 113 from Camp Morton, and 316 from Camp Douglas. Only Johnson's Island, surrounded by the waters of Lake Erie, had a better record, with only 12 prisoners successfully absconding.[27]

September 1863 was the worst month for escapes at Camp Chase. Nineteen prisoners got away, making it and September 1862 the only months that the number of escapees exceeded seven. No surviving camp records provide any details. The only apparent reference to the matter appears in a November 3, 1863 letter from Brig. Gen. Speed S. Fry. Writing from Camp Nelson, Kentucky, Fry informed Brig. Gen. J. L. Boyle, commanding the District of Kentucky, that "several rebel prisoners who recently escaped from Camp Chase" were confined in Fayette County, Kentucky. They had reportedly informed friends that they escaped by bribing their guards. "They also boast," Fry continued, "that there is a *fund* subscribed by Rebel sympathizers in this state and else where, for the purpose of bribing the guard at Camp Chase and Camp Douglas to allow prisoners to escape." Writing home on October 18, a Camp Chase guard conceded that one of his comrades had been charged with accepting a bribe from a prisoner and helping him escape. He was quick to point out that this incident was an exception. "The attempt is not often successful," he emphasized, "as the guards 'can't see it' in that light."[28]

Thomas A. Sharpe, a citizen prisoner from Walker County, Georgia, wrote in his diary on September 8, 1864 that the morning had opened with the shout of "Fresh fish!" Normally this meant that a new batch of prisoners had arrived. On this occasion it marked "the return of some of our boys that thought they had a couple of the sentinels *bribed* to let them over the wall." Instead the guards had armed men waiting on the ground beneath the parapet. One of them "batted" the first one to clamber over and marched the entire group of five back into the prison.[29]

The most common method of attempting to escape was by digging a tunnel. Most were found by camp officials. Others were foiled by simple bad luck. On one occasion, recalled Maj. J. Coleman Alderson, a group of prisoners had a tunnel nearly completed when heavy rains caused it to cave in. Reminiscing about an 1864 escape attempt, former prisoner R. M. Gray recounted a similar bit of bad fortune. "But for an accident," he recalled, a tunnel he had worked on with his fellow prisoners "would have doubtless opened the outside world to our longing eyes." Unfortunately for Gray and his comrades, the tunnel passed under a road used for daily deliveries of wood by wagon. The weather was rainy, and one of the wagon's wheels broke through and betrayed their plans.[30]

More often the men were betrayed by their fellow prisoners or by spies planted among them by camp officials. One prisoner who believed he had been the victim of such a scoundrel was Henry C. Mettam of the First Maryland Cavalry. In late 1864 Mettam joined a committee of men "getting a little tired of the confinement." After some discussion the group decided to remove the bricks in front of a stove in the barracks, dig down four feet, and head for the fence. Being quartered close to the fence, the men felt their chances of success were good. They dug with case knives. Once the tunnel had advanced far enough, one man could lie on his back and dig with two knives. Another would remove the dirt in a small box and hand it up to a man at the opening. He, in turn, handed the box to yet another, who packed the dirt under a bunk.[31]

Mettam's group worked this way for two or three weeks. The men believed they were near the fence when, at about midnight one evening, the officer of the guard suddenly arrived with a squad of soldiers. The prisoners were required to reverse the process and fill in the tunnel "with the threat that we should not have a mouthful of food until it was finished." The men concluded that someone had turned them in for pay or other privileges, although they never determined who it was. "Even in prison," Mettam concluded, "there were traitors."[32]

Maj. Alderson concurred in that sentiment. "Many attempts were made to escape by tunneling at night," he wrote in 1912, "but we were always betrayed by some Judas, whom we called 'razorbacks,' or a spy from the outside." On one occasion, he recalled, a tunnel had been completed, and the men started on what they hoped would be their journey to freedom. Col. J. E. Josey of the Fifteenth Arkansas led the contingent. He and two others made it though, but as the fourth man stuck his head above the ground he saw those who had preceded him in the hands of the camp guard. "The order of procession was immediately reversed," Alderson wrote, "and the disappointed prisoners returned to their bunks."[33]

Former prisoner James W. A. Wright recalled that a shaft had been in progress in his barracks in March 1864 when he and a number of other officers were transferred to Fort Delaware. Tunneling, he noted, was "a popular enterprise for several months in Camp Chase after all hopes of early exchange were destroyed." Only the most trusted men were welcomed into the fold when these groups were plotting escapes. "Spies were kept among us," Wright insisted, "and it was hard to identify them." As with Mettam's committee, the men in Wright's barracks started in the area of the stove. They began the operation by moving the stove and removing some loose boards. "A file was obtained by careful management," Wright recalled, "then a 'strap hinge' was taken from the outhouse." Using the file, the men cut apart the two straps of the hinge. They then heated the two sections, bent and sharpened them, and attached them to small wooden handles with screws taken from the hinges. As the men went to the sinks, they carefully emptied the dirt from their pockets. Although he described in careful detail the procedure of the "popular enterprise," Wright did not record any successful escapes.[34]

Two escape attempts were made by charging the sentries, according to the accounts of two prisoners. Both occurred in 1864, and both ended in failure. Pvt. James W. Anderson, a Tennessee soldier, recorded in his diary that "a squad of forty or fifty" prisoners determined one night to make the attempt. "When the slightest demonstration was made," he wrote, "shots were fired and soon the whole Federal Guard was on the look out." One prisoner was shot in the thigh. Many of the others involved had their "greenbacks and fine cloths" confiscated in consequence. Considering what had been attempted, the casualties were surprisingly light.[35]

After the wood wagon betrayed his group's plans, R. M. Gray wrote, a coterie of Camp Chase prisoners organized a secret society "with grips, signs, passwords, and oaths." Their goal was to form a band of one thousand men who would break out by force and keep going until they reached Virginia. Gray and his comrades "were approached cautiously" by members of the group. "We readily embraced their desperate scheme," he recalled, "were introduced to the leaders, and after a strict examination were admitted into all of their secret designs." The group formed into companies of one hundred men, and each company was assigned a position of attack. They selected the evening of December 10, 1864 to make their escape. Armed with rocks, they planned to knock the sentinels from the walls with a geological volley. Then they would open the gate and somehow seize the arms of the relief guard. "Once armed," Gray remembered, "we thought 1000 desperate men an overmatch for any force which could be marshaled immediately against us."[36]

They never had the chance to test this theory. As the time of attack approached, the plotters discovered their prison surrounded with a large force of Union soldiers and a daunting display of artillery. The men had been betrayed, although they never learned by whom. Writing many years after the war, Gray concluded, "Twould not be safe even now for him to be known."[37]

By limiting the number of men who knew about his plan, W. S. Whiteman of the Tenth Tennessee Cavalry managed one of the rare escapes from Camp Chase. Rather than tunneling out from his own barracks, as he related to his daughter in a postwar letter, Whiteman befriended the prisoners in a barracks set aside for wounded men. Even if so tempted, these men could not get out to inform prison officials. The barracks had the added advantage of being located only ten or twelve feet from the prison wall. To avoid the danger of a cave-in, he proposed to dig down five feet before starting horizontally. Whiteman selected a handful of men he thoroughly trusted to help him with the project.

The only thing that came close to ruining the scheme was Whiteman's own trepidation. He and three comrades selected a dark, rainy night to make their break. Whiteman ventured through the tunnel first. "When I got to the end I peeped out at the guard," he recalled. "I could see everything so plain that I could not understand why my head would not be shot off if I undertook to pull though the hole to Terra Firma. My courage failed," he confessed, "and I crawled and pulled myself back." One of his fellows chided him for his loss of nerve and offered to start through himself. He, too, soon returned, insisting that his shoes had hindered him in the narrow tunnel. Taking them off, the man again headed down the shaft. Whiteman and two others followed. Those three remained together, but the shoeless escapee was nowhere to be found. "I think he must have run like a scared dog," Whiteman concluded, "as I have never seen or heard of him since that memorable time."[38]

On May 30, 1864 a detail of prisoners was doing landscaping work outside Prison 3. Seven of them received permission to go to a nearby pump, accompanied by a single guard, for a drink of water. The men jumped the guard, wrested away his gun, and bolted for the woods adjacent to the camp. Four were quickly recaptured, but the others apparently made good their escape. One of them, Pvt. John W. Gentry, was a member of the Twenty-sixth Alabama Infantry. The others, Hiram Hyden of Kentucky and John McBride of Virginia, were civilian prisoners. Reporting the incident to Hoffman, Col. William Richardson, then the commander of the camp, placed the blame on the negligence of the officer in charge of the work detail in permitting seven prisoners to go to the pump under the supervision of just one guard.[39]

Just a few weeks later, a group of prisoners came close to staging what would have been Camp Chase's most daring escape. As with previous attempts, bad luck played a large role in denying freedom to the prisoners. According to R. H. Strother of the Fourth Kentucky Cavalry, the men in Prison 3 organized themselves into military units as the summer of 1864 approached. After carefully instructing their recruits on the plan of attack, the leader decided to make the attempt at 10:00 a.m. on July 4. The prisoners had learned that many of the guards were planning to celebrate Independence Day at a picnic to be held a few miles from the camp, evening the odds considerably. The chosen time coincided with the scheduled arrival of the bread wagon, when the gate would be thrown open.

"The morning designated came bright and beautiful," Strother recalled. "The prisoners were jubilant over the prospect of escaping." One hundred men had been selected to make the initial charge, and they cautiously took their positions. Prison rules prohibited the men from gathering in large groups, so they clustered in parties of three or four, standing as near the gate as they could without attracting suspicion. As the wagon departed the men planned to follow it as closely as possible. When it passed through the gate, the leader of that first wave of attack was to shout, "Fresh fish!" That was the signal for the men in the barracks closest to the gate to fall in at the rear of the lead group. Successive waves of men, armed with rocks, were to follow. "Everything seemed to be working all right," Strother wrote, "and there was no indication that the officers in charge of the prison had suspected anything wrong."[40]

Indeed, camp officials suspected nothing. Neither spies nor "razorbacks" had discovered the plot. The plans were disrupted—quite inadvertently— by the driver of the bread wagon. Like the Union soldiers, he was looking forward to the picnic—so much so that he arrived at Camp Chase an hour early that day. The men outside the barracks made the charge as planned, but those waiting inside were not yet prepared to move out. About twenty-one prisoners made it through the gate, where they were met by several guards, mounted and preparing to depart for the picnic. All were easily recaptured. One, Pvt. Ezekiel A. Cloyd, was shot in the arm. The wound required amputation. Strother wrote that a guard was also shot, as was a cow grazing nearby—casualties not mentioned in the official report of the incident.[41]

Although the escape attempt was unsuccessful, Richardson's report left Hoffman indignant. The commissary general was anything but a bloodthirsty individual, but he nevertheless wrote, "It appears to me as something very remarkable that twenty-one prisoners could in the daytime rush through the prison guard and make their escape without injury to but one of them." He demanded a full report on "the organization of your prison guard, the number on post at a time, the orders given to sentinels, and the special duties of the guard, with a view to the safe custody of the prisoners."[42]

The most dramatic Civil War escape from the Columbus area—at least in terms of the attention it garnered—did not occur at Camp Chase. It did, however, involve personnel from the post. On the night of November 27–28 1863, seven Confederate military prisoners broke out of the

Ohio State Penitentiary, located in downtown Columbus, just a few miles from the camp. Any escape from Ohio's main prison was likely to make news. This one quickly found its way into folklore because the leader of the escapees was Confederate cavalry commander John Hunt Morgan.

On July 2, 1863 Morgan and some three thousand horsemen crossed the Cumberland River near Burkesville, Kentucky. Six days later they reached the Ohio at Brandenburg, sixty miles downstream from Louisville, and crossed into Indiana, thus launching one of the most legendary raids of the war. For the next two weeks Morgan and his men led their Union pursuers on a wild chase through Indiana and Ohio. Along the way they destroyed bridges and railroads, robbed and looted, and spread terror as they crossed the counties of southern Ohio. On July 19 a hastily arranged force blocked Morgan's crossing of the Ohio River at Buffington Island. He got many of his men across the river a few miles upstream, but for Morgan and the nine hundred men still with him, the game was up. The raiders turned north, as much fleeing felons at that point as a fearsome enemy force. Morgan remained elusive, however, prolonging the inevitable for a week and not giving up until he had reached Columbiana County in northeastern Ohio. He made it a point to surrender to a local militia officer he had captured along the way. In reversing their roles, Morgan enacted paroles for himself and his men. His pursuers repudiated the deal, as did their civil and military superiors.[43]

On July 12 Tod called militia companies in southern Ohio to service. Those in the southeastern section of the state were to report to Camp Marietta, and those from the southwestern counties were summoned to Camp Dennison. Camp Chase was the rendezvous for companies from six counties in central Ohio. Some fifty thousand men answered the governor's call, although fewer than half ever got within fifty miles of the action. Those at Camp Chase were mainly there as a preventive measure. Tod credited them with discouraging Morgan from attacking Columbus and perhaps looting the state treasury. The camp itself was also a potential target. As a further precaution, many of the prisoners were shipped to Fort Delaware as the raiders entered the state.[44]

In Morgan's raiders Union officials had several hundred prisoners. In Morgan himself they had a celebrity. Most of the former were soon bound for prison camps, including Camp Chase, Camp Douglas, and Camp Morton. Morgan found himself in the penitentiary, along with sixty-seven of his officers. The order sending them there came from Gen.

Halleck, with Tod's hearty approval. Officially, the high-profile prisoners were being held as hostages for Col. Abel Streight, a Union raider, who was allegedly being held in a Confederate jail. Word eventually reached the North that Streight and his men were being treated as prisoners of war. When it did, Morgan and his men were not accorded the same privilege. Instead they became hostages for Gen. Neal Dow, the prohibition crusader, who had been accused of recruiting slaves in Florida for Union service.[45]

Morgan and his officers arrived in Columbus on July 30 and, under Gen. Mason's supervision, were marched to the penitentiary. There they were turned over to Nathaniel Merion, warden of the prison. Before being taken to their cells, Morgan and his men were bathed and their hair and beards were closely trimmed. Such treatment was considered improper for prisoners of war, and for Southern officers, facial hair was worn as a badge of personal honor. Mason later claimed that he objected to the procedure. At the time, however, he defended Merion and his staff when Burnside suggested that such treatment was not advisable. "The cells to be occupied by them were new, sweet, and clean," Mason explained, adding, "The warden was desirous of keeping them so."[46]

It was not the last time that penitentiary policies would conflict with military practice. Treating Morgan and his officers like criminals had seemed a good idea to top civil and military leaders. Sending them to the state prison, however, created a dual responsibility shared between lower-level state officials and military officers. Eventually the results of this division of responsibility would prove embarrassing to both institutions. At first the confusion arising from this arrangement seemed innocuous. For example, Merion lost Mason's order for the delivery of a portion of the prisoners. In requesting a second copy, the warden suggested that one of Mason's officers had inadvertently carried the first off with him. Later communications reveal much more friction between a prickly warden and the military officials who, he felt, were interfering with the operations of his institution. When Capt. Robert Lamb, aide-de-camp at Camp Chase, inquired about "the conditions on which the prisoners of war . . . are held," Merion replied curtly, "They are held by virtue of an order from Gov. Tod, of which, if you require, I will send you a copy." He added that maintaining discipline among the military prisoners had been "a source of more vexation than the government of all state convicts."[47]

Morgan and his men were segregated from the other prisoners in the institution. During the daytime they could gather with each other in their cell block. At night they returned to their individual cells. Except for receiving coffee and sugar, they were treated much as the other prisoners. Occasionally the officers allegedly violated prison rules and ended up in solitary confinement in what Morgan referred to as "the dungeon," a dank, moldy, unlit cell. Thomas B. Webber found himself in solitary confinement, although not in the dungeon, after a letter he wrote was intercepted and sent to the War Department. Webber had written, "I hope all negroes captured in arms and their officers may be hung. I am willing to accept the consequences." A subsequent letter he wrote to Confederate secretary of war James Seddon concerning his punishment also ended up in Washington. With it came an endorsement from Mason reporting that the order to isolate Webber had come from Stanton.[48]

Not all of Morgan's men found life in the North objectionable. On August 16 Capt. Edwin Webber, commanding the prison at Camp Chase, forwarded to the War Department a list of "about one hundred" of the general's men in his custody who had applied to take the oath of allegiance. "I have talked with each personally," Webber noted, "and explained to them that they would be subject to the same laws as other citizens with respect to the draft &c. They were very anxious and seemed honest in their desire." The list, he added, represented "only a few of the many" eager to take the oath.[49]

Lt. Thomas W. Bullitt viewed his time at the penitentiary as an opportunity for intellectual and spiritual nourishment. "To say the truth I am very well satisfied with this [place]," he wrote in an August 29 diary entry, "and if we are to be prisoners [I] would as willingly remain here as at any place, for separate cells give us a retirement [and] an opportunity for study and reflection which I fear we cannot gain elsewhere." He added, "My Bible I have endeavored to study more closely than ever before, and I trust to be able to give to the subject of Religion a steady thorough and prayerful reflection." For a time Bullitt and his comrades had their physical needs richly met as well. "Had quite a handsome table set out from the boxes sent from Ky to certain of our number," he noted on August 30. This proved temporary. When word reached Washington that Morgan and his officers were being generously provisioned by friends, relatives, and admirers, Hoffman instructed Mason to put a stop to the deliveries.[50]

For their first three months in the penitentiary, Morgan and his men were the sole responsibility of Merion and his staff. A military guard of twenty-seven men was stationed at the prison, but they were under the warden's instructions and were mainly there as a reserve force in case of emergency. This changed on November 4, when the army assumed a larger role during the hours when the prisoners were outside their cells. Sgt. John Moon became the steward of the cell block in which the military captives were housed. Merion would later assert that he turned over to Moon full control of the cell block at Gen. Mason's insistence. Mason would claim that Moon was placed under Merion's authority.[51]

With nobody ultimately responsible, certain security details were overlooked. Among them was the daily inspection of the cells. This was the opportunity Morgan needed. With table knives stolen from the cafeteria, the men dug through the floor toward an air shaft they had discovered beneath one of the cells. Once they had reached it, they tunneled up to six other cells and outward toward the prison yard. On the night of November 26 Morgan and six others emerged from the end of the shaft just short of the prison wall. They scaled the wall with a rope made of bedding.[52]

The next morning William Wallace, in command of Camp Chase, informed Hoffman of the escape. He also sent notices to chiefs of police in Cincinnati, Pittsburgh, Sandusky, Detroit, Cleveland, Wheeling, and Indianapolis. Tod sent word to Stanton. "The warden and his guards are alone to blame," the governor asserted. Two days later he amended that opinion. As Merion and the military officers exchanged accusations, Tod concluded, "Both were certainly to blame, for between the two no inspection was had for the last twenty days." Tod offered a reward of $1,000 for Morgan's recapture. Stanton not only approved the measure but on December 2 urged Tod to increase the figure fivefold. At that point the war secretary believed Morgan was likely still in Columbus, "secreted with some copperhead." The same day Tod received a dispatch from Toronto assuring him that Morgan was not in the Canadian city. Based on what he termed reliable information, Tod had believed for three days that the general had indeed headed north.[53]

By that time Morgan, who had taken a passenger train from Columbus to Cincinnati the night of his escape, was well into Kentucky and safely on his way to the Confederate lines. Two captains who escaped with Morgan were recaptured near Louisville, a consolation prize of sorts for Union officials. In hopes of preventing future escapes, Col. Wallace ordered a search of all the military prisoners remaining in the penitentiary and their cells. The search lasted three days and uncovered Confederate and Union money, gold and silver watches, and pocketknives. The soldiers also confiscated "some thirty-five saws, very fine, and tempered to cut steel or iron." The saws, the inspecting officer explained, had been provided by one of Mason's guards "to assist [the prisoners] in making rings and trinkets." A February 1864 inspection followed the disclosure by a prisoner that several men were planning to attack the guards with homemade weapons. The inspectors discovered seven dinner knives filed to a sharp point. According to Col. Richardson, the escape plan extended to the prisoners at Camp Chase. Richardson implicated Morgan's brother-in-law, Gen. Basil Duke, who was confined at Camp Chase, in the plot. This was the last straw for federal officials. On March 18 Hoffman ordered all of the prisoners at the penitentiary transferred to Fort Delaware.[54]

The Ohio State Penitentiary was free of prisoners of war. The same month Camp Chase's prison population stood at 1,183. By the end of the summer it would exceed 3,000. Despite Hoffman's wishes, Camp Chase would remain a Union prison for the duration of the war; and despite frequent transfers to other camps, the number of prisoners would eventually approach 10,000.[55]

5

The Search for Stability

It is not clear when Union officials decided that Camp Chase would remain a Union prison. Indeed, there is no evidence that they ever consciously reached such a conclusion. The end of prisoner exchanges following the collapse of the cartel simply limited their options. As the number of captives in federal hands shot up rapidly, new places had to be found to put them. Point Lookout, Maryland, one of the Union's largest prison camps, was pressed into service after the battle of Gettysburg, receiving its first prisoners in July 1863. Rock Island, Illinois, followed in December, and the prison at Elmira, New York, began housing Confederate captives in July 1864. With so many major prison camps opening, it was unlikely that any would be closed.[1]

As circumstances conspired to dictate Camp Chase's evolution into a permanent Union prison, the depot finally achieved a measure of stability in its command structure. On June 23, 1863, Col. William Wallace of the Fifteenth Ohio assumed command of the camp. He owed the job to his immediate superior. On June 3 Gen. Mason had informed Gen. Rosecrans, then commanding the Department of the Cumberland, "Col. Wallace . . . is here too unwell to take the field. I would like him to command Camp Chase temporarily." Rosecrans gave his consent. On November 23 Mason recommended Wallace to Hoffman "as the permanent commander with a command reporting only to you."[2]

Wallace remained in command until February 10, 1864, when he was ordered to rejoin his regiment. His successor was Col. William Pitt Richardson. A Pennsylvania native, Richardson had served with the Third Ohio Infantry in the Mexican War. After returning from that conflict he was admitted to the bar, settling in as prosecuting attorney of Monroe County, Ohio. When war again broke out in 1861, Richardson raised two companies, which were accepted as part of the Twenty-fifth Ohio. The veteran soldier received an appointment as major and within a few weeks was promoted to lieutenant colonel. On May 10, 1862 Richardson earned promotion to colonel and took command of the regiment.

On May 2, 1863 Richardson suffered a serious wound to his right shoulder during the battle of Chancellorsville. The Twenty-fifth Ohio was part of the Second Brigade, First Division of the ill-fated Eleventh Corps, which bore the brunt of Stonewall Jackson's devastating flank attack during the Virginia battle. In his after-action report, Brig. Gen. Nathaniel C. McClean, commanding the Second Brigade, wrote that the First Brigade had quickly given way to Jackson's onslaught. McClean ordered Richardson and his regiment to "wheel to the right in column, and deploy on the double-quick into line facing the approaching enemy. This was done with as much precision as if on parade," McClean boasted, "and as soon as possible the regiment opened fire, and remained firm until ordered back." The wound Richardson suffered in trying to help stem the Union rout deprived him of the use of his arm. His next duty did not come until January 1864, when he was detailed as president of a court-martial that was convened at Camp Chase. His appointment to command the following month brought a stability that was long overdue. Richardson would remain in the post for the remainder of the war.[3]

In June 1864 a Camp Chase guard wrote of Richardson, "He is the most capable, efficient, and popular commandant we have ever had." The colonel had just been nominated for the office of state attorney general. "His election," the man feared, "will rob us of an almost father." Richardson declined the honor, and over the following months he proved worthy of the soldier's endorsement. He supervised major projects to rebuild the prison barracks and addressed long-standing drainage and health issues. He also earned a reputation among the prisoners as a humane commander. Writing in 1912, Maj. J. Coleman Alderson remembered Lt. Alexander Sankey, who commanded the guard and the prisoners, as being "cruel, even brutal in his treatment of the prisoners. Sometimes, when we were able to reach Colonel Richardson . . . our wrongs were righted." Former prisoner John F. Hickey, who worked in the camp hospital, concurred with Alderson's view of both men. Richardson, Hickey recalled, "at once stopped, in a measure, the inhumanities of Sankey, and inaugurated a pacific and humane course of treatment." Richardson's humanity, Hickey admitted, extended to permitting access "to a bottle of good old Kentucky bourbon." A woman had been allowed to send the bottle to her allegedly ailing husband, and twice a week the man visited the hospital "for treatment of his throat trouble." After one such session, Richardson told Col. William S. Hawkins, Hickey's supervisor at the hospital, "Colonel, if Sankey knew what you and Mr. Hickey are allowed to do, he would call out the guard and hang every mother's son of us around these headquarters."[4]

Indeed, Richardson seemed to be more understanding of the prisoners than he was of individuals who challenged his prerogatives as commander. After the battle of Chancellorsville Richardson had accused his division commander of being drunk during the fight. At Camp Chase he displayed a similar willingness to take on superiors. When Hoffman received a report from one of his inspectors stating that the muddy condition of the camp was "a disgrace to the service," he asked the camp commander for a reply. "To police mud," Richardson shot back, "is not practicable— I have tried it." Instead, the colonel suggested, "If you will authorize me to make the proper, and I think, *necessary* improvements in the grounds to prevent this overflow of mud, I will agree after they are completed, that it is my fault that the quarters and grounds are in bad condition if they are found so."[5]

On another occasion Richardson became indignant when Inspector General James Hardie ordered him to turn over to another officer all money belonging to the prisoners. Richardson felt his honesty was being questioned, and he resented it. He brusquely informed Hardie that he was "not unknown as an officer to the Secretary of War himself." Even members of Congress did not intimidate the prickly officer. Representative S. H. Boyd of Missouri learned this when he demanded the return of money belonging to a Dr. Boyd, a former Camp Chase prisoner and perhaps a relative of the congressman. Dr. Boyd had been transferred to Fort Delaware, Richardson explained. Even if he were still at Camp Chase, the commander was not permitted to turn over such funds to third parties. Richardson continued, "You betray a want of knowledge of the duties of officers in charge of prison posts that should have induced caution and polite inquiry instead of blustering and angry demand." Not mincing words, the colonel concluded, "Neither can I for a moment recognize your right to *demand* my reasons for any official act, and can only explain your conduct in this affair by inferring that you are [as] ignorant of your own powers and duties as you have demonstrated yourself to be of those of others."[6]

Although it took most of the war for Camp Chase to find a capable, permanent commander, the same was not true of its guard force. On October 27, 1862 the First Battalion of Governor's Guards, Ohio Volunteer Infantry, was mustered into federal service. The outfit was immediately assigned to duty at Camp Chase. The following July it was brought up to regiment strength as the Eighty-eighth OVI. Lt. Col. George W. Neff, commander of Camp Dennison and a former Confederate prisoner, was promoted to colonel and put in command of the regiment. Except for a foray to Cincinnati in the fall of 1863, the Eighty-eighth would serve as the permanent guard at Camp Chase. According to the unit's official postwar history, "The hope was cherished by the officers and men that they would be afforded a chance to display their acquirements at 'the front.' This hope was soon dissipated, orders having been received for the regiment to remain on duty at Camp Chase." This may have been true of many of the personnel. However, a recruiting notice placed in Ohio's *Delaware Gazette* when the outfit was being increased to the regimental level contradicts the notion. "This regiment is designed exclusively for guard duty at Camp Chase," potential enlistees were informed, "and in no event [is] to be taken out of the state." The ad continued, "Here is an opportunity to get into a very desirable branch of the service, to which young men liable to be drafted would do well to avail themseles."[7]

Among the men who did avail themselves of the opportunity was DeWitt C. Lugenbell, who, at age thirty-three, joined the regiment on July 10, 1863. Through a series of letters to the *Gazette*, Lugenbell, a veteran newspaper writer, kept Delaware readers informed of the adventures of their hometown regiment. If his views were representative of his comrades, the men of the Eighty-eighth harbored a very low opinion of the soldiers they guarded. In August 1863 several groups of prisoners were transferred to Camp Douglas. "Men are detailed from our regiment to guard them safely to [Camp Douglas]," Lugenbell wrote, "but the journey is not looked upon by the guards as a very envious one, from the fact their being while *en route*, in such close proximity to the lousy, dirty, filthy rebs, and thus invariably return well covered with 'grey-backs,' a class of vermin that cling to a person with a disagreeable tenacity." According to Lugenbell, several applications of a lye and water compound was the only way to remove them.[8]

"Sometimes a prisoner refuses to work at cleaning up in the prison," Lugenbell wrote in October, "but a little moral suasion in the shape of hand-cuffs and ball and chain with no rations soon brings him to his senses." The sergeant added, "They are furnished well by Uncle Sam at a great expense. Some say they live much better than they did at home. Still they are not satisfied, but want to get out so they can do more mischief." Lugenbell was particularly disgusted by a detachment of prisoners brought to camp during the spring of 1864. "The last batch bought in were a portion of [Gen. Nathan Bedford] Forrest's command," Lugenbell wrote, "who indulged in the gentlemanly pastime of inhumanely butchering negroes at Fort Pillow." He added, "They are a devilish looking set, and would undoubtedly cut a man's throat for a five cent Treasury note."[9]

The ball and chain that Lugenbell spoke of so highly was, of course, not viewed in such a positive light by at least one of his regiment's prisoners. W. C. Dodson of the Fifty-first Alabama Cavalry recalled that he and several of his messmates found themselves thus encumbered after addressing an unspecified protest to the commander. Among those punished was Capt. S. F. Nunnellee, who was much older than the other men and was suffering from a hip wound. "The shackles rendered him practically helpless," Dodson recalled, "and we younger ones had to wait on him like he was a child."[10]

Dodson had been captured near what was soon to become the Chickamauga battlefield on September 9, 1863. He wrote that he received much kinder treatment at the hands of his original captors. "I remained with . . . the rear guard for several days, and could not have been treated with more courteous consideration." A teamster loaned him a blanket, and the commissary issuing his rations said, "Now, Johnny, when you eat that up come back and get some more." Dodson noted that the home guards he encountered upon reaching Louisville were much less friendly, as were the guards at Camp Chase. Dodson attributed the difference to the experiences of the "brave men on the front," contrasting them with the guards, who had never been close to a battle.[11]

Col. George H. Moffett, who was captured in West Virginia in December 1863, concurred with Dodson's views. "I had no reason to complain of the treatment received from our captors," he wrote. "They were veteran soldiers who had seen a great deal of service. Consequently they were respectful in their behavior." By contrast, at Camp Chase: "The slightest infringement of prison rules often brought lamentable consequences." As an example, Moffett cited the case of a newly arrived prisoner who was unaware of the rule requiring fires and lights to be extinguished at night.

The man attempted to kindle a fire in the stove to warm himself. A sentinel saw the light and fired into the barracks, killing the prisoner.[12]

Although Moffett's story, published in 1905, might be dismissed as an example of postwar prison propaganda, it is not the only account concerning allegedly trigger-happy guards at Camp Chase. "A gun was fired last night diagonally into one of the houses below the window passing inside, but hurt no person," Georgia prisoner Thomas Sharpe recorded in his diary on August 4, 1864. He added, "Said to have been done because a stone was thrown at the Sentinel." Former prisoner James W. A. Wright recalled that one night a light was left burning a few minutes after taps were sounded. "Merely calling once, 'Put out that light,' a guard on the walls sent a ball whizzing through the thin partitions of the room." Although the ball passed close to some of the occupants of the barracks, none were hit. Maj. Alderson remembered two similar incidents that resulted in fatalities. One, similar to Moffett's account, involved a prisoner who was shot and killed after he lit a fire in the stove to keep warm one night. On another occasion, Alderson wrote, "the moon was shining through a back window in barracks No. 2, on the opposite side from the guard, who called, 'Lights out;' and as the moon did not go out, he killed two men sleeping together in their cold, narrow bunks."[13]

According to his account, Alderson himself narrowly avoided being shot shortly after his arrival. Knowing nothing of the prison rules, the major approached too close to the wall, crossing the "dead line." Hearing a "click, click," he looked up to behold a guard with his weapon leveled directly at him. "Raising his gun," Alderson related, "he asked me if I was a 'fresh fish.' He then asked if I had come in with the batch of prisoners that afternoon." Alderson replied that he had. The guard then informed him that he had orders "to shoot any d——n Rebel who came within ten feet of the prison walls." Alderson thanked the guard for the information and returned to his barracks, a valuable lesson learned.[14]

The dead line was actually a small ditch that, depending on various accounts, was between four and ten feet from the wall of each prison. "If an unfortunate 'Rebel' but passed over this line ignorantly he was instantly shot by the sentinels who lined the parapet above us," former prisoner R. M. Gray wrote in his postwar memoirs. Gray claimed to have witnessed several such shootings. Both Wright and Lt. James Taswell Mackey, the latter belonging to the Forty-eighth Tennessee Infantry, recorded instances of prisoners nearly being shot while engaged in the game of "fox and geese." According to Wright's postwar account, two players were grappling when they fell into the ditch. The sentinel took aim at them but was stopped by an officer who knocked the muzzle of the weapon into the air. On February 9, 1864, Mackey noted in his diary that a participant "unthoughtedly ran across the ditch which the prisoners are forbidden to cross." He, too, was immediately in the guard's sights. On this occasion it was a surgeon who saved the man from injury or death.[15]

Confederate prisoners were not the only ones who questioned the actions of Camp Chase guards. In January 1864 the commissary general of prisoners became concerned following a series of four shooting incidents that occurred between September 17 and December 19, 1863. Three of the shootings resulted in the death of a prisoner. Hoffman asked Wallace to investigate the incidents personally and report his findings. Instead of following those instructions, Wallace asked Lt. Col. August H. Poten, assistant commandant of prisons, to report on the shootings. He then forwarded Poten's reports to Hoffman.[16]

Wallace's inaction left Hoffman indignant. The commissary general had by that time received a copy of a disturbing report submitted to the surgeon general by Lt. Col. Lewis Humphreys, a medical inspector. According to the report, there had been cases of prisoners who had been shot by guards after dark not receiving medical attention until the following morning. "Such treatment of prisoners, whatever may be the necessity for wounding them, is barbarous and without possible excuse," Hoffman wrote. As for Wallace's delegated report, Hoffman fumed, "My telegram . . . required you to make a detailed report yourself and not turn it over to subordinate officers." Terming Poten's brief reports "vague or general, and without any evidence to support them," Hoffman demanded affidavits from witnesses. Until the matter was investigated satisfactorily, Hoffman ordered Wallace to relieve Poten from duty. "The rebels have outraged every human and Christian feeling by shooting down their prisoners without occasion," Hoffman lectured, "and it is hoped that Union soldiers will not bring reproach upon themselves by following their barbarous example."[17]

In relieving Poten, Wallace lost the services of an officer upon whom he had come to rely. Poten had arrived at Camp Chase in October 1863 as part of a detachment of the Fifteenth Regiment, Invalid Corps. Formed in April 1863, the Invalid Corps was composed of soldiers disabled because of wounds or disease. Later renamed the Veteran Reserve Corps, the organization performed a number of noncombat duties, freeing able soldiers needed in the fighting lines. Poten's outfit relieved the Eighty-eighth Ohio, which had been temporarily sent to Cincinnati for garrison duty. When the Fifteenth Regiment was transferred to Camp Douglas in December, Wallace requested that Poten be allowed to remain. In a telegram to the War Department, Wallace wrote, "He has become familiar with his duties and is almost indispensably necessary to me."[18]

Three of the four shootings in question came at the hands of guards under Poten's supervision, and two of them involved members of his regiment. His reports gave Hoffman reason to question Wallace's judgment and Poten's fitness for duty. On one occasion a guard had fired into a barracks because the prisoners failed to extinguish a light. The ball struck Henry Hupman of the Twentieth Virginia Cavalry in the arm. "He was put directly under treatment of the surgeon in charge of the prison hospital," Poten claimed. Surgeon G. W. Fitzpatrick remembered the incident differently. Fitzpatrick reported that he did not see the wounded man until late the next morning "while making my usual visit to Prison No. 1." Equally disturbing was Poten's rationalization of the whole affair. "As sad as this case may be," Poten wrote, "to wound a perhaps innocent man, . . . it has proved to be a most excellent lesson, very much needed in the prison—No. 1—as the rebel officers confined in that prison showed frequently before a disposition to disobey the orders given to them by our men on duty. They have since changed their minds and obey."[19]

Whether this chain of events had anything to do with Wallace being removed from command is not clear. His removal left Col. Richardson responsible for determining exactly what had happened. In the case of the Hupman shooting, three prisoners testified that they had extinguished the candle in their barracks when the sentinel first called "Lights out!" All insisted that the light the guard saw came from the stove, the door of which was broken off. The sentry who fired the fatal shot conceded that one of the prisoners had shouted that all the lights were out. The guard further admitted that he had "heard a cry" after he fired. The prisoners then requested permission to light a candle so they could treat their wounded comrade. The guard at first denied this request, although he relented several minutes later.[20]

The November 17 shooting of prisoner Hamilton McCarroll also involved a light from a stove, although the circumstances in this case came closer to justifying the guard's actions. McCarroll was a prisoner in Barracks 49 of Prison 3. It was one of a group of barracks from which a number of escape attempts had recently taken place. The sentries were alerted to pay particularly close attention to that section of the prison and to enforce strictly the rule against burning lights after dark. McCarroll did not have a blanket, and his messmates reported that he had kept a fire in the stove all night despite their warnings to the contrary. Sometime between 1:00 and 3:00 a.m., another prisoner opened the door to find a kettle to make some coffee. Prisoner H. P. J. Hathcock admitted that the stove "threw considerable light." The guard, John W. White, said he ordered the light out three times before firing, and his fellow sentinels supported his claim.[21]

The other two cases involved prisoners who allegedly approached too close to the fence. One was Samuel Lemley, shot on the night of September 17. The only witness Richardson produced was Thomas Reber of the Eighty-eighth Ohio, who was officer of the guard that night. According to Reber, the prisoners had gotten into the habit of running behind the sink, putting them beyond the limits of the dead line. He said he had warned a group of prisoners against this practice a few hours before the shooting occurred. Reber added that he distinctly heard the guard order Lemley to halt before he fired. Prisoner William L. Pope was shot on the night of November 5 after approaching closely to the fence. Two prisoners supported the guard's assertion that he shouted repeated warnings before firing. One added that Pope had been attempting to ask permission to burn a light to help care for a sick prisoner.[22]

Following the shootings at Camp Chase, Hoffman issued new instructions for all prison camps. "Rigid discipline must be preserved among the prisoners," the commissary general noted, "but great care must be observed that no wanton excesses or cruelties are committed under the plea of enforcing orders." Hoffman called for a board of officers to be convened after every shooting and its reports forwarded to him. He also insisted that both guards and prisoners be fully informed of camp regulations. Sentinels who fired upon prisoners would be required to justify their action under those regulations. At Camp Chase, Richardson took further action to limit the chances of prisoners being shot. In a set of instructions issued April 1, 1864, rules against allowing prisoners to congregate or burn lights after dark were reiterated. However, if prisoners ignored a guard's orders in those situations, the sentinel was to summon the sergeant of the guard instead of firing. Guards would be justified in firing only if the prisoners made an attempt to rush the fence.[23]

Despite these strictures, two more shootings occurred at Camp Chase in July 1864. On the 7th Tennessee prisoner Junius Cloyd was shot in the leg during roll call. Writing forty-eight years later, J. Coleman Alderson insisted that Cloyd's only offense had been to step forward when he mistakenly believed his name had been called. According to Richardson's report, which was written twelve days after the shooting, Cloyd refused to remain in his proper place after stepping forward but attempted to return to his original place in line. He was shot, the commandant added, after repeated warnings. The bullet struck Cloyd in the left leg below the knee, producing an injury that required amputation. Three days earlier Cloyd's father had lost his right arm after being shot during the Fourth of July escape attempt.[24]

Richardson did not specify the date of the other incident, which grew out of a violation of a rule against "throwing water or offal of any kind" in the ditch of Prison 3. When ordered to stop, the offending prisoner, Joseph W. Rutter, refused and "used much abusive language toward the sentinel." The guard fired. The ball passed through Rutter's arm, then struck another prisoner, Mahlon Hurst, in the left thigh. Hurst's wound required amputation of his leg. "Hurst had no connection with Rutter," Richardson conceded, "and is an entirely innocent sufferer." Although the guard violated Richardson's orders against firing upon a prisoner, the commanding officer noted that a "very insubordinate spirit has prevailed among the prisoners for four or five weeks." Because of this he went no further than to reprimand the guard. There is no record of Hoffman responding to the two reports.[25]

Unlike many of the earlier shootings, these came at the hands of the Eighty-eighth Ohio. The regiment returned in December 1863 after Governor Tod asked Stanton to send them back from Cincinnati. On December 4 he told the war secretary that the number of effective men at Camp Chase was far too small to handle the increasing prison population. Lt. Col. Samuel W. Beall of the Invalid Corps agreed. Five days before he had reported to Wallace, "This command of the Corps is overworked. Their duties are promptly performed, but their ranks are being gradually and constantly thinned. The fatigue and exposure is too great—much more so than if in the field." Beall's plea likely did not matter, but Tod's did. On December 9 the Eighty-eighth was ordered back from Cincinnati. It would remain at Camp Chase until the end of the war.[26]

Although Camp Chase's permanent guard regiment was back, it was not the sole outfit guarding prisoners. Men from the Seventh Regiment, Invalid Corps, arrived the same month. They remained through May 1864. In September 1864 a detachment of the Thirty-seventh Iowa Regiment was stationed at Camp Chase. Raised under the authority of Iowa's governor, Samuel J. Kirkwood, the outfit included no men younger than forty-five. One member reportedly was eighty. It was generally known as the Greybeard Regiment, and it also served at Alton, Rock Island, and Camp Morton. Although the regiment's members were obviously patriotic volunteers, they left at least one Camp Chase officer less than impressed. Visiting the guard stations on October 27, 1864, Capt. Robert Lamb reported that the Iowa soldiers were "doing very lax duty. A number of the guards were allowed to congregate together on the parapet and engage in conversation, some of them with their guns at an order arms, while others carried arms in various positions." Some of the guards were facing away from the camp's prisons, "gazing over the camp." If the Greybeards were lax, they were not the only ones. On March 3, 1865 Sankey reported that Camp Chase guards had lost nineteen Remington revolvers in seven months. The Thirty-seventh Iowa had been responsible for only one. The men of the Eighty-eighth Ohio had misplaced the other eighteen.[27]

Guards were not the only Union soldiers at Camp Chase. Although the facility's role as a prison had evolved into a permanent one, it continued to be a training camp for recruits. Among the thousands passing through was Sgt. John D. Axline. Like those of his predecessors, Axline's views of camp life were mixed. "Plenty to eat, plenty to wear, and to day got plenty of straw to sleep on, so I have prospects of a good night's rest if only the boys keep still," was his assessment on November 8, 1862. Indeed, the noise he had to endure in the barracks was his most constant complaint. Often he sought out the solitude of the officers' quarters to avoid it. He also disapproved of his comrades' habits, including card playing and the performances of "vulgar mouthed songsters." The training he was receiving also left Axline less than impressed. "The drill masters we have are not worth a curse," he wrote on November 14.[28]

Although not part of the original outpouring of enlistees, Axline was a volunteer. As such he was part of a vanishing breed of young men. As the war dragged on and casualties mounted, volunteers became increasingly rare. Because of this, on March 3, 1863, Congress passed the first draft law in the nation's history. The lawmakers enacted the measure out of necessity, but it resulted in soldiers who were far less eager to serve than the wide-eyed volunteers who had rushed to their country's defense in 1861. Many deserted, and many others tried to. Especially unreliable were men who had accepted cash to go as substitutes for draftees. Such substitutes were allowed under the conscription law, but many of them took the money and ran. Officials at Camp Chase were forced to deal with these "bounty jumpers" as well as other deserters. In April 1863 Gen. Mason addressed the problem by prohibiting the sale of civilian clothing to soldiers. When a new fence went up around the camp in the autumn of 1864 its purpose was to keep in Union soldiers rather than prisoners. Sgt. Lugenbell wrote that only patients of the hospital could come and go at will. "The new recruits learning this fact," he added, "many of them made slings for their arms or crutches, and by this means get out, and then skedaddle for parts unknown."[29]

Not all deserters were drafted men. On April 16, 1864 Lugenbell reported that three members of the Eighty-eighth Ohio had "skedaddled." One of them left with $100 he had borrowed from his comrades. "The most degraded rebel in our prisons here be a gentleman by the side of [any] of them," the sergeant observed. In August he informed his readers that the number of deserters from his regiment had reached twenty-seven.[30]

Other occupants of the deserters' prison came from a variety of regiments and were charged with a number of ancillary offenses. One, an apparent bounty jumper, had deserted from the Third Ohio and subsequently joined the Fifth Ohio Cavalry. Somehow, according to the provost marshal at Newark, Ohio, he had managed to report regularly to his original outfit for pay although he was not otherwise present. A member of the Forty-sixth Ohio had deserted while awaiting court-martial on the charge of selling forged furloughs to soldiers. The wife of a substitute with the Twelfth Ohio followed her husband all the way to Baltimore, where she slipped him some civilian clothing. He was arrested in Harrisburg, Pennsylvania, and taken to Camp Chase in September 1864. His wife visited him at the camp, where she stole $100 from a soldier confined in the guardhouse for drunkenness. Maj. John W. Skiles of the Eighty-eighth

Ohio, who was commanding Tod Barracks, a rendezvous for recruits in Columbus, urged Richardson to guard the deserter carefully. "[He] is a most slippery case and will desert you," Skiles warned. Richardson apparently did not heed the warning—on the night of November 18 the prisoner again escaped.[31]

Perhaps the greatest influx of recruits arrived in May 1864. John Brough had recently succeeded Tod as Ohio's governor, and he had an ambitious idea that he hoped might end the war by the end of 1864. Brough proposed organizing regiments of one-hundred-day volunteers. The men would largely perform garrison or guard duty behind the lines, freeing regulars for service at the front. Brough's fellow governors approved of the plan, as did President Lincoln, and each state was soon assigned a quota. Ohio called upon its recently organized National Guard to fill its portion. In sixteen days the state had 35,982 men to offer the national government.[32]

Several of the hundred-days men found themselves at Camp Chase, although only for a few days of training in most cases. B. R. Cowen, Ohio's adjutant general, sought Richardson's assistance in organizing the flood of recruits into companies of eighty-three men, which would then be formed into ten-company regiments. Cowen made the request on May 8. Seven days later Richardson had fifteen regiments organized. Through Cowen, Brough offered Richardson his "warmest thanks for the very valuable assistance you have rendered the State in organizing and forwarding our National Guard, and to the nation in expediting the addition of such liberal re-enforcemnts."[33]

The camp was alive with activity. "Regiments have been constantly arriving and others departing as soon as mustered and equipped," wrote "Palo Alto," a member of the 162nd Ohio. The anonymous soldier added, "A fine noble looking set of men they are, full of that patriotic ardor which gives assurance that the love of liberty and hatred of treason still lives in the hearts of the American people." There were, however, limits to the men's ardor. The process of consolidation was unpopular with many. Men found themselves separated from their original companies, and some officers found themselves suddenly without a command. This produced, Palo Alto observed, "a feeling of distrust and the impression among many that partiality and favoritism is shown to some companies."[34]

The men's other complaints had a familiar ring to them. John Harrod of the 132nd Ohio informed his wife that there were not enough woolen blankets to go around when his company arrived. He also continued a Camp Chase tradition by complaining about the mud. "There is nothing here to write about except rain and mud," he told his wife on May 16. When the 132nd moved from their tents to barracks, the men asked and received permission to delay the move until they could clean out their new quarters. Joseph L. Brown, a member of the 180th Ohio, an outfit that trained at Camp Chase during the autumn of 1864, found conditions no better. The roof of his barracks leaked badly. "We do not have very much to eat now," he told his sister, "frequently one slice of bread about an inch thick & coffee as much as we want is all we get at a meal."[35]

Across the camp these complaints would have struck a familiar chord with the increasing number of Confederate prisoners arriving at the camp. The difference, of course, was that the trainees were there only a few days or weeks. With the collapse of the cartel, the prisoners would remain for months or years. Despite this, in the world of Civil War prisons, these men were relatively lucky. Camp Chase, as one prisoner put it, was "in many respects . . . the most comfortable of all the Northern prisons." On the other hand, "relatively lucky," in the world of Civil War prisons, was a term with the emphasis on "relatively."[36]

1. Columbus photographer Manfred M. Griswold took four known photos of Camp Chase during its days as a prisoner of war camp. This one shows Prison 3. Courtesy of National Archives, Washington, DC.

2. Another view of Prison 3 from the Griswold collection. Courtesy of National Archives, Washington, DC.

3. The headquarters building at Camp Chase. Courtesy of National Archives, Washington, DC.

4. The prison camp made up only a small portion of Camp Chase. This view shows the barracks for Union recruits. The second building from the left is the sutler store. The third building from the left is the post office. Courtesy of National Archives, Washington, DC.

6

The Lives of the Prisoners

For prisoners arriving in Columbus, the recent days or weeks had already been trying. Capture, layovers in jails that were often filthy, and long marches and rides in freight cars proved difficult for all and debilitating for many. After all this they reached the Ohio capital only to learn that a four-mile march from the depot to Camp Chase still lay ahead. Under the best of circumstances it was an unpleasant prospect. Inclement weather made it much worse. George Moffett recalled stepping off the train very early in the morning of New Year's Day 1864 to a temperature of twenty-four degrees below zero with a stiff gale blowing. Although his memory may have exaggerated the circumstances a bit, the winter of his arrival was undeniably bitter. "The four-mile tramp across the bleak Scioto [River] bottoms to Camp Chase in the face of that cutting cold wind was an event in our prison experience never to be forgotten," he wrote. Upon reaching the camp, the "fresh fish" stood in the cold for nearly an hour as officials took down their names, ranks, and units. "It was not cheerful tidings," Moffett recalled, "when the officials informed us that two of the sentries had frozen to death on their posts that night."[1]

Pvt. James W. Anderson was among a group of prisoners who arrived on April 3, 1864. The men were first formed into a rank and ordered to give up all valuables. Anderson had a federal $10 bill, which he did not attempt to conceal. He surrendered it, receiving a receipt for the greenback the next day. The prisoners were then searched. "It was really amusing," Anderson wrote, "to see the prisoners working to smuggle in money, and other things such as pocket knives, etc. which were reported contraband." Anderson received a less thorough search than many of his fellow prisoners, a courtesy he attributed to the fact that he did not complain when the search was announced. James Taswell Mackey of the Forty-eighth Tennessee noted a similar procedure in his diary after arriving at Camp

Chase on January 18, 1864. He added, "Receipts are given for greenbacks, but none for Confederate [money]."[2]

Once the men had been searched and their names recorded, they headed for their new homes. For enlisted men, the overwhelming majority of Camp Chase prisoners, this meant Prison 2 or 3. "We had had nothing to eat all day," Pvt. Anderson wrote, "and I for one wanted none. I rolled myself in my shawl and stretched my weary bones out on the cleanest bunk I could see and slept until morning." Upon awaking, Anderson talked to some veteran prisoners, learning that he was an inmate of Prison 3. "It was an enclosure of about four acres," he recorded, "and contained 69 mess rooms which, with a forced effort, could be made to bunk twenty men." Anderson was apparently better educated than many of his fellow enlisted men. Looking around, he concluded, "I don't think a much ruffer set of fellows could be found." Although most officers were soon transferred to other prisons, a few remained at Camp Chase. They were housed in Prison 1, along with the political prisoners still remaining. "Within these limits, between three and four hundred officers of all ranks, up to a Brigadier-General, were confined," noted prisoner James W. A. Wright.[3]

The collapse of the cartel brought the realization that, despite Hoffman's wishes to the contrary, Camp Chase was to remain a Union prison for the duration of the war. It also meant increasing numbers of prisoners, far beyond what the camp was ever intended to hold, that would soon tax the capacity of the three prisons. As Camp Chase evolved from a temporary to a permanent depot for Confederate prisoners, it became obvious that the temporary measures of temporary commanders would no longer suffice. Soon after assuming command, Col. Richardson noted, "The original structures, having been put up in the spring of 1861 in a very temporary manner [are] nearly, if not quite, worn out and useless." He proposed an extension and at least the partial rebuilding of Prisons 1 and 2 and the relocation of Prison 3 "to put the prisons and camp in a sense of thorough repair." The plan was intended to increase the capacity of the prisons to hold "at least 7,000 prisoners." Richardson informed Hoffman, "I am also . . . changing the form of the camp, putting the barracks on three sides of a square, rendering it more compact and easily guarded." Under the plan Prison 1 remained the destination of Confederate officers. Civilians were removed to Prison 2. The wall for the new Prison 3 was completed in June 1864, and the prison was occupied on the 21st of that month. Since the new structures were built largely of lumber from the original buildings, the prisoners were temporarily housed in wall tents.[4]

On August 11, 1864 Thomas Sharpe recorded in his diary, "We hear today the work mess hammers tearing down the houses in Prison No. One . . . of course to put up others." By September 1 the noise had been replaced by "the hammers and saws of carpenters . . . sounding loud and quick all this week erecting more buildings inside Prison Two." As the term *work mess* indicates, prisoners performed much of the labor. Under orders from Hoffman only prisoners who had taken the oath of allegiance could be so employed. The labor earned the men extra privileges, including the right to purchase apples, bread, and other items.[5]

On January 16, 1865, soon after the work was completed, Pvt. Anderson recorded his observations of the renovated prisons. Prison 1, he wrote, had been enlarged to one and one-half acres. It contained two barracks, each with five mess rooms. There was space, he noted, for six more barracks of the same size. Prison 2 adjoined it on the south. In it were eighteen barracks that were twenty-four by one hundred feet, each capable of housing two hundred to three hundred men. Prison 3, Anderson wrote, "is entirely new and joins number 2 on the south." He had not seen it, but he wrote, "It is said to be very nicely laid out and kept." The enclosure contained seven acres. The parapet, he added, was "about 18 feet high around all and sentinels walk on the top at distances from one another of 40 yards."[6]

Old or new, the quarters at Camp Chase were Spartan. One blanket per man was the only bedding provided for the wooden bunks. "Some poor fellow's bony hip bones wore through the skin sleeping on the naked plank," recalled M. A. Ryan. In some barracks each bunk would accommodate three men. According to Col. Moffett, this allowed trios of prisoners sharing bunks to use one blanket as a thin mattress and the other two for covering. The bunks were generally three high, and Pvt. Anderson believed it was advantageous to seek out the top bunk. "First," he explained, "it's warmer because as science teaches heated air rises. So when the stove below gets warm we who bunk near the roof keep very comfortable. Second, having to climb seven or eight feet, lazzy fellows rarely ever have energy to climb so high to lounge, hence we can keep our blankets cleaner, and third, it's more private and not so much crowded."[7]

"Each man has his chair, stool, or box to sit on," Anderson wrote of the furnishings. Both Moffett and Wright recalled a "rough pine table" for dining. Wright added that some prisoners were fortunate enough to secure barrels, from which they manufactured chairs. One stove per barracks provided both heat and a place to cook. The prisoners received tin plates and cups plus cooking and eating utensils. James Mackey recorded that his mess of twenty prisoners had to share six plates, knives, and forks. However, Joseph Mason Kern of the Eleventh Virginia Cavalry recalled being housed in a barracks in which each of the thirty-six men had his own plate, cup, knife, and fork. The mess, Kern wrote, was also furnished with an ample supply of pots, frying pans, and coffeepots.[8]

The prisoners received their rations of food and wood daily and did their own cooking. Generally they delegated details of men on a rotating basis to do the cooking. The rations typically included beef or pork and bread or cornmeal. Potatoes were a frequent supplemental item, and occasionally the men received hominy, beans, or rice. Although M. A. Ryan would later assert, "There was just enough to keep us ravenously hungry all the time," his was a minority view, at least in the days before the War Department ordered the rations reduced. At the other extreme was Pvt. Anderson's view: "We lived too well for prisoners. Indeed, we could scarcely realize that we were in prison at all." Joseph Kern expressed a similar view in his postwar memoirs. "They were generally of good quality and enough to supply our wants," he wrote of his prison meals. Col. Moffett agreed to a point. "The diet was plain," he recalled, "yet the only fault we ever found was the scarcity of it." When Thomas Sharpe's mess received spoiled beef, the men were able to get it exchanged. Sharpe's conclusion about prison food at Camp Chase was that the captives got "enough to eat of [a] coarse diet."[9]

This changed during the spring and summer of 1864. On June 10 Sgt. Lugenbell wrote, "An order has been received . . . from the War Department to put the chivalry [Southern prisoners] on half rations. Of course they will crow at this," he predicted, "but it is much better than our boys get while in their hands."[10]

In that brief passage Lugenbell summarized the Union policy of retaliation—and the motivation behind that policy. Union retaliation was first subjected to scholarly analysis by historian William Best Hesseltine. In his landmark 1930 study, *Civil War Prisons: A Study in War Psychology,* Professor Hesseltine asserted that a wartime "psychosis" came to infect Northern thinking early in the conflict. It grew out of wildly exaggerated reports of "barbarities" perpetrated by the Confederates upon their prisoners. Northern newspapers became "the fomenters and agents for the dissemination of this psychosis." Before long they were not only spreading accounts of Confederate abuse but contrasting these stories with the allegedly generous treatment afforded Confederate prisoners. Stories of Camp Chase prisoners waited on by their slaves and enjoying visits to Columbus played into this thinking. The result, Hesseltine concluded, was a public outcry for retaliation, to which the Lincoln administration willingly responded.[11]

That a policy of retaliation was put into effect is beyond doubt. That it grew out of a "psychosis" is more difficult to prove. The earliest evidence that such a policy was taking shape dates from November 1863. Hoffman requested permission to have new barracks erected at Camp Douglas to accommodate an expected influx of prisoners. To this James A. Hardie, the assistant adjutant general of the army, replied, "The Secretary of War is not disposed at this time, in view of the treatment of our prisoners of war are receiving at the hands of the enemy, to erect fine establishments for their prisoners in our hands." He added, "Whatever is indispensable, however to prevent suffering, whether from the effects of weather or other causes, will be provided by commanding officers of prison establishments."[12]

Actual evidence of the suffering of Union prisoners at the hands of the Confederates came the following autumn when paroled prisoners began reaching the North. Adrian Root, commanding Camp Parole in Annapolis, reported that one contingent "arrived here in a pitiable condition of mind and body, having experienced extreme suffering from a want (apparently) of proper food." Five had died en route from City Point. An incensed Stanton demanded of Maj. Gen. Ethan A. Hitchcock, the Union commissioner of exchange, a report on the treatment of Union prisoners. "You are directed to take measures," Stanton added, "for precisely similar treatment toward all the prisoners held by the United States, in respect to food, clothing, medical treatment, and other necessaries." This Hitchcock advised against. His objection arose from security rather than humanitarian concerns. If the Northern prisoners' treatment was as bad as early reports indicated, Hitchcock feared that similar treatment would result in mass uprisings at Camp Chase and Camp Morton, "where the means of security are very slender." In his annual report, issued November 15, 1863, Halleck simultaneously endorsed and condemned the idea of retaliation. Such a policy, he wrote, was justified by the laws of warfare and by the treatment of Union prisoners. "Nevertheless," Halleck immediately added, "it is revolting to our sense of humanity to be forced to so cruel an alternative."[13]

The alternative first employed fell short of cruelty. On December 1 prisoners at all Union camps were forbidden from purchasing anything from the camp sutlers. Hoffman issued the order, but he would not have done so without Stanton's approval—or insistence. At the same time Hoffman informed the camp commander that prisoners could no longer receive shipments of clothing from anyone other than members of their immediate families. Even then they could be sent only items that were absolutely necessary. On March 3, 1864, for reasons never explained, the sutler stands were reopened. Hoffman sent all commanders a list of items permitted for sale. Socks, underclothes, and caps were allowed, but no other articles of clothing. The list also included several food items, but this proved temporary. Circular No. 4, issued by Hoffman at Stanton's direction on August 10, prohibited the prisoners from purchasing any food or clothing. Prison sutlers could sell only writing materials, postage stamps, tobacco, cigars, pipes, matches, combs, soap, toothbrushes, hairbrushes, clothes brushes, scissors, needles, thread, handkerchiefs, towels, and pocket looking glasses. The circular reiterated the limitations on prisoners receiving clothing. Family members could send food only in cases of illness.[14]

By then Hoffman and Stanton had put into effect a plan that reduced the prisoners' rations by approximately 20 percent. The war secretary was careful to protect his political flanks before acting. On May 4 he wrote to Senator Benjamin Wade, a powerful Radical Republican and chairman of the Joint Committee on the Conduct of the War, urging the senator and his fellow committee members to visit Annapolis, where released Union prisoners had recently arrived. "The enormity of the crime committed by the rebels toward our prisoners for the last several months is not known or realized by our people," Stanton wrote, "and cannot but fill with horror the civilized world when the facts are fully revealed." The next day the busy secretary reported to Lincoln, "Our prisoners are undergoing ferocious barbarity or the more horrible death of starvation."[15]

On May 19 Stanton presented Hoffman's plan for reduced rations to top military officials. Gen. Halleck, forgetting his assertion that retaliation was a "cruel alternative," approved the reductions and further suggested that tea, coffee, and sugar be eliminated. At the recommendation of Surgeon General J. K. Barnes, those items were restored for sick prisoners. With that exception, retaliation had become the policy of the War Department. Hoffman issued the circular that put the system into effect on June 1. The savings from the reduced rations were to be placed in a "prison fund" to purchase items needed by the prisoners that did not otherwise fit into the camp's budgets. The frugal Hoffman had already ordered camp commanders to establish similar funds. This sounded like a generous addendum, but at the end of the war the unspent prison funds totaled $1.8 million. The surplus at Camp Chase was $120,734.[16]

Historians have long discussed the motives of this policy and its effects. For the prisoners the question of retaliation was anything but an academic debate. The earliest surviving complaints from Camp Chase prisoners concerning short rations are from August 1864. "For several days our rations have been short in meat, less than 2 lbs. bacon and about 3/4 lbs. fresh beef," Sharpe wrote on the 25th. Sharpe seldom complained about his fate, but on October 13 he noted, "Bread rations are short, and we are all the time hungry." He added, "Some healthy men are actually suffering for lack of food." Maj. Alderson recalled, "The order was rigidly enforced, and our suffering thereafter cannot even be imagined." Even James Anderson, who generally was remarkably positive about his treatment, complained in his diary, "What's left on my plate would starve a snow bird. A cat tried it in here, but passed away of starvation." He added, "If any body should ever read these notes they will worry over my complaints of hunger, and, for all I speak, often yet I do not tell half the suffering I see."[17]

Not only was the quantity of the prisoners' rations reduced, so too, in the opinion of many prisoners, was their quality. "For two days we have had a new sort of ration, salt fish, said to be the white fish of the lakes," Sharpe noted on September 3. Over the next two months fish reappeared frequently on the menu, much to his disappointment. Although the prisoners viewed the fish rations as evidence of further Union retaliation, Richardson insisted that it was issued because of a difficulty in obtaining beef or pork. Still, Maj. Alderson pronounced the fish "unsound" and recalled, "Sometimes when the head[s] of the barrels were knocked out we smelled them in any part of the prison." After the prison officials began issuing fish, Marylander Henry Mettam recalled, "We were in a quandry for a while how to cook it." Calling upon all his culinary creativity, Mettam suggested boiling the fish and removing the bones, then mixing it with cornmeal and boiled potatoes before boiling the entire mixture again. The final step was to bake the resulting concoction. "It was beautiful and brown," the proud chef wrote of his improvised dish, "and we divided it between us six [messmates], and each had a square meal or fill, and kept a little over for our evening meal."[18]

Other means of combating hunger were less appetizing. Men made daily searches of the prison grounds for bones or any rare scrap of refuse. They also gathered whatever they could from the open sewer that ran through the middle of the camp. According to M. A. Ryan, the sewer was flushed daily by water from a tank at the head of the ditch. "Our boys would be strung along the sides of the ditch, and as [the contents] came floating by they would grab it and eat it like hungry dogs," he wrote. Beef bones were particularly sought after. The men broke them, boiled them, and carefully skimmed off the grease. They called it "bone butter" and considered it a delicacy when spread on bread. Meanwhile, the prisoners' hunger provided the guards with a strange form of amusement. From the parapets they tossed apple cores or melon rinds and watched the prisoners scuffle for them.[19]

"Our mess were so near out of anything to eat," Sharpe wrote on October 10, "that 3 of them made their breakfast on a big *grey rat* caught in a dead fall." Another group of men had a rat salted down for a future meal. As the rations at Camp Chase decreased, rat became a more common supplemental dish. Generally the rodents were fried in grease, and usually the prisoners spoke highly of the taste. One compared it favorably with squirrel. As Col. Moffett explained, "Fresh meat, regardless of species, was too much of a rarity among these hungry men to be discarded on account of an old prejudice." According to Henry Mettam, that attitude also applied to the feline species. Some members of his mess were walking near the commissary when they spotted "a good sized cat, looking nice and fat and apparently . . . filled with food that should have been ours." Possessed by both jealousy and hunger, they captured the animal and slaughtered it. After soaking it in saltwater overnight, they added onions and potatoes before cooking. The result, Mettam wrote, was a dish reminiscent of rabbit stew. He enjoyed the meal but admitted, "I have never been able to eat rabbit since."[20]

For many prisoners, the closing of the sutler stand was as troubling as the reduced rations. These were men who had the means of purchasing items to supplement their diets. Like any society, a prison camp had its "haves and have-nots." With this situation came a certain cultural Darwinism that often caused more affluent prisoners to feel that they had as little in common with their poorer comrades as they did with their Yankee captors. William Cary Dodson referred to one of his messmates as a "damphool," a play on words to which he appended the explanation, "No profanity intended." Dodson added, "He was nearer the 'missing link' than any human I ever saw." He recalled with disgust how the "damphool" became so filthy that another prisoner, a "French steamboat cook," was detailed to wash him.[21]

Although he did not go into detail, James Wright recalled that he and his fellow officers received more privileges and less severe treatment than the enlisted prisoners. It was not rank alone, however, that determined social class. Pvt. Anderson, who felt he had never seen a "ruffer set of fellows" than those in his original mess, rejoiced when a friend somehow found a mess room "on the citizen row." He invited Anderson and carefully chosen other men, including a railroad executive, to join him. Of his former messmates, Anderson wrote, "It was not my misfortune to have to stay long in this miserable dirty squad."[22]

A few of the men took pity on their less fortunate fellow prisoners. Horace Harmon Lurton had a friend in Kentucky who kept him well supplied with money and tobacco. He was concerned, however, for those not so fortunate. On at least two occasions he asked his benefactor if he would send clothing to "some of the prisoners who are without money or friends." He pleaded, "I wish that you would see that clothing . . . is sent [because] the parties whom I named are really needy and are particular friends of mine." In July 1864 members of the Masonic Lodge formed an association "for the purpose of relieving the wants of sick brethren and needy cases outside of the hospital." They appointed a secretary, an executive committee, corresponding secretaries, and a treasurer. The group collected monthly contributions from its members to purchase "tobacco and other small articles" for prisoners in need."[23]

Whatever the motive for limiting sutler sales might have been, one of its effects was to put all the prisoners on a more equal footing when it came to suffering. "We have met with a great misfortune within the last few days," Lurton wrote when the stand was first shut down. "Now," he lamented, "we will have to do without a great many luxuries I have been accustomed to." The normally unflappable Sharpe became agitated when foodstuffs were eliminated from the sutler's inventory. He reacted almost as if he was a dissatisfied customer at the prison. "[It has been] just five months since we were introduced to a settled prison life," he wrote on

September 14, 1864, "and if we were treated as well now as we were for the first 5 or 6 weeks the case would be much more tolerable." Limited purchases were not the only problem prisoners had with the sutler's stand. Shortly after the war George Washington Nelson recalled that a fellow prisoner had traded $10 for sutler's checks when he arrived at the camp. Later, when the man was transferred to Johnson's Island and wished to redeem the paper, the sutler was nowhere to be found."[24]

The limitations on receiving items from friends and relatives addressed a concern that Union officials had long held. As early as February 28, 1863, Webber had sought guidance for dealing with prisoners who received large sums of money from home. They wished to spend it on extra clothing and boots of a quality not readily available in the South. Replying on Hoffman's behalf, Capt. Wilson T. Hartz said prisoners should be limited to receiving or purchasing clothing and footwear "of the commonest quality" that would be of little use if they were exchanged. On March 11, 1864 Hoffman formalized the policy. In orders sent to commanders of all Union prisons, he wrote that "boxes containing nothing hurtful or contraband" could be delivered. Among the items considered contraband were any articles of clothing beyond what the prisoners immediately needed.[25]

The addition of foodstuffs to the list of contraband items, of course, was the most severe blow to the prisoners. It was also the least justifiable portion of the Union's retaliation policy. Reductions in rations, it could be claimed, put Confederate prisoners on a par with Union captives. It could also be justified, moral questions aside, on grounds of economy. Limitations on clothing prevented prisoners who might be subject to future exchanges from returning home better supplied. Banning the delivery of food sent from friends or relatives addressed no such concerns. Its only effect was to make certain that all Southern prisoners would remain hungry. Although Camp Chase officials told prisoners that they were only carrying out policies over which they had no control, at least one incident suggests otherwise. On November 18, 1864 Pvt. R. H. Geyer, a guard, found himself in the guardhouse for "attempting to furnish a prisoner apples while on duty."[26]

Although food was off-limits, other items did make it through to the prisoners. Lt. Tom Wallace informed a friend that the edibles she had sent him were confiscated, but he did receive the cigars that were enclosed. "They are splendid, & I was very much obliged." He intended to smoke them all despite being warned not to because of "an attack of palpitation of the heart" he had recently suffered.[27]

The Union's policy of retaliation was limited to sins of omission rather than commission. No surviving account from Camp Chase speaks of abuse of any type beyond limiting supplies of food and clothing. Even though the Civil War grew less civil as time wore on, there were limits beyond which the guards did not appear to pass. Indeed, the captives had few responsibilities. Among them was the requirement that they keep themselves clean. Pvt. Anderson wrote that, upon their arrival, he and his fellow prisoners had received an ample supply of soap accompanied by orders that every man "wash and clean himself up properly." One prisoner refused to comply and found himself in a tiny, solitary cell. Upon locking the man up, the guard remarked, "There now, let him stay without anything to eat. He is too lazy to live." The man had received the opportunity to clean himself, Anderson recorded, and the private fully supported the punishment.[28]

Besides doing their own cooking, the only other duties the prisoners had were to attend a daily roll call and police their quarters. Roll call was at 8:00 a.m. and was conducted at one mess at a time. A sergeant called the roll, supervised by the provost marshal, who held the rank of lieutenant. "The duties being light," prisoner Joseph Kern recalled, "there was plenty of idle time." Filling that time was one of the most vexing challenges the prisoners faced. Even those who rarely complained of their circumstances found it a depressing prospect. As Sharpe noted, "Imprisonment is hard to bear—however mild the treatment may be."[29]

The "idle time" of which Kern complained was a constant in Civil War prisons. Beyond that, there were significant differences from camp to camp that affected the level of suffering the Confederates endured. Chicago's Camp Douglas, for example, had, like Camp Chase, begun housing prisoners as a result of the fall of Fort Donelson in February 1862. It had also seen the prison population fall dramatically as exchange progressed under the cartel. The condition of its buildings deteriorated dramatically as a result of the Union parole policy. Unruly paroled soldiers were shipped there to prepare for departure to the Minnesota Indian wars. The angry men started fires and otherwise destroyed much of the camp.

The result, according to one historian of the camp, was a "battered, ramshackle collection of huts, festering latrines, and sagging fences." Unfortunately for prisoners destined for the Windy City, Hoffman's request to rectify the problem resulted in Stanton's tirade against "erect[ing] fine establishments" for Confederate prisoners. This meant those at Camp Douglas would have to endure bitter Chicago winters in barracks totally inadequate to protect them from the elements. The situation was complicated by administrative incompetence that left the prisoners poorly clad and often without blankets. Complicating it even more was administrative cruelty. Attempting to address a rash of escapes, Col. Charles De Land, the camp's commander, in 1863 ordered the floors of the barracks removed. "This will undoubtedly increase the sickness and mortality," he conceded in a message to Hoffman, "but it will save much trouble and add security."[30]

Prisoners confined at the camps pressed into service after the collapse of the cartel also generally fared poorly. Point Lookout, located on a peninsula between the Potomac River and Maryland's Chesapeake Bay, was established as a prison in July 1863, largely to handle the tremendous influx of prisoners captured at Gettysburg. Within three months there were nearly seven thousand prisoners in the camp, and more were on their way. Many arrived with smallpox. Others developed scurvy thanks to the lack of vegetables at the prison.[31]

Because the facility did not have barracks, Point Lookout prisoners were housed in tents that had been rejected for use by Union soldiers. The lack of barracks made Point Lookout unique among Union prisons. It was not a fact that the prisoners appreciated. Pvt. C. W. Jones of the Twenty-fourth Virginia Cavalry recalled after the war that he had been one of sixteen men assigned to a single tent when he arrived in December 1863. "I was thrown in company with prisoners of every nationality, kindred and tongue." Another Virginian, Charles Warren Hutt, was among a group of prisoners who pitched their tent on wood taken from cracker boxes, "which adds greatly to our comfort," he noted in his diary. As the winter of 1864–65 approached, Hutt observed a number of cracker-box huts going up to provide a bit more protection against the elements. They also provided more protection against thieves. Many prisoners cut into tents at night and absconded with what little property their fellow prisoners possessed.[32]

Tents also dotted the grounds during the early days at Elmira, New York's prison, which was established in July 1864. A number of the camp's first prisoners were men transferred from Point Lookout. Unfortunately, officials had not had sufficient time to prepare for them, and the captives found themselves trading canvas homes in Maryland for those in New York. Camp Chase was muddy, and Point Lookout was marshy. Elmira had a worse problem. Foster's Pond, a putrid body of water, bordered the camp. It created difficulties with drainage and bred disease at a frightening rate. A number of doctors, commanders, and inspectors complained of its ill effects. Nevertheless, the situation was not remedied until December 1864.[33]

Much farther west, the Rock Island prison, located in the middle of the Mississippi opposite Rock Island, Illinois, received its first prisoners in December 1863. Most had been captured by Grant's forces a month earlier at the battle of Chattanooga. Under instructions from Hoffman, the barracks were constructed quickly and cheaply. The budget-conscious administrator did not even allow a hospital to be built. The first result, exacerbated by a bitter winter, was much suffering. The next result, when smallpox broke out, was nearly two thousand deaths over the next twenty months.[34]

Any analysis of Civil War prisons winds up becoming a macabre comparison of horrors. Many such comparisons, at least of Northern camps, end at Fort Delaware. The camp was located on Pea Patch Island in the Delaware River opposite Delaware City. It was, in the opinion of one historian, "dreaded above all other Federal prisons." The water was so bad that camp officials eventually used boats to bring in fresh water from Brandywine Creek. The ground was so marshy that the barracks actually began to sink. A. J. Hamilton, a guard at the camp, wrote in his diary that "the stench is intolerable." Perhaps more revealing was the September 1863 testimony of Samuel Galloway. Morgan's raid had led officials at Camp Chase to transfer the political prisoners to Fort Delaware. Galloway, who was examining their cases, departed with them. After a few weeks, terming Fort Delaware "a very loathsome and unhealthy place," he requested that the prisoners be returned to Ohio.[35]

Although fewer negative accounts emerged from Camp Morton, Johnson's Island, and Camp Chase, that should not be taken to mean that they were pleasant places. Poor rations, a lack of clothing and blankets, and uncomfortable quarters were constant complaints at every camp. So were the twin problems of loneliness and boredom. The prisoners at Camp Chase filled the time as best they could. Outdoor activities included walking or running for exercise. Occasionally the men would engage in a game of "fox and geese." Cards, checkers, and chess, the latter two played with homemade boards and pieces, were common indoor amusements. Like most military camps, Camp Chase had a post band. Henry Massie Bullitt, a member of Morgan's cavalry, later recalled that he and his fellow prisoners "greatly enjoyed" the musicians' afternoon concerts.[36]

As at other Civil War prisons, carving was popular with many Camp Chase captives. It not only passed the time but also served as a way of earning money. A file, a knife, a clamp, and some sandpaper were all a man needed to set up shop. All could be obtained from the sutler, at least when the stand was in operation. Rings and small trinkets were the items the prisoners most commonly produced. However, Horace Lurton informed a friend that several men turned out violins, flutes, guitars, and other musical instruments. R. M. Gray recalled that he was penniless when he arrived at the camp and was eager to find a way to make some money. After observing a member of his mess whittling a spoon from a piece of maple, he decided to go into business for himself. Gray converted an old knife into a crude saw and went to work. "For a whole week," he remembered, "I sawed and whittled and finally succeeded in making a spoon to my taste." After producing about a dozen, he offered his wares for sale at 10¢ apiece. Soon he had earned about $5. By then, though, others had caught on to the potential profit, glutting the market. Gray turned his attention to pipes, which sold "tolerably well." Before long he had a comfortable nest egg saved. It was, however, largely for naught because Union officials then issued the restrictions on what the sutler could sell.[37]

As with the 1862 prisoners, many of the more literate men found solace in reading. "He who was so fortunate as to get a book or paper was very much envied," recalled Joseph Kern. Added James Wright, "Much time was spent in reading such books as we could buy, or as some were fortunate enough to receive from outside friends." On February 13, 1864 James Mackey happily recorded in his diary that a supply of novels and magazines had arrived at his mess, although he did not note the source of the windfall. According to Thomas Sharpe, some of the prisoners attempted to improve their education by reading law or physics texts. Over the course of about five weeks, Pvt. Anderson read the Old Testament. Newspapers, the Tennessean noted, were not allowed, but the prisoners occasionally received them by means of what he termed an "under ground railroad."[38]

The prisoners also attempted to publish their own newspaper. R. H. Strother, recalling the sheet some thirty-six years later, wrote that it was known as the *Rebel Sixty-four-Pounder, or Camp Chase Ventilator.* According to Strother, the paper included a number of writers who later "ranked high in the literary world." One series of articles, he recalled, contrasted the characteristics of natives of the various Southern states. Strother may have exaggerated, or perhaps Camp Chase prisoners produced more than one newspaper: on October 10, 1864 prisoner John Shields informed his sister that he could not send her a copy of the paper. "The boys finding that it would not pay," he explained, "issued one copy and quit."[39]

Sometimes the men found intellectual stimulation in general conversation or in associations they formed. "The mess frequently get into animated discussions sometimes on interesting subjects," Sharpe recorded. This he attributed to the fact that there were three lawyers in the group. The topics ranged from grammar to religion to "whether the moon has any effect on animal or vegetable life." In September 1864 what Sharpe termed "the literary gentlemen of this prison" formed the Jeff Davis Club or Literary Association. The association sponsored debates and recitations on various subjects. According to Horace Lurton, the debate association to which he belonged also functioned as a glee club.[40]

Although their access to news was limited, the prisoners took a great interest in Northern elections. In 1863 Clement L. Vallandigham was the Democratic Party's candidate for Ohio governor. Vallandigham was, depending upon one's point of view, a stalwart Peace Democrat or a notorious "Copperhead." Either way, his candidacy offered Ohioans a clear choice, as the Republicans nominated John Brough, who was loyal to the Lincoln administration. On October 18 the inmates of Prison 3 conducted their own election. Guard DeWitt Lugenbell reported the results. Vallandigham ended up with 1,081 votes, while Brough tallied only 2. "After this election by his friends," Lugenbell suggested, "Val ought to be appointed to some position in the prison." The next year Sharpe recorded in his diary the nomination of George McClellan as the Democratic candidate for president. "We hope [McClellan] will be elected," he wrote, "and pray that the hearts of the U.S. rulers may be disposed to acknowledge our Independence."[41]

In March 1864 the inmates of Prison 2 held a mock election. At stake were the offices of governor and lieutenant governor of Camp Chase as well as various legislative and judicial positions. Competing for the top job were Gen. Robert Vance of North Carolina and Col. William S. Hawkins of Tennessee. Hawkins, who worked in the prison hospital, often preached at Sunday services for the prisoners. He gained a certain measure of postwar fame for his poem "The Letter That Came Too Late," about a dying prisoner who longed to hear from his sweetheart. According to James Mackey, Vance had been nominated by a convention, while Hawkins ran as "the people's candidate." Since the prisoners were not allowed to cluster in groups, they had to receive special permission to gather and listen to the speeches. This was granted. On the day of the election a number of Union soldiers and civilians also showed up to hear the candidates. When the ballots were counted, Hawkins had carried the day. According to one witness, a deciding factor was the fact that Hawkins had ended his speech with a song of his own composing.[42]

For many men, elections and other diversions were not enough, and they sought comfort in faith. According to Pvt. Anderson, prayer meetings were held in his mess virtually every night. Rev. John E. Peterson, a prisoner from Mississippi, served as the leader. In addition to the joint glee club–debating association, "religious associations" also met in Horace Lurton's barracks. Thomas Sharpe joined a Bible class that was organized in September 1864. Of the two hundred men approached, twenty-five joined, "but there are many more no doubt that will join us," Sharpe optimistically wrote. The group began its study with the fourth and fifth chapters of the book of Matthew. The prisoners went beyond merely discussing the spiritual aspects of the text. "Those of the class who had classical education," Sharpe explained, "discussed the meaning of certain words of the text, giving the root and derivation of some of them." Regarding Camp Chase's nominal spiritual leader as too doctrinaire, Sharpe concluded, "I would like to see more than one class formed for there is some men here that I would rather be instructed by than by Col. Hawkins."[43]

For one class of prisoners, the Camp Chase experience was quite different, as were the potential problems such prisoners presented to camp officials. On January 2, 1863, the post commandant at Louisville, Kentucky, ordered thirteen prisoners transported to Camp Chase. Three of them were women dressed in military uniforms. They ended up in Prison 1, which was otherwise unoccupied at the time. In reporting the situation to Hoffman, Edwin Webber, then serving as the prison commander, said they were a mother and her two daughters. Arrested along with the woman's son, they were charged as spies and with smuggling contraband. Hoffman suggested that Webber place them in the city jail, but they remained at Camp Chase for two months. Money from the prison fund was used to purchase a number of items for them, including a coffeepot, two teapots, plates, saucers, cups, window blinds, a washtub, a washboard, and a clothesline.[44]

On April 15 two more female prisoners arrived. Miss Fannie Battle and Miss Harriet Booker, both of Davidson County, Tennessee, were charged with spying and smuggling goods through the lines with passes they had allegedly forged. Apparently, five women were too many for Webber. He had all of them taken to the home of "a loyal female" in Columbus and placed under strict guard. Miss Battle turned out to be the daughter of Col. Joel E. Battle, a Confederate. The colonel requested the assistance of Governor Isham Harris of Tennessee to secure both women's release. Harris, in turn, appealed to Confederate secretary of war James A. Seddon, who pronounced their arrest "another shameful outrage of the enemy" and referred the case to Robert Ould, the Confederate agent of exchange.[45]

Apparently Ould was able to secure quick action in the case. On April 23 Samuel Galloway reported on his interrogation of the pair. Of Miss Battle he wrote, "The prisoner is affable and attractive and well qualified by manners and mind to be influential for evil to the loyal cause." In Galloway's opinion, "There can be no doubt from the manner of the prisoner in replying to inquiries that she has been engaged in smuggling." Miss Booker he pronounced "less intelligent," adding, "She has obviously been under the control of Miss Battle." He recommended that both be exchanged and, if possible, kept separated. Five days later Hoffman ordered all five of Camp Chase's female prisoners forwarded to Washington, along with the charges against them. No further disposition of the cases was recorded. For camp officials, the departure of these prisoners was likely a source of relief. Housing male prisoners was difficult enough, and any additional complications made their challenges all the more difficult.[46]

7

The Health of the Prisoners

During Camp Chase's four years as a Union military camp, the most common complaint from soldiers there was about the ubiquitous mud. The nuisance produced by wet weather, freezing and thawing ground, and the camp's poor drainage garnished diaries and letters home, whether their writers were Union or Confederate. Recruit Jonathan Harrington, writing on February 2, 1862, informed his parents that the camp was "nothing but a regular mortar bed, the mud is from four to six inches deep." Prisoner Timothy McNamara agreed. Upon his arrival on February 26, 1862, McNamara's first observation of his prison was "a wooden wall enclosing about 1/2 acre of the wettest mudiest ground." Andrew Jackson Campbell termed Prison 3 "the filthiest, muddiest place I ever saw human beings in." Time apparently did not improve the situation. Writing in February 1863, Lt. J. K. Ferguson noted, "It has become so muddy that it is almost impossible to get about the prison." The problem still persisted in May 1864, when John Harrod, a Union recruit, attempted to describe the muddy scene to his wife. "It is the allfiredest time for rain and mud I ever seen. Just imagine a tent pitched in the middle of the road in the mudiest place between our house and Huntsville this spring and a thousand men walking around it constantly and in and out and not a dry inch of ground in sight to clean their feet on, and you can have some idea of our fix."[1]

As the first large wave of military prisoners arrived, Col. Moody, then commanding, made some attempt to correct the problem. He ran into an obstacle in the form of George B. Wright, Ohio's quartermaster general. When Moody applied for funds to open ditches in the camp, Wright responded, "I have already expended since the Fort Donaldson prisoners came over $400 in improvements and it is hard to see where all the money has gone." Still, Wright agreed that "every thing *necessary* should be done and a wise & prudent discretion must be exercised by you and it will be approved by the governor." Tod's prudence became less pronounced when federal dollars came into the picture. On July 10 he urged Hoffman to build a new prison between Camp Chase and Columbus. The governor was less worried about mud than about the potential problems created by keeping prisoners and recruits at the same facility. Regardless of Tod's reasons, his plan was rejected by Stanton. The exchange cartel had just been signed, and the war secretary felt Camp Chase would not be required much longer as a prison.[2]

This was not the last time the question of moving the camp arose. On August 3, 1863 Dr. D. Stanton, military superintendent of hospitals in Columbus, informed Gen. Mason, "The selection of ground [for Camp Chase] was a most unfortunate one. It is low, flat, and not susceptible of drainage." The location of the hospital, in the doctor's opinion, was even more unfortunate. Much of the camp drainage, he explained, accumulated near the hospital. In addition, its location between the highway and the parade ground left it susceptible to dust from both. Stanton concluded, "The occupation of a camp so situated for so long a time, chiefly by prisoners and paroled forces, with whom it is almost impossible to enforce police regulations, has made Camp Chase a very unhealthy place." Once again, Governor Tod appealed to Washington to have the camp moved, this time to a location near the Scioto River. Secretary Stanton forwarded Tod's proposal to Quartermaster General Meigs, who suggested that the project would be much more expensive than the governor had estimated. That was apparently all Stanton needed to know; nothing more was heard of relocating the camp.[3]

Instead, prodded by federal officials, Camp Chase commanders did battle with mud. When Capt. Lazelle made his July 1862 inspection trip at Hoffman's behest, he attributed much of the "terrible stench" that pervaded the camp to poor drainage. He called for an extensive program of grading the grounds and digging drains and ditches along walkways and roads. Returning in December, Lazelle found the prison to be "quite well drained." He did, however, suggest that the walks and roads be covered with gravel, a suggestion that Hoffman put into the form of an order. Capt. Webber, then commanding the prisons, put the orders into effect the following month. It was part of an overall improvement program that also saw cavalry quarters, barracks, and stables erected. A kitchen for the post hospital and an addition to the post quartermaster's office went up at the same time.[4]

More projects were undertaken during the summer of 1863. Among them was an eighteen-by-twenty-five-foot frame building for the quartermaster, the earlier extension apparently not being sufficient. Also built were a fence to enclose the quartermaster and commissary departments, a new headquarters building, a stable for the use of the commissary, and an addition to the commissary kitchen. In October Prison 2 was extended to allow for the construction of new sinks. Still, there remained limits to the improvements camp officials were allowed to construct. In October 1863 Gen. Mason proposed extensive improvements to the prison. Writing to Hoffman, he sought permission to move Prison 3 away from the center of the camp. Despite the changes already made, that area, Mason wrote, was "very foul from want of sufficient drainage." Further, relocating the prison would place it in closer proximity to the other two enclosures, making it easier to guard the prisoners. The general also wished to have a chapel and reading room built as well as a new prison hospital. "This matter [of constructing a hospital] has been delayed," Mason explained, "as we had hoped to get Camp Chase moved ere to this. Having failed in this it becomes absolutely necessary to increase the hospital accommodations largely." Hoffman approved each request. Such was not the case with the secretary of war. At first Stanton forbade the entire project. He later relented somewhat, allowing the hospital to be built. As it went up during December 1863, a medical inspector Hoffman sent to the camp reported that the new facility "is unfit and will not be comfortable when completed."[5]

The most extensive improvement project was done during the summer of 1864 under Col. Richardson. In making the proposal to Hoffman to move Prison 3, Richardson repeated Mason's arguments concerning health and increased efficiency in guarding the prisoners. As added ammunition he included a report from surgeon Albert Longwell endorsing the project. Richardson's plea was strengthened by Hoffman, who stated that the project was necessary to preserve the health of Union soldiers at the camp. However grudgingly, Stanton finally gave his approval to the project.[6]

Richardson boasted that his changes, in addition to improving the appearance and capacity of the camp, had also made it a healthier place. "I have adopted a plan for the sinks," he informed Hoffman, "by which the contents will be discharged outside the prison and [the sinks] can be kept thoroughly washed and clean at all times." As Pvt. Anderson described it,

Richardson's plan involved construction of a large reservoir, several hundred gallons in capacity. Each day it was filled, then opened so the rushing water could "carry away the filth that accumulates in a deep plank ditch thereby keeping all things quite clean." Richardson noted that he had employed a large force of men to construct drains. To support his contention, the colonel forwarded to Hoffman a report from the camp inspecting officer. With much of the work still to be completed, the inspector nevertheless reported, "The prisoners present a healthy appearance, being very much improved since their arrival at this post."[7]

The personnel situation in the medical department during much of Camp Chase's existence, like the command structure, was characterized by inconsistency. Between February and August 1863, four different individuals were listed as post surgeon. It seems likely that, as was the case with camp commanders, these doctors served until their regiments received orders to report to the field. On February 1 Dr. R. Schallern of the Fifty-eighth Ohio held the job. One month later Dr. Jonathan Morris was listed as post surgeon. In July L. C. Brown used the title in addressing correspondence to Col. Allison, then in command, although Morris's name still appeared on reports into August. Dr. Alex McBinn assumed the post on August 20.[8]

All these physicians had in common the duty to perform a difficult task with very little help. On April 1, 1862, Col. Moody ordered the post quartermaster to erect a hospital at the northeast corner of Prison 3 "for the use of diseased prisoners of war confined in said prison." Surviving records give no indication that the order was carried out. In his July 1862 inspection report, Lazelle indicated that hospital accommodations were woefully inadequate. Even if the hospital was built, constructing it was a less daunting task than staffing it. Such was the shortage of labor in the hospitals that individuals then representing very diverse groups were pressed into service. A March 5, 1862 special order announced, "Dr. Morris is hearby authorized to employ the Negroes in all the military prisons at Camp Chase in the hospital within the prison enclosure and the small hospital near Prison No. 1." At the same time Hoffman paroled six Confederate medical officers at Camp Morton. Their regiments had been transferred to Camp Chase, and Hoffman allowed them to follow and assist with their care.[9]

According to prisoner John Henry Guy, prisoners handled much of the medical care of their fellows. "The Yankee surgeons confine themselves to the Hospitals & intrust the care of the sick in the Prisons chiefly to our own surgeons, several of whom are Prisoners." In addition to medical care, at least one of the prison doctors kept the men up-to-date on war news and rumors. "This makes him always a welcome visitor," Guy noted. The fact that he was as "firm as one could wish in his Southern Sentiments" also endeared him to the occupants of Prison 3.[10]

Camp Chase's medical officials agreed that assistance was badly needed. On August 14, Dr. Morris complained to Allison that he was the only surgeon at the post hospital. Five hundred furloughed men were awaiting examinations, the doctor continued. Further, medicines had not been prescribed for the men in the hospital because Morris did not have the authority to do so. Upon assuming the post one week later, McBinn expressed similar complaints. "The labors to be done are of almost Herculean magnitude," he wrote, "when the small force employed to do it is considered." Examinations of the furloughed and invalid soldiers at the camp would take a month, he predicted. Meanwhile the bookkeeping and record-keeping systems "are quite in disorder." McBinn concluded, "I intend no reflections on any predecessors, for the institution has never had force enough since I have known it."[11]

The surgeon general of Columbus agreed with McBinn's bleak assessment. On August 14 Gustav C. E. Weber complained to W. A. Hammond, surgeon general of the United States Army, about the situation. There were sixteen hundred ill prisoners and three thousand sick Union soldiers at Camp Chase, Weber wrote. Over five hundred of the latter were awaiting examination. Regimental surgeons, who were busy meeting the needs of their outfits, were not available. Paroled surgeons had been pressed into service, but many of them were heading back to their units. "A first-class man with five good assistants ought to be appointed for this post at once," Weber urged. No record exists of Hammond responding to the appeal.[12]

The exchange cartel greatly eased the hospital crisis at Camp Chase. An inspector sent to the camp by Hoffman in October 1862 was unconcerned by the situation. Capt. Henry W. Freedley reported, "I found the hospital well arranged, well ventilated, and comfortable." There were only twenty-four patients. By that time exchange had reduced the total number of prisoners to 1,051, most of these political prisoners. Two months later Lazelle reported, "The hospital is well supplied with wholesome food, cooking utensils, fuel, medicine, and bedding." In a prison of nearly 800 inmates, the average number of sick was "about eighteen." This, Lazelle noted, made the prison healthier than the rest of the camp.[13]

As for the paroled Union soldiers who then populated Camp Chase and Camp Lew Wallace, there is virtually no record of any medical care they may have received. Although this is not conclusive evidence, it suggests that Union officials ignored these men's medical needs in the same way they ignored their welfare in general. Only a July 2, 1862 message from L. C. Brown to Col. Allison discusses the medical situation of the parolees. In it the surgeon informed the commander that he had detailed two hospital stewards "to prescribe and administer to" the sick parolees.[14]

The return of large numbers of prisoners in July 1863 after the collapse of the exchange cartel did not result in a significant increase in the number of prisoners who became ill. Between July 1863 and July 1864 the prison population was generally between two thousand and three thousand. According to monthly returns, the number of sick prisoners never exceeded seventy-four. The greatest number of deaths in a month was twenty-six, a total reached in both October 1863 and May 1864. Illness during this period peaked during January, February, and March 1864. This confirmed Pvt. Anderson's view that Ohio's harsh winters were difficult for his fellow Southerners. On December 11, 1864 he noted in his diary that it had been a particularly cold day. Three inches of snow covered the ground. "It's a hard time on Prisoners born and raised in Southern lands." Writing long after the war, Maj. J. Coleman Alderson recalled that winter temperatures often fell below zero. "We had never experienced such intensely cold weather," he explained, adding that the rule against fires at night led to severe suffering. The prisoners were not the only ones who suffered. On February 18, 1864 James Mackey noted in his diary, "No sentinel stalks on the parapet; the extreme cold has compelled them to crouch behind the wall."[15]

Sgt. Lugenbell suggested another cause of illness and death. In one of his frequent letters to his hometown newspaper, this one penned in August 1863, he reported, "Much sickness is prevailing among the rebs, which is not to be wondered at when we take into consideration the filth amid which they live." Lugenbell claimed that some actually died because of "grey backs" (lice) and other vermin that covered their bodies. The hospital in Prison 2, the sergeant added, was in the charge of a Confederate surgeon. "They say if any liquor is sent in for use in the hospital, he drinks it and rubs the bottles on the sick under his charge."[16]

The job of post surgeon continued to change hands, and sometimes the true occupant of the position was difficult to discern. A medical inspector sent by Hoffman in October 1863 reported that Dr. A. L. Fitzpatrick held the post. Another inspector dispatched in December identified Dr. G. W. Fitzpatrick as post surgeon (a version that later dispatches corroborate). Before the end of the month, Dr. Thomas McFadden succeeded Fitzpatrick, but his tenure was brief. On January 7, 1864 Dr. A. M. Clark, Hoffman's medical inspector, reported that McFadden had neglected to inform the post commander of an outbreak of varioloid, a potential harbinger of smallpox, among the Eighty-eighth Ohio. Further, he had failed to obtain enough medicine to vaccinate the entire regiment. "In this connection," Clark wrote, "I would again suggest the impropriety of intrusting the medical management of these posts to comparatively irresponsible contract surgeons." Although it is not clear if this report led to McFadden's dismissal, Dr. S. S. Schultz replaced him on February 6. Schultz was still serving in August when Dr. C. T. Alexander, another medical inspector sent by Hoffman, described him as "capable, but not attentive." Between those two dates, Dr. Albert Longwell signed at least one report as post surgeon, on April 11. A March 1864 letter from a Camp Chase guard also places Longwell in the job. A veteran of the Fourth Ohio, Longwell had been honorably discharged in 1862. He reenlisted in the summer of 1863, joining the Eighty-eighth as its surgeon. Dr. Longwell died at the camp in March 1865, a victim of what was listed as "Typhus Malaria."[17]

Regardless of the officer in charge of medical care at Camp Chase, inspectors sent by Hoffman and Secretary Stanton filed ambivalent reports concerning the state of such care at the post. After his November 7, 1863 inspection, Dr. Clark wrote that the general condition of the prisoners was good. He complained strongly, however, of poor drainage in the camp and a total lack of ventilation in the barracks. The hospital, he reported, was "utterly insufficient in capacity, poorly ventilated, and in need of repair." While blankets and bedding were sufficient and clean, the overall condition of the hospital Clark found "not very good." William W. Orme, dispatched by Stanton the following month to inspect a number of prison camps, concurred with Clark's findings. "The sanitary condition of the camp is very good," Orme reported. He quickly added, "The hospital is not as clean and neat as it should be." Clark returned in January, after construction of the new facility, and was more favorably impressed. In the same inspection report that faulted McFadden's procedures, Clark noted, "I found the sanitary condition of the prisoners' quarters and hospital quite satisfactory." In his August 11, 1864, inspection report, Dr. Alexander also gave the sanitary condition of the hospital high marks. Medical and surgical treatment he listed as fair.[18]

Both Clark and Alexander noted that nursing chores in the hospital were handled exclusively by prisoners. Among the volunteer nurses was John F. Hickey. In a postwar memoir, Hickey recalled that he and Col. Hawkins assumed the position only after giving their word of honor not to escape, nor to aid others attempting to escape. Among their duties was dispensing food and clothing sent by family members to the patients. According to Thomas Sharpe, members of the Masonic Lodge extended their charitable work to the hospital for a short time. They secured permission to visit the facility to distribute tobacco and other small items and to see that "the sick and wounded are attended through the day [and] the flies kept off." After his first visit, Sharpe wrote in his diary, "The sick I think are kindly and carefully nursed, and the surgeon in charge is a very agreeable gentleman." This good work ended in August, when Sharpe and his fellow Masons were removed from Prison 2, where the hospital was located, and transferred to Prison 1.[19]

Two outbreaks of smallpox in 1864 threatened the health of the camp. The first occurred in January. Dr. Clark was there at the time on one of his inspection trips. On the 7th he ordered that enough vaccine be secured to vaccinate "every person in or connected with, or who may hereafter become connected with the prison camps." The next day the surgeon of one of the regiments training at the camp announced that the disease had broken out in one of his unit's barracks. "It is imperatively necessary for the future health of that company," he wrote, "that the floor and bunks of that quarter be removed, the ground within thoroughly sprinkled with lime, a new floor laid, and new bunks erected, also that *every* part of the inside walls and roof be whitewashed with two good coats of white lime." Col. Wallace, then commanding the camp, immediately gave orders to have the work carried out.[20]

Despite the precautions, cases continued to be reported into February. On January 29 Lt. Mackey recorded in his diary that two prisoners had been taken to the "pest house" with the disease. On February 20 he reported that another three had been removed. Writing home on February 5, Sgt. Lugenbell said there were about ninety cases in the camp, "and the list is daily increasing." Few had died from the disease, but among those who had was a man from Lugenbell's company.[21]

The next outbreak was far worse. The first mention of it appears in the diary of Capt. A. S. McNeil of the Forty-fifth Virginia. On August 9, 1864 McNeil made the stark entry: "Smallpox raging." On September 6 Thomas Sharpe wrote, "Some uneasiness among us on account of small pox." He was aware of one prisoner who had been removed from Prison 1 to the pest house. According to the rumor mill, about twenty had gone from the other prisons. Lugenbell was soon writing home with the blunt report, "The prisoners have the small-pox quite bad, and many of them are dying." On October 14 Richardson reported to Hoffman, "The smallpox is prevailing in the prisons to a considerable extent, averaging this month ten cases pr day." There were 168 men in the pest house, which the commander noted was located outside the camp at "a considerable distance." Hoffman replied, "You will appreciate the necessity of doing all in your power to abate and remove the smallpox from the camp, and by every means to prevent its spreading." The commissary general ordered that no prisoner be transferred from the camp without a thorough medical examination. Otherwise he offered no assistance in dealing with the problem that he demanded be abated and removed.[22]

On November 26, after it had claimed 105 prisoners in a two-month period, Richardson reported that the disease was abating. Ten days later he informed Brig. Gen. Henry W. Wessells, who had temporarily replaced Hoffman on November 11, "Measures now adopted will soon eradicate smallpox." This optimism proved premature. In reports of December 16 and January 21, Richardson was forced to admit that the disease had not been eradicated at the camp. In the latter report he noted, "The smallpox is still prevailing to some extent, but vaccination is still going on and very soon all will have been favored with this means of prevention." The prisoners were somewhat less positive. As late as December 21, Pvt. Anderson recorded in his diary, "The air here if perfectly impregnated with small pox, and no man knows at what hour he is to be struck with this loathsome disease." A member of his mess had been taken to the hospital that day, and Anderson feared that the man would go from there to the pest house. "If so, we may bid him farewell." According to one prisoner, even the vaccine did not guarantee safety. "We were vaccinated with poisonous vaccine matter," Maj. Alderson later recalled, "and many arms became terribly swollen. The arms of some in Prisons 2 and 3 were amputated."[23]

Many of the dead were buried in a cemetery established solely for Camp Chase prisoners. According to Sgt. Lugenbell, it was located "a short distance in the rear of the camp on the banks of a run, in a quiet place." It eventually became the resting place for over twenty-two hundred men. Although granite markers were later provided, the graves at first were marked only by boards, on which were written the name, rank, company, regiment, branch of service, and date of death of the deceased. One exception was a marble monument erected by a family member. At first it bore a message, but according to Lugenbell, "[S]ome ruthless hand has entirely obliterated it." The marker read, "This stone was placed here by an only brother, who, at Shiloh and Perryville, met his brother in mortal combat; I a Federal, he a Rebel. Friends respect this stone for my sake.— W. W. Ranny."[24]

In November 1864 Col. Richardson reported to Wessells an even more serious matter of desecration. On the night of the 24th three men, including one listed as a doctor, had been arrested and charged with stealing the bodies of six prisoners from the Camp Chase cemetery. Richardson referred the matter to the Department of the Ohio. The judge advocate replied that the situation was a civil matter and instructed the commander to turn the men over to the state attorney general.[25]

The Camp Chase cemetery filled quickly as 1865 arrived. In addition to the continuing smallpox epidemic, a sudden large influx of prisoners presented camp officials with a different sort of health crisis. The prison population jumped dramatically in January, going from 5,523 the previous month to a total of 9,423. The number of prisoners remained over 9,000 in February before dropping to 7,861 in March.[26]

Many of these prisoners were members of Gen. John Bell Hood's Army of Tennessee. They went to Camp Chase after being captured by Gen. George H. Thomas's forces in Tennessee, and they arrived demoralized, weak, and ill. "About 2,400 prisoners have arrived here since Thomas' recent victories and more are expected soon," guard J. P. Preston wrote on January 4. He added, "They are the most destitute and spiritless of any perhaps that have ever arrived here, many of them being entirely barefoot and others suffering from scarcity of clothing." The camp commander agreed. Reporting to Wessells on January 21, Richardson noted,

"The prisoners received from Thomas' army have been very much exposed, and great mortality prevails." Although many of Hood's soldiers were sent to Camp Douglas and Johnson's Island, the saddest cases apparently went to Camp Chase, which was closest to the fighting front. On December 27 Hoffman, who had been sent to oversee prisoners captured in the western theater, informed Stanton that hospitalized prisoners would be sent to Camp Chase when they were able to travel. Prisoner Samuel B. Boyd witnessed the arrival of one such group. "Thirty five officers of Hood's army received here today, legless and armless," he wrote on March 12, 1865. "Many in a pitiable condition." Three days later he observed, "Another [body] carried out this morning," adding, "The prisoners pay no more, if as much, attention to a dead body as they would to a dead dog."[27]

An unnamed Camp Chase guard, writing in early February, noted of the prisoners, "They are as ragged as ever." The mortality rate he placed at between ten and eighteen men per day. Two hundred prisoners were in the hospital, while another two hundred smallpox patients resided in the pest house. Officially the number of prison deaths reached 293 in January, 499 in February, and 309 in March. These were the only three months of Camp Chase's existence that the death toll exceeded 160. Pneumonia was the most common cause of death, accounting for 180 in January and 357 in February. As for the decrease in deaths in March, Capt. Edward K. Allen, Camp Chase's inspecting officer, offered a blunt explanation on March 11. "A very large decrease in numbers of sick and deaths is attributable to the fact that those brought here in an almost dying condition have died."[28]

While the poor health of the prisoners arriving at the camp was a major factor in the higher number of deaths, at least one medical inspector placed a portion of the blame on both camp and federal officials. Lt. Col. Richard H. Coolidge visited the camp in March. After reading Coolidge's report, Col. Charles Tripler, medical director of the Northern Department, asserted, "The mortality at Camp Chase [is] due to bad police & overcrowding." Tripler went on to report, "The barracks are in the worst possible condition (save that they have not been used as sinks) and no system of police has been enforced." He placed a greater blame on the crowded condition of the camp. In addition to the large influx of prisoners, several thousand recruits and paroled Union soldiers were arriving at the camp. All this was occurring "at a season of the year when inflammation of the lungs, fever of severe type, all aggravated by foul air, are very prevalent."

Tripler urged that a large portion of the recruits and parolees destined for Camp Chase be sent elsewhere and that camp officials receive orders "to organize immediate police squads & enforce the *immediate* & thorough police of all barracks & of sinks & grounds as soon as *practicable.*"[29]

Responding to the report on April 1, H. E. Warner, post surgeon, conceded that "the general police of the hospital and surrounding grounds . . . have been greatly neglected." Despite that, he placed the blame for the "frightful mortality of this post" on the crowding of the hospital wards. The six wards, Warner reported, had a total of 217 patients. He reported that he had been forced to press three hospital tents into service. Twenty-two prisoners were being treated in them. "As long as Camp Chase is a rendezvous for recruits and paroled forces," Warner concluded, "I would respectfully suggest that the hospital accommodations be increased."[30]

Officials had the luxury of debating the causes of Camp Chase's high mortality rate. For the prisoners, the battle to remain alive went well beyond a topic of discussion. Among the saddest cases was that of Washington Pickens Nance. A member of the Tenth Alabama Cavalry, Nance was captured on December 23, 1864 during a skirmish in Madison County, Alabama. Following brief stays in Huntsville and Stevenson, Nance and a group of some fifty prisoners arrived in Nashville on December 31. There they were lodged in a prison for three days before being transferred to Louisville, where they remained for a week. On January 9 the prisoners were ferried across the Ohio and put on railroad cars. Two days later they arrived at Camp Chase.[31]

Six inches of snow covered the ground, and the temperature was very cold, although the sun was "shining very nice." Four days after arriving Nance spent his first Sunday at the camp reading his Bible. Many prisoners did the same, while others played cards, told stories, and made rings and other items to sell for money to purchase pepper, tobacco, and writing paper. In early February the prison was "all excitement about exchange." With the war winding down, the cartel was back in operation. By February 11 some men in Nance's brigade had been called. "I have been here one month," he wrote that day, "and have no prospect of leaving before some time in March but expect to have at that time."[32]

The weather remained cold, but one advantage of the men leaving on exchange was a more abundant supply of blankets. On February 23 Nance expressed gratitude in his diary for continued good health. "Many of the prisoners are Sick." Five men from his command had died. Over the next month Nance devoted a great deal of space in his diary to the continuing exchange. Five hundred left on March 4. "The boys are marching out in a glow of spirits," he wrote, "although it is very cold."[33]

It was among his last entries. On March 18, less than a month before Appomattox and three months short of Nance's fortieth birthday, David Branson, a fellow prisoner, made the final entry in Nance's diary. Nance had taken ill on March 10, Branson wrote. He went to the hospital five days later and died on March 18. "He Died perfectly Eassey," Branson noted, "without a groan." Branson continued, "He said he new he would soon take his Exit that he would soon meet the Grate Judge of the universe but he said he was not afraid to finish the Battle." Nance asked that Branson and another friend get the news to his family. Branson concluded, "He said it would be Tidings to his Family to know that he had no fears for Death."[34]

8

"i think i feel a change"

The case of Washington Pickens Nance was not unique. Among the saddest ironies of Camp Chase's four years of service is the fact that the number of deaths peaked in February 1865, two months before Lee's surrender and five months before the facility was virtually empty of prisoners. Camp officials were not entirely to blame. Indeed, if the stories of two captives who arrived during the winter of 1865 are typical, the most surprising fact may be that more men did not die.

William H. Young of the Fifth Mississippi Cavalry was captured near Nashville on December 6, 1864. He and his comrades had dismounted to engage Union soldiers in a skirmish. When the fighting went against the Confederates, the men who stayed behind to hold the troopers' horses fled the scene. Young was attempting to mount a civilian's horse to make his escape when he looked up and saw a group of Yankees surrounding him. "Surrender or I'll shoot says Yank which you may suppose I did," Young explained in a letter home.[1]

"They treated me very kindly," Young wrote of his Union captors, "[and] spoke to me as if we had been friends of long standing." Despite that, the food the Yankees promised the prisoners after they stopped for the night never arrived. The next morning Young and twenty-one other captives were marched eight miles over muddy roads to Nashville. "Oh I was tired when I got there," Young wrote, "[but] this was only the beginning of trouble to us." The men were forced to remain in a rock quarry for five days and nights, exposed to rain and snow. They received little to eat and had "no fire of consequence." Young reported that several died before the men were taken to the penitentiary. Although he offered no details, Young described his trip from Nashville to Columbus as "long and miserable." He reached Camp Chase on January 4. Of the fifteen men from his regiment that arrived with him, seven or eight soon died, he informed his family on March 18. Another had been left behind at a Nashville hospital. "I guess [he] has died," Young wrote, "as we have heard nothing of him since."[2]

Samuel Beckett Boyd, a civilian clerk of the "Ordinance Dept., C. S. A.," was among a group of prisoners captured by Union forces at Bristol, Tennessee, on December 14, 1864. The captives were marched to Knoxville, a distance of over one hundred miles. Heavy rains marked the journey, and camping in the open added to the suffering. So, too, did the men's lack of coats and boots. "My boots gave out the first day," Boyd informed his uncle, "and I was almost barefoot." A woman along the route took pity on him and gave him an old shoe. This allowed him to discard the worse of his boots.[3]

From Knoxville the prisoners traveled by rail to Chattanooga, where they were put in a military prison. On January 5 Boyd and about one hundred other prisoners climbed aboard boxcars for the trip to Nashville. Along the way Boyd's car jumped the tracks. Nobody was injured, but the damaged car could not be repaired. As a result he and several others had to ride on the roof of another car through a soaking rain the last sixty miles to the Tennessee capital. Upon their arrival the men had to wait another two hours before gaining admission to the penitentiary. Even inside the walls of the prison Boyd and the others gained no relief from the weather. Instead of being placed in cells, they spent two days in the prison yard before starting out for Louisville. Boyd found the Louisville prison more comfortable. The rations were also better, and the surgeon was "very attentive."[4]

After six days in Louisville, Boyd and the others began the rail journey to Columbus. Most of the men were eager to make the trip. Boyd spoke for many when he noted in his diary, "[My] own desire is for change, hoping to get to the good place always just ahead."[5]

At first he did not find that good place at Camp Chase. Arriving on January 14, Boyd wrote, "Put in Prison No. 2 and spent a miserable night in the midst of all that was disagreeable in locality and conduct." He was one of 250 men in the barracks, which was heated by three stoves. The next day Boyd and three friends were transferred, at their request, to Prison 1. There they found life better. Twenty men occupied a barracks, and there was a sufficient number of blankets and a good stove with plenty of wood for heating and cooking. A relaxation of the restrictions placed on the sutler also made life better for Boyd and his comrades. Apples were available on February 18, and Boyd reported that there was "quite a rush to get them." The scene was repeated nine days later. The sutler had apparently acquired a large quantity because he was by then offering the apples for 40¢ a dozen. On March 20 coffee, sugar, "and all eatables" were offered for sale. Of course, access to them depended on a man's means.[6]

In late 1864 Robert Ould, the Confederate agent of exchange, attempted to do something for those prisoners who did not have money. On October 30 Ould asked Gen. Grant, now general in chief of the Union army, if his government would allow a shipment of cotton to be sent from a Southern port to a Northern city. Under Ould's plan, proceeds from the sale of the cotton would be used to purchase blankets and other supplies for Confederate prisoners. Grant responded favorably to the proposal and quickly gained approval from government officials. On November 11 Ould informed Grant that one thousand bales of cotton would be delivered to Mobile Bay. He asked that Maj. Gen. Issac R. Trimble, a prisoner of war at Fort Warren, be given a parole to receive and sell the cotton and purchase and distribute the supplies.[7]

Problems almost immediately surfaced. Stanton rejected Trimble as the agent for the transaction, terming him "the most dangerous rebel in our hands." Brig. Gen. William N. R. Beall was selected in his place. He was to be accompanied by a Union representative, Brig. Gen. Halbert E. Paine. Although Stanton at first indicated that Gen. Beall would be acceptable, the secretary later ordered Paine, for reasons not explained, to suspend Beall's parole. The Confederate agent soon found himself in a cell at Fort Lafayette, in New York Harbor. There he was to remain until the cotton was delivered, which made it impossible to make prior arrangements for its sale and the purchase of supplies. Poor communications between Union and Confederate officials at Mobile, meanwhile, delayed the shipment of the cotton. It arrived at New York on January 24, some two months later than originally planned—and far too late to alleviate the suffering of the prisoners as winter set in.[8]

This was especially true at Camp Chase. Long before the cotton arrived, orders went out from Wessells's office to prison commanders to cooperate with Paine and Beall when they arrived at their respective camps. Officers were to be selected from among the prisoners to receive and distribute the supplies. At Camp Chase Col. Hawkins, Col. John E. Josey, and Capt. C. T. Smith served as the camp's representatives. On December 27, nearly a month before the cotton arrived in New York, Hawkins sent word to Beall that twenty-five hundred prisoners were on their way to Camp Chase from Tennessee greatly in need of blankets and clothing. Beall responded by seeking permission to purchase supplies on credit in anticipation of the shipment. If that could not be done, he requested that Richardson be directed to furnish necessary supplies, with Beall agreeing to reimburse the government. Both requests were denied, forcing Beall to suggest weakly to Hawkins that he "look to making those prisoners to arrive comfortable. Get other prisoners to divide with them," he asked, "with the full understanding that I will furnish all late arrivals when they are destitute first."[9]

A total of 828 bales of cotton reached New York. After expenses it brought $331,789.66. With the proceeds Beall purchased 16,983 blankets, 16,216 jackets and coats, 19,888 pairs of pants, 19,000 shirts, 17,000 shoes, and several other items. Camp Chase's allotment arrived in early March. "Col. Will Hawkins distributed some very nice clothing to the prisoners," Washington Pickens Nance observed on March 7. More was issued three days later. On the 12th Nance wrote in his diary, "The prisoners look considerably improved dressed up in the new clothing Col. Hawkins distributed."[10]

That the items purchased with the proceeds of the cotton sales made the prisoners more comfortable is beyond doubt. It is likely that their distribution also saved many lives during the final winter of the war. Despite that, Stanton ordered a halt to the operation after the first shipment. His pretext was that Beall had purchased only clothing and blankets, not foodstuffs. "The result," Halleck wrote to Grant by way of explaining Stanton's objections, "is that we feed their prisoners and permit the rebel Government to send cotton within our lines, free of all charge, to purchase and carry back the means of fitting out their own men for the field."[11]

From a purely practical standpoint, Stanton's argument was correct. Many of the Confederates were indeed carrying the newly purchased supplies back to the South. As Nance had observed, prisoner exchange had finally been resumed. On January 24, 1865 Ould made an offer to Grant to begin a general exchange. "I propose that all of them [prisoners in Confederate hands] be delivered to you in exchange, man for man and officer for officer, according to grade, for those of ours whom you hold." The offer dealt with the problematic question of race by ignoring it. On February 2 Grant informed Stanton that he was "endeavoring to make arrangements to exchange about 3,000 prisoners per week." On the 16th

Grant sent formal word through Lt. Col. John E. Mulford, federal assistant agent for exchange, that he accepted Ould's proposal.[12]

Even before the agreement was official, word of the impending exchange reached Camp Chase. On February 5 Samuel Boyd noted in his diary that an announcement of the news had interrupted the prisoners' Sunday services. To this Boyd added two words: "Great joy." Even before that, Boyd had heard rumors of the resumption of the cartel. Such prison "grape" was common, and it had often led to great disappointment. This time the captives apparently gave credence to the reports. "Prospect of exchange creates quite an excitement," Boyd wrote on January 24. Seven days later the possibility was still a major topic of conversation. Boyd wrote, "*Willing to be exchanged for Negroes.*"[13]

Washington Pickens Nance mentioned five departures of five hundred prisoners between February 12 and March 4. DeWitt Lugenbell confirmed those figures. On March 8 he wrote that "five installments of Johnnies of 500 each" had recently left for exchange. On March 18 Boyd recorded the departure of another five hundred. Included were thirty officers "and all the Citizens who wished to go."[14]

Not all citizen prisoners did wish to go. The same was true for a number of captives from the Confederate army. This created a dilemma for Union military officials. In early February, according to local press accounts, Gen. Richardson, who had received a brevet promotion in December, received orders to make out an exchange list of three thousand prisoners. Those who did not want to be exchanged were to be excluded. Richardson called out a detachment of prisoners and asked those desiring to remain to step five paces forward. Only six prisoners did so. That evening, however, the commandant "received notes innumerable from prisoners, begging to be retained." Richardson repeated the process the next morning, informing the men that this time the decision would be final. The result was that 260 came forward. Most, according to the report, were from Hood's army.[15]

This procedure did not sit well with Gen. Grant. "I see it stated in the papers," Grant informed Hitchcock on February 16, "that where some prisoners in the West were paraded to be sent forward for exchange, those who preferred Northern prisons to a return to the rebel service were invited to step to the front." Grant considered this a mistake. "Those who do not want to go back are the ones whom it is most desirable to exchange," he explained. Those not wishing to return to the Confederate army, Grant noted, could desert and return to the North after they had been exchanged, depriving the Confederates of their services.[16]

Stanton referred the question to Halleck, who had become, at least informally, the Union's leading authority on questions of military law. Halleck responded on February 17. "It is contrary to the usages of war," he wrote, "to force a prisoner of war to return to the enemy's ranks. If he declines to return, he is, in regard to his own Government, a deserter, and desertion from an enemy is always to be encouraged." Halleck feared that the return of such men would "expose them to punishment by their own authorities for having offered to desert their cause." He pointed out further that no Confederate prisoners had been returned against their will during the course of the war. To begin such a practice, Halleck suggested, would go against Lincoln's policy of amnesty. Although he generally favored the practical over the merciful, Stanton sided with Halleck on this matter. On February 24 Hoffman informed the commanding officers of all Union prisons, "Please let all understand that [no prisoners] will be sent for exchange who do not wish to go."[17]

In March a recruiting officer from the Northern Department arrived at Camp Chase to muster into federal service two companies for deployment "in the northwest and on the plains." The men were to be enlisted for three years and were to receive no bounties. According to J. P. Preston, a Camp Chase guard, the companies were filled by March 21. The former prisoners, he reported, were on their way to Chicago for assignment. "They seem well pleased with their new situation," Preston wrote, "but were quite anxious to know whether they would get enough to eat."[18]

Among those who did wish to be exchanged was Henry C. Mettam of the First Maryland Cavalry. In early March Mettam was part of a contingent of paroled Confederates that started by rail for Baltimore. Upon their arrival the men were taken to Fort McHenry. Mettam had written to his father, who lived nearby, and the pair enjoyed a brief visit. The next morning Mettam and his fellow parolees boarded a steamer "and started for old Virginia." They got as far up the James River as Aiken's Landing. President Lincoln was arriving for a conference with Grant, Sherman, and Adm. David D. Porter, and Mettam's ship had to anchor until the president had passed. Mettam got a good look as the *River Queen* sailed past with its prominent passenger. "Lincoln was out in the stern," he recalled, "and passed right by our old ship, and he had such long legs, as he sat all cramped up his knees were about his ears."[19]

The excitement was soon over, and the men resumed their voyage to City Point. There Col. Ould looked them over as a band played "Home Again from a Foreign Shore." Then, Mettam recalled, "We gave a yell and off we went into a double quick and we were soon aboard the steam tugs &c., and ladies [were there] to wait upon us with good things to eat as we steamed up to the [Richmond] city dock." The men's stay in Richmond was brief. They soon marched to Camp Lee, a short distance from the city, where they received their paroles. Mettam took no chances, locking his paper in a tin box.[20]

After a few days in Virginia, Mettam and five others decided to head for Maryland, secure horses and money, and return to the army. As they prepared to leave, Richmond fell. Their cause was on the verge of being lost, and time was too short for the men's plans to come to fruition. Mettam made it to Maryland. He was at the home of a friend when he received word from his father of President Lincoln's assassination. Union cavalrymen were pursuing John Wilkes Booth through Maryland, and Mettam's father urged him to stay put, at least until the excitement died down. Mettam took the advice seriously, taking to the woods and remaining secluded for a month. He then headed for home to resume his life, but at least one effect of his service in the Confederate army, including his time as a prisoner, stayed with him. "It was quite a while before I could sleep on a feather pillow."[21]

As Confederates prepared to depart Camp Chase, Union soldiers arrived to take their place. Many were recruits, members of regiments that were being quickly organized in the hope that they might hasten the end of the war. They began arriving in January, before exchanges were resumed, just as the prison population reached its peak. Their presence added to the crowded conditions with which Richardson had to contend. The new men were troublesome in other ways. On January 25 Richardson reported to Ohio's adjutant general that of the 469 recruits who were supposed to be in the camp, 130 were absent without leave. The commander had only 676 men to guard over 9,000 prisoners, leaving him with virtually no force to prevent "this whole sale desertion or bounty jumping." By February 15 the number of recruits had reached 3,419. Two weeks later Richardson placed the number at over 6,000. By then the camp's guard force had been reduced further as detachments of the Eighty-eighth Ohio were dispatched to guard prisoners being sent away for exchange.[22]

If they were a headache for Richardson, the recruits were fair game for the veteran soldiers in the camp. Some were merely the victims of pranks, venturing to headquarters to "trade boots" or secure nonexistent items. Others paid up to $50 for $3 watches or purchased forged passes for $15.

"In the hands of the 'old 'uns,' their big bounties are disappearing like the due of the morning before the hot sun," one Camp Chase guard observed.[23]

In addition to the recruits, paroled Union soldiers began arriving soon after the exchange cartel was resumed. On February 28 Richardson reported that "nearly two thousand" of them were present in camp. On April 8 Maj. George Blagden, an assistant to Hoffman, informed Richardson that several more would soon arrive from Vicksburg. Six days later the number was set at six thousand. After Ohio's adjutant general requested funds to build barracks to accommodate the influx, officials at the War Department decided to send half of the parolees to Camp Parole.[24]

The paroled soldiers returned hungry and ill. James F. Johnson, one of the Union recruits at Camp Chase, expressed his disgust at their condition in a letter to his sister. "You cannot imagine the difference between our Starved, and Sick Soldiers, then the Rebels, that we Exchange for them, their men are well fed, and go away from the camp, well and hearty. Ours are most all sick, and the cause [is] starvation." The chapel was converted into a hospital to care for the returning parolees. The wife of a captain from the Eighty-eighth Ohio, assisted by her two daughters, operated the facility. Through the pages of their hometown newspaper, the women appealed to their neighbors to send packages of food for the men. "Government rations are sufficient for the sustenance of well men, but are not suitable for the sick," they explained. "They need something of a more delicate nature."[25]

Among the many paroled prisoners arriving at Camp Chase were nine officers and 213 enlisted men who were survivors of America's worst maritime tragedy. They had been aboard the steamer *Sultana*, which had been transporting nearly 1,900 parolees north from Vicksburg when its boilers exploded in the early morning hours of April 28. About one-third of the passengers were killed. The 222 survivors sent to Camp Chase arrived on May 3. "The men are in good condition and will be well cared for," Richardson promised Hoffman. He also said he would immediately muster them for two months' pay.[26]

The explosion of the *Sultana* was one of many emotional events that marked the waning days of the war. In addition to receiving the contingent of survivors of that tragedy, Camp Chase was at least marginally involved in two other significant events. On April 5 a salute of one hundred guns was fired in honor of the fall of Richmond. Meanwhile, Samuel

Boyd noted that the news had "spread a general gloom over the prisoners." Seventeen days later Richardson received orders from the Northern Department to "hold all your force in readiness to receive the remains of the late President on his arrival." Columbus was one of many stops on the circuitous journey of the Lincoln funeral train. Gen. Richardson's superiors wanted him to prepare his men for duty as an honor guard. "They should be at the Depot in the best possible condition," the order read, "and should be drawn up in line at least an hour in advance of the time announced in the program for the arrival of the remains, and held in readiness to be employed either as guards or escort while the remains are in the city."[27]

Camp Chase's days as a Union prison were nearing an end. On April 26 Richardson informed Hoffman that all prisoners in the camp were willing to take the oath of allegiance. Richardson sought permission to make out the rolls accordingly. Maj. Wilson T. Hartz, an assistant to the commissary general, responded. Stanton, still seeking a measure of revenge, had ordered that only those prisoners who had offered to take the oath before the fall of Richmond be released. Despite this limitation, Richardson started a number of captives south. On May 17, just nine days after his communication from Hartz, Richardson announced that he had released 1,470 men under the terms set down by the secretary of war. This represented the total number of Camp Chase prisoners meeting that condition.[28]

The War Department eased the requirements on June 8. Under the terms of General Orders 109 all enlisted prisoners of war were to be released upon taking the oath of allegiance. Officers not above the rank of captain in the army or lieutenant in the navy could be released if they were not graduates of the U.S. service academies or commissioned officers in the United States military at the start of the war. On June 14 Hoffman ordered Richardson to send all officers not eligible for release to Johnson's Island. Three days later orders went out to release all political prisoners willing to take the oath of allegiance if serious charges were not pending.[29]

Guard J. P. Preston reported on June 5 that only seventeen prisoners remained unwilling to take the oath. That did not mean, however, that all the rest had accepted the situation. "The prisoners here seem pretty well imbued with that Southern vindictive spirit which will not allow them to brook an insult, hence an occasional fight," Preston wrote. To support that assertion he cited a recent altercation in which one prisoner had been stabbed to death. Richardson reported the incident to Hoffman, seeking guidance as to his proper course of action. The commissary general referred the matter to the War Department, whose attorneys suggested it was a problem for local criminal courts.[30]

On June 27 Grant recommended to Stanton that "general direction for the discharge of all remaining prisoners be given." Grant cited the expense of continuing to hold the men as his reason. Perhaps this reasoning persuaded the war secretary, or perhaps the capture of Jefferson Davis and other Confederate officials allowed him to redirect his sense of vengeance. Whatever the reason, the commanders of all Union prisons soon received orders to release all their remaining prisoners. The order extended even to those who had defected to the Confederates after being first captured. On July 5 Hoffman announced that all prisoners had been released from most Union prisons, including Camp Chase. The largest contingent was the 150 officers still confined at Johnson's Island, and Hoffman suggested that they be transferred to either Fort Warren or Fort Delaware.[31]

If Confederate prisoners were eager to be done with Camp Chase, so, too, were the thousands of Union soldiers sent to Camp Chase to be mustered out of the service. It was the final role played by the training camp turned prison turned parole camp; and like all its previous duties, Camp Chase's tenure as a mustering-out facility was marked with difficulties.

Discharge of federal troops began in May. For the first few months Tod Barracks was the primary mustering-out point, although many units reported to Camp Chase. A committee of citizens formed to arrange receptions for the returning soldiers. These were generally held at Goodale Park, the original site of Camp Jackson. Governor Brough and former governor Tod addressed many of the gatherings. Other speakers included Samuel Galloway, who had heard the claims of Camp Chase's political prisoners, former commander Granville Moody, and a number of politicians eager to welcome home the thousands of soldiers who were destined to become thousands of voters. By the end of August Tod Barracks and Camp Dennison, near Cincinnati, had been disbanded as military posts. Camp Chase then became the primary mustering-out point. Although distant regiments would continue to arrive until August 1866, most units were mustered out by the end of 1865. On June 17, 1865 a Columbus newspaper insisted that the returning soldiers had been well behaved. Few, the *Ohio Statesman* asserted, were seen loitering about the city. "While civilians are daily arrested and fined for drunkenness and disorderly conduct, it is rare, indeed, that a soldier is found at the morning [mayor's] court."[32]

Camp Chase guard J. P. Preston offered a somewhat different view. In a June 5 letter to the *Delaware News,* Preston wrote that the veterans were eager for discharge and less than happy with "their circumscribed sphere of action" at the camp. On one recent occasion, he noted, several of them charged the fence and a few broke through despite the firing of warning shots by the guards. According to Aaron S. Turner of the Ninety-fourth Ohio, another attempt was made a few nights later. On June 10 Turner complained in his diary that the men had been allowed to roam at will while waiting in Washington, DC to return to their various states. "Now," he wrote, "when we are in a manner at home we are put as one might say in a bullpen under guard." He added, "Wont stand it." Apparently he was not the only soldier who felt that way. The next day Turner reported, "Well the boys made an attact on Camp Chase last night tore down some fence and made a raid on the sutler shop."[33]

The impatience of the war-weary soldiers was understandable. Col. James Wilcox, Ohio's chief mustering officer, suggested that Richardson send only fifty men per day to Wilcox's office. Slowing the process even further was the fact that only one mustering officer was stationed at the camp. On May 31 Richardson complained to Lt. Col. Samuel Buck, Ohio's assistant adjutant general, that this sole officer was responsible for four thousand men who had arrived at Camp Chase. The situation became even more complicated the next day when, Richardson reported, the mustering officer was under arrest for drunkenness.[34]

Despite the problems, many men were able to start for home. Among them was Aaron Turner. Just four days after "the boys" made their attack, Turner received his pay and "struck out for home immediately." He apparently did not have far to go because he reached his home at about dark that evening. "So ends the chapter i am a citizen now," Turner wrote. Then he penned an addendum that thousands of former Camp Chase prisoners would have happily echoed: "i think i feel a change."[35]

Afterword
Keeping Alive the Memory

On July 14, 1865 Gen. Richardson sold "the prison property of Camp Chase" at public auction. There was little in which anybody would have been interested, windows perhaps being the most valuable offerings. The sale brought in $3,200. Richardson reported to Hoffman that another $1,000 worth of property did not sell.[1]

In addition to serving as a rendezvous for soldiers awaiting discharge, Camp Chase performed a few other duties during its last months as an active military camp. Courts-martial were held there in November 1865 and January 1866. In early September 1865 two deserters who had been convicted of murder were hanged at the camp. According to press accounts, Hiram Oliver and his brother-in-law, J. W. Hartup, had recently purchased adjoining farms in Illinois. They became nervous, fearing that J. B. Cook, a deputy provost marshal who lived in Cambridge, Ohio, was on their trail. So great was their paranoia that the pair traveled to Ohio and shot Cook in his yard.[2]

By the middle of April 1866, all government property had been removed from the camp, leaving rows of vacant, windowless buildings. On May 1 a reporter from the *Ohio State Journal* visited Camp Chase, recording the following observations of the once-bustling post:

> It is no longer a military centre, no more a living thing; the city is deserted; the giant form a skeleton. Hundreds and thousands of armed men paraded as the guardians of the living thing; a single man unarmed keeps watch and ward over the remains of the thing dead waiting for burial. Two years ago you entered the precincts of Camp Chase armed with passes signed and countersigned; were directed by shortspoken orderlies; warned by straight up-and-down sentinels; received with punctilious standoffishness by offi-

cials; and came away duly impressed with the military power of the country.

Now, you drive up to the gate as you would to that of a cemetery; the guardian presents himself in his shirtsleeves; you tell him your desires; he kicks away a huge stone; opens the gate; cautions you a little, and you enter unchallenged and unheralded to the mighty presence of the great solitude of lonliness.[3]

In 1872 five members of a Quaker settlement purchased 460 acres of the land that had been the site of Camp Chase at a price of $87.50 per acre. A sixth member purchased the remaining 63.5 acres two years later. Other members of the sect joined them in the years that followed. By then the walls and barracks of the camp had been razed and the lumber used to construct a wall around the Confederate cemetery. Figuratively, at least, Camp Chase's military swords had been beaten into plowshares. In 1879 Congress paid $500 for the cemetery, the only surviving portion of the camp. A stone wall replaced the wooden one, but otherwise the location was ignored for the next decade and a half.

That changed in 1894, thanks to the single-handed efforts of William H. Knauss. A Union veteran, wounded at Fredericksburg, Knauss seemed an unlikely champion of the Confederates buried at Camp Chase. As he explained it, the seed of what was to become an obsession was planted in 1868. A business trip took Knauss to Virginia, where he befriended a Confederate veteran who served as his guide. The Southerner, Knauss learned, had lost a leg on the same field where he had been wounded. "Through a bond of friendship then formed," Knauss recalled years later, "we mutually agreed to assist the comrades of the other, as best we could, whenever opportunity occurred."[4]

A few months later Knauss discovered a Confederate cemetery near the Antietam battlefield. It was the veteran's first opportunity to make good on his promise, and he took advantage of it. Knauss hired a local farmer to enclose the resting place with a log fence. In doing so he "became impressed with the belief that some good might be done, and, perchance, some persons made happy should they learn that a stranger respected the resting place of their loved and lost."[5]

In 1893 Knauss moved from New Jersey to Columbus. He soon learned about the neglected Confederate cemetery west of the city. It would prove to be the greatest test of his agreement, a challenge that would become a crusade. "The gate and gateposts of the stone wall inclosing the cemetery were down," he later wrote, "the ground overrun with briers, bramble bushes, and weeds, and it had become a resort for animals." Knauss arranged to have a farmer living nearby clean the site. The following spring Knauss and some friends planted a few flowers at the cemetery.[6]

This was only the beginning of the efforts of the man erstwhile Confederate general John B. Gordon would call the "Golden-Hearted Col. W. H. Knauss." In 1895 Knauss met with ex-Confederates living in Columbus. The group made plans to refurbish the site and agreed to inaugurate an annual memorial service. About fifty people attended the first one, held on June 5, 1896. Despite the small turnout, *Confederate Veteran* magazine announced that the event "was successful in every way." Knauss, the publication declared, was a "noble patriot."[7]

Not everybody north of the Mason-Dixon Line agreed. The era of the "bloody shirt" had not yet reached its end, and Knauss endured bitter opposition to his efforts. Three individuals who had agreed to share the expenses of the ceremony "backed out, thinking best not to do it." The local post of the Grand Army of the Republic voiced its opposition, as did a committee of the state legislature. Knauss reported that he had received nasty letters and "rude cartoons . . . sent by anonymous persons." Still, he remained undeterred. "I considered the sources and took fresh courage with an approving conscience."[8]

Gradually the persistent Knauss won over most of his opponents. Soon the ceremony was attracting an audience of several hundred. A drill corps from the Columbus Grand Army of the Republic participated in the 1898 ceremony. One of its members, Knauss claimed, returned to the post and declared, "Comrades, I went there, and I am converted, and I thank God I have lived to see this thing done. I thank God that Knauss kept at it." That same year a Confederate from Kentucky saw to it that half the flowers sent by his state were placed on the graves of Union soldiers at a nearby cemetery. By 1902 the ceremony had gained such acceptance that Republican governer George K. Nash of Ohio appeared to deliver a brief address.[9]

Nash's presence helped stifle any opposition to what Knauss considered the crowning achievement in his efforts to honor the memory of his former enemies. The highlight of the 1902 ceremony was the unveiling of a large stone memorial arch at the entrance to the cemetery. It was presented by a Union veteran, Judge David F. Pugh, and received by ex-

Confederate congressman David E. Johnson. Threats to blow it up had been received during the construction of the arch, and a guard had been posted as the work continued, but the threats came to nothing. Elizabeth May Gamble, Knauss's daughter, unveiled the memorial. Engraved in it was one word: "Americans."

Nash likely spoke for all assembled when he said, "We are not here as federals, we are not here as Confederates; we are all here as Americans to honor our heroic dead."[10]

With the unveiling of the memorial arch, Knauss considered his work at Camp Chase complete. He turned responsibility for the annual ceremony over to the United Daughters of the Confederacy, who conducted it for the next ninety-three years. Although he was no longer in charge of the affair, Knauss did occasionally return as a speaker. In 1906 he published *The Story of Camp Chase*. The book combined reminiscences of former prisoners with an account of his efforts to restore the cemetery. Accounts of the memorial ceremonies were also included, as were tales of Johnson's Island. *Confederate Veteran* urged its readers to "expend the small sum of $2.20 necessary to meet the outlay of its cost." The magazine continued, "This is an important work by Colonel Knauss and his colaborers, and every Southern person who would honor the patriot and benefactor should be diligent to procure it."[11]

In 1905 the stage was set for Camp Chase's ultimate transition. That year a real estate company purchased much of the original site and divided it for housing. In 1936 the Works Progress Administration, a New Deal agency, replaced the wooden headstones at the cemetery, although it is uncertain that there is a body to match each individual stone.[12]

Today, along busy Sullivant Avenue on the west side of Columbus, the lush green spot with its uniformly straight rows of simple white markers stands out among the homes and businesses of the Hilltop neighborhood. It remains the final resting place for 2,260 soldiers in gray who died in a hostile place a long way from home. In 1986, its members growing old, the Daughters of the Confederacy asked the Hilltop Historical Society to assist with the annual memorial ceremony. Nine years later the society assumed sole responsibility for the event, held annually on the Sunday nearest June 3, the birthday of Jefferson Davis. Thus the society keeps alive the memories of men who, in death, are thought of no longer as enemies, but as honored veterans.

Notes

Abbreviations

ADAH—Alabama Department of Archives and History, Montgomery
CWMC—Civil War Miscellaneous Collection
CWTI—Civil War Times Illustrated
Duke—Manuscripts Department, William R. Perkins Library, Duke
    University, Durham, NC
Filson—Filson Historical Society, Louisville, KY
LC—Library of Congress, Washington, DC
MARBL, Emory—Manuscripts, Archives, and Rare Book Library,
    Emory University, Atlanta
MDAH—Mississippi Department of Archives and History, Jackson
Memphis—University of Memphis Libraries, Special Collections
    Department
NA—National Archives and Records Administration, Washington, DC
OHS—Ohio Historical Society, Columbus
OR—U.S. War Department, *The War of the Rebellion: A Compilation
    of the Official Records of the Union and Confederate Armies*, 128 vols.
    (Washington, DC: Government Printing Office 1880–1901). Unless
    otherwise noted, all references will be to series 2. Citations will be to
    volume and page number(s).
RG—Record Group
SHC, UNC—Southern Historical Collection, University of North
    Carolina, Chapel Hill
TSLA—Tennessee State Library and Archives, Nashville
USAMHI—United States Army Military History Institute, Carlisle
    Barracks, PA
VHS—Virginia Historical Society, Richmond

Introduction

1. *OR,* 3:8.
2. Ibid., 3:271.

Chapter 1

1. Jacob Dolson Cox, *Military Reminiscences of the Civil War,* 2 vols. (New York: Charles Scribner's Sons, 1900), 2:1–2.

2. Ibid.

3. Ibid., 2–3; Eugene H. Roseboom, *The Civil War Era,* vol. 6 of Carl Wittke, ed., *The History of the State of Ohio* (Columbus: Ohio State Archaeological and Historical Society, 1944), 379–80.

4. Phillip Shaw Paludan, *"A People's Contest": The Union and Civil War, 1861–1865* (New York: Harper & Row, 1988), 15–18; *Hancock Courier* (Findlay), April 26, 1861; William Kepler, *History of the Fourth Regiment Ohio Volunteer Infantry in the War for Union* (Cleveland: Leader, 1886), 17.

5. Letter to the *Cincinnati Enquirer,* reprinted in *Hancock Courier* (Findlay), April 26, 1861; *Stark County Republican* (Canton), April 25, 1861; *Fayette County Herald* (Washington Court House), May 9, 1861.

6. *Ohio State Journal* (Columbus), April 25, 1861; Kepler, *History of the Fourth Regiment,* 18; *Stark County Republican* (Canton), April 25, 1861; Thomas Thomson Taylor to wife, April 28, 1861, Thomas Thomson Taylor Letters, Louisiana State University Library, Baton Rouge.

7. *Cleveland Herald,* quoted in *Belmont Chronicle* (St. Clairsville), May 2, 1861; *Lima Gazette,* April 29, 1861; *Stark County Republican* (Canton), May 8, 1861.

8. *Hancock Courier* (Findlay), April 26, 1861; Kepler, *History of the Fourth Regiment,* 17–18; *Marysville Union Press,* May 1, 1861.

9. *Hancock Courier* (Findlay), April 26, 1861; *Ohio State Journal* (Columbus), April 24, 1861; *Lima Gazette,* April 29, 1861.

10. Whitelaw Reid, *Ohio in the War: Her Statesmen, Her Generals, and Soldiers* (Cincinnati: Moore, Wilstach, & Baldwin, 1868), 1:28–30.

11. Alfred E. Lee, *History of the City of Columbus, Capital of Ohio* (New York and Chicago: Munsell, 1892), 2:96; *Mt. Vernon Republican,* May 2, 1861; *Marysville Union Press,* May 1, 1861; *Wyandot Pioneer* (Upper Sandusky), May 16, 1861; *Ohio State Journal* (Columbus), May 16, 1861.

12. *Fayette County Herald* (Washington Court House), May 23, 30, 1861; *Marysville Union Press,* May 1, 1861; *Wyandot Pioneer* (Upper Sandusky), May 2, 1861; Lee, *History of Columbus,* 2:95.

13. *Marysville Union Press,* May 1, 1861.

14. *Mt. Vernon Republican,* May 2, 1861; *Fayette County Herald* (Washington Court House), May 16, 1861; *Belmont Chronicle* (St. Clairsville), May 2, 1861.

15. *Ohio State Journal* (Columbus), May 28, 1861; Lee, *History of Columbus,* 2:97.

16. *Ohio State Journal* (Columbus), July 22, 1861; William M. Lamers, *The Edge of Glory: A Biography of William S. Rosecrans, U.S.A.* (New York: Harcourt, Brace,

& World, 1961), 26; William S. Rosecrans, Camp Chase, General Orders 1 and 2, June 18, 1861, RG 249, NA.

17. Rutherford B. Hayes to Lucy Webb Hayes, June 10, 14, 1861, in Charles Richard Williams, ed., *Diary and Letters of Rutherford Birchard Hayes, Nineteenth President of the United States* (Columbus: Ohio State Archaeological and Historical Society, 1922), 2:23, 25; entries for June 20, 23, 1861, William McKinley Diary, in H. Wayne Morgan, ed., "A Civil War Diary of William McKinley," *Ohio Historical Quarterly* 69, no. 3 (1960): 276–77.

18. James A. Garfield to Lucretia Garfield, August 22, 30, October 27, 1861, Garfield to "Dear Friends," August 31, 1861, in Frederick D. Williams, ed., *The Wild Life of the Army: Civil War Letters of James A. Garfield* (Lansing: Michigan State University Press, 1964), 28, 30, 35, 43.

19. *Cleveland Leader,* June 19, 1861; Alvin Coe Voris to wife, January 17, 1862, Alvin Coe Voris Papers, VHS.

20. *Highland Weekly News* (Hillsboro), July 11, 1861; *Marietta Intelligencer,* October 2, 1861; Capt. B. Eggleston to Headquarters, September 7, 1861, Capt. N. Buck to Headquarters, October 22, 1861, Camp Chase, Letters Received, RG 249, NA; W. M. Kaull to John B. Rice, February 2, 1862, Dr. John B. Rice Papers, LH 30, Rutherford B. Hayes Presidential Center, Fremont, Ohio.

21. *Chardon Democrat,* June 7, 1861; *Scioto Gazette* (Chillicothe), July 7, 1861; entry for July 24, 1861, Andrew J. Duncan Journal, William L. Clements Library, University of Michigan, Ann Arbor.

22. *Highland Weekly News* (Hillsboro), August 1, 1861; Camp Chase, Proceedings of Garrison Courts-martial, RG 249, NA.

23. Entry for June 11, 1861, Duncan Journal, William L. Clements Library, University of Michigan, Ann Arbor; *Ohio State Journal* (Columbus), May 15, 16, 20, 1861; Memoirs of Henry Otis Dwight, Henry Otis Dwight Papers, microfilm edition, OHS; *Chardon Democrat,* October 25, 1861.

24. Jonathon F. Harrington to parents, February 2, 1862, Jonathon F. Harrington Papers, Rutherford B. Hayes Presidential Center, Fremont, Ohio; *Cleveland Leader,* June 7, 1861; *Chardon Democrat,* October 17, 1861; *Fayette County Herald* (Washington Court House), August 29, 1861.

25. Headquarters, Ohio Militia, Special Orders No. 655, RG 249, NA; *Chardon Democrat,* November 15, 1861.

26. Headquarters, Ohio Volunteers for U.S. Service, General Orders No. 3, RG 249, NA.

27. *London National Democrat,* January 2, 1862.

Chapter 2

1. Alfred E. Lee, *History of the City of Columbus, Capital of Ohio* (New York and Chicago: Munsell, 1892), 2:102; *Ohio State Journal* (Columbus), July 6, 1861.

2. *West Union Democratic Union,* July 12, 1861; John A. Smith to family, December 25, 1861, John A. Smith Papers, Bentley Historical Library, University of Michigan, Ann Arbor; Garfield to "Dear Friends," August 31, 1861, in Frederick D. Williams, ed.,

The Wild Life of the Army: Civil War Letters of James A. Garfield (Lansing: Michigan State University Press, 1964), 35; Mungo P. Murray to family, September 15, 24 1861, Mungo P. Murray Letters, *CWTI* Collection, USAMHI.

3. *Fayette County Herald* (Washington Court House), August 29, 1861; *London National Democrat,* December 19, 1861; Harrington to "Friend Sarah," February 15, 1862, Harrington Papers, Rutherford B. Hayes Presidential Center, Fremont, Ohio; Murray to family, September 15, 1861, Murray Papers, *CWTI* Collection, USAMHI.

4. *OR,* 2:39, 219.

5. Ibid., 4:348, 358, 380, 416, 425.

6. Ibid., 4:690; *Zanesville Courier,* April 8, 1872; Camp Chase, Register of Cases of Prisoners Who Were Tried by the Special Commissioner, RG 249, NA.

7. Correspondence between the Special Commissioner and Judge Advocate General relating to the Release of Confederate Political Prisoners, RG 249, NA.

8. Ibid.

9. R. J. McKenzie to Samuel Galloway, n.d., R. H. Hanson to Galloway, n.d., Samuel Galloway Papers, OHS; Reuben Hitchcock to "Gov. Robinson," September 6, 1861, United States Army, Office of the Judge Advocate General, Records, 1862–63, LC.

10. Correspondence between the Special Commissioner and Judge Advocate General relating to the Release of Confederate Political Prisoners, RG 249, NA.

11. Lee, *History of Columbus,* 2:116; *OR,* 3:169, 270, 277, 280, 288, 317, 417.

12. *East Liverpool Mercury,* March 6, 1862.

13. *Delaware Gazette,* March 7, 1862.

14. *London National Democrat,* February 13, March 13, 1862; *Columbus Journal,* quoted in *Marietta Intelligencer,* May 21, 1862; Lee, *History of Columbus,* 2:117.

15. Charles Barrington Simrall to wife, September 10, 1862, Charles Barrington Simrall Papers, SHC, UNC.

16. *Ohio State Journal* (Columbus), March 21, 1862.

17. *OR,* 3:410–11.

18. Ibid.

19. Ibid., 3:412, 420, 427–28.

20. Ibid., 3:337, 428.

21. Ibid., 4:504.

22. Camp Chase, Special Orders No. 277, March 1, 1862, RG 393, NA; Jill Knight Garrett, ed., *The Civil War Diary of Andrew Jackson Campbell* (Columbus, TN: privately printed, 1965), 27; Sylvester Weeks, ed., *The Civil War Memoirs of Bvt. Brig. Gen. Granville Moody* (1890; repr., Columbus: General's Books, 1998), 115; *Morgan County Herald* (McConnelsville), June 5, 1862.

23. *Clinton Republican* (Wilmington), July 4, 1862; Camp Chase, General Orders No. 1, June 29, 1862, RG 249, NA; *OR,* 4:197, 205; Maj. Peter Zinn to Gen. Lew Wallace, September 26, 162, RG 249, NA.

24. *OR,* 1:815.

25. Ibid.

26. Camp Chase, Report of the Officer of the Day, August 25, 29, September 8, October 28, 1861, RG 249, NA.

27. Camp Chase, Special Orders No. 87, October 10, 1861, Special Orders No. 116, October 26, 1861, Special Orders No. 120, October 30, 1861, RG 393, NA.

28. Ohio Militia, Special Orders No. 104, RG 249, NA.

29. Col. Granville Moody, General Orders for the Government of Prisoners at Camp Chase, n.d., RG 393, NA.

30. Garrett, *Diary of Andrew Jackson Campbell*, 20–22.

31. Ibid., 22–25.

32. Ibid., 25; *OR*, 4:198–99.

33. Garrett, *Diary of Andrew Jackson Campbell*, 26–30.

34. Ibid., 26–35.

35. Entries for February 18, 21, 1862, James Calvin Cook Diaries, vol. 593, OHS.

36. Entries for March 1, 2, 3, 7, 1862, ibid.

37. Mack Curle, ed., "The Diary of John Henry Guy, Captain, Goochland Light Artillery," *Goochland County Historical Society Magazine* 33 (2001): 16.

38. Entry for March 23, 1862, Timothy McNamara Diary, MDAH; Curle, "Diary of John Henry Guy," 11.

39. Joseph Warren Westbrook's Story, unpublished memoir, CWMC, USAMHI; C. Wallace Cross, "The Incarceration of a Regiment," *Tennessee Historical Quarterly* 56, no. 2 (1997): 90; entry for March 31, 1862, McNamara Diary, MDAH.

40. William H. Knauss, *The Story of Camp Chase* (1906; repr., Columbus: General's Books, 1994), 140, 177.

41. J. P. Jackson to William Jackson, April 22, 1862, Charles Ray to parents, April 20, 1862, W. A. H. Shackelford to family, April 20, 1862, W. J. Rogers to Mrs. L. W. Malone, April 21, 1862, M. S. Miller to Maria Miller, April 21, 1862, Z. M. Hall to Mrs. S. S. Griffen, April 21, 1862, M. B. Locke to Mrs. John F. Allen, April 21, 1862, S. M. E. Russell to family, December ?, 1862, J. W. Haywood to family, December ?, 1862, Camp Chase Papers, VHS.

42. A. S. Levy to Ella Levy, April 21, 1862, Charles A. Ray to brother, April 21, 1862, John B. Stuart to Sarah Stuart, April 21, 1862, Camp Chase Papers, VHS.

43. J. R. Rush to wife, April 19, 1862, J. R. Rush Letters, Confederate Miscellany Collection, MARBL.

44. *London National Democrat*, March 13, 1862.

45. Camp Chase, Report of the Officer of the Day, August 29, November 15, 1861, Report of the Officer Commanding the Guard, January 13, 16, 1862, RG 249, NA; Thomas M. Covert to wife, March 8, 1862, Thomas M. Covert Papers, USAMHI.

46. Camp Chase, Report of the Officer Commanding the Guard, October 14, 1861, January 3, 17, 1862, RG 249, NA.

47. John A. Smith to family, December 25, 1861, Smith Papers, Bentley Historical Library, University of Michigan, Ann Arbor; Thomas M. Covert to wife, May 9, 1862, Covert Papers, USAMHI.

48. Official Report of Colonel H. B. Carrington, 18th U.S. Infantry, to the Governor of Ohio, June 1, 1862, OHS.

49. *OR*, 3:605; Official Report of Colonel H. B. Carrington, 18th U.S. Infantry, to the Governor of Ohio, June 1, 1862, OHS.

50. Camp Chase, Special Orders No. 21, July 8, 1862, Special Orders No. 23, July

10, 1862, Special Orders No. 14, October 16, 1862, RG 393, NA; *Clinton Republican* (Wilmington), July 18, 1862.

51. Lee, *History of Columbus,* 2:117; *OR,* 4:545.

52. *OR,* 3:121; Lonnie R. Speer, *Portals to Hell: Military Prisons of the Civil War* (Mechanicsburg, PA: Stackpole, 1997), 2–3.

53. *OR,* 3:49, 54–58, 135–36, 317.

54. Ibid., 3:337.

55. Ibid., 4:198–99.

56. Ibid.

57. Ibid., 4:199.

58. Ibid., 4:205.

59. Ibid., 4:200–4.

60. Ibid., 4:203.

61. Camp Chase, Prison Orders No. 4, July 16, 1862, RG 393, NA.

62. Camp Chase, Prison Orders No. 5, July 17, 1862, RG 393, NA.

63. *OR,* 4:304–5, 341–42.

64. Ibid., 4:305, 369, 371, 677–87, 5:3–5.

65. Ibid., 3:348, 367–68, 375.

66. Ibid., 3:360, 4:110–11.

67. Ibid., 4:112–13, 130–31, 256.

68. Ibid., 4:763–64.

69. Speer, *Portals to Hell,* 100–2; William Best Hesseltine, *Civil War Prisons: A Study in War Psychology* (1930; repr., Columbus: Ohio State University Press, 1998), 70.

70. *OR,* 4:414, 420–21, 428–29; Camp Chase, Special Orders No. 97, August 25, 1862.

71. Lee, *History of Columbus,* 2:120; Camp Chase, Special Orders No. 22, October 27, 1862, Special Orders No. 34, November 5, 1862, Special Orders No. 55, November 19, 1862, Special Orders No. 57, November 20, 1862, Special Orders No. 70, December 2, 1862, Special Orders No. 75, December 8, 1862, Special Orders No. 89, December 23, 1862, RG 393, NA; *OR,* 4:514.

72. *OR,* 4:370.

Chapter 3

1. William Best Hesseltine, *Civil War Prisons: A Study in War Psychology* (1930; repr., Columbus: Ohio State University Press, 1998), 76–77.

2. *OR,* 4:499.

3. Ibid., 4:94, 499.

4. Ibid., 4:499, 522, 529.

5. Lew Wallace, *Lew Wallace: An Autobiography* (New York, Harper & Brothers, 1906), 2:632–34.

6. Gen. Lew Wallace to Gen. Lorenzo Thomas, September 21, 1862, Letters Sent from Headquarters, U.S. Paroled Forces, RG 393, NA.

7. Ibid.

8. *OR,* 4:545–48.

9. Ibid., 4:569–70; Alfred E. Lee, *History of the City of Columbus, Capital of Ohio* (New York and Chicago: Munsell, 1892), 118.

10. *OR*, 4:570–71; Headquarters, U.S. Paroled Forces, General Orders No. 7, September 29, 1862, RG 393, NA.

11. Wallace to Thomas, October 18, 1862, Letters Sent from Headquarters, U.S. Paroled Forces, RG 393, NA.

12. Camp Lew Wallace, General Orders No. 1, October 4, 1862, RG 393, NA; Wallace to Thomas, October 18, 1862, Letters Sent from Headquarters, U.S. Paroled Forces, RG 393, NA; Camp Lew Wallace, General Orders No. 5, December 20, 1862, Special Orders No. 149, December 4, 1862, Special Orders No. 211, December 23, 1862, RG 249, NA.

13. Camp Lew Wallace, General Orders No. 2, October 4, 1862, Special Orders No. 9, October 19, 1862, Special Orders No. 54, November 5, 1862, Headquarters, United States Paroled Forces, Circular, January 21, 1863, Col. William Richardson to Lt. Col. S. H. Leathrop, May 22, 1864, Camp Chase, Letters Sent, RG 393, NA.

14. *OR*, 4:569–70; William Horner to Stanton, September 4, 1862, Camp Chase, Letters Sent, RG 249, NA; Abner Royce to parents, October 3, 1862, Royce Family Papers, Mss. 1675, Western Reserve Historical Society Library, Cleveland.

15. *OR*, 4:570, 670.

16. *Springfield Republic*, November 26, 1862.

17. Ibid.

18. Entries for August 13, 25, September 1, 18, 26, 30, October 21, November 4, 1862, William L. Curry Diary, William L. Clements Library, University of Michigan, Ann Arbor.

19. Entries for September 4, October 6, 16, 30, November 6, 1862, William L. Curry Diary, William L. Clements Library, University of Michigan.

20. Wallace to Thomas, October 18, 1862, Wallace to Edwin M. Stanton, October 27, 1862, Letters Sent from Headquarters, U.S. Paroled Forces, RG 393, NA; *OR*, 4:695–96, 5:113–14; Camp Lew Wallace, Special Orders No. 76, December 20, 1862, RG 249, NA; Headquarters, U.S. Paroled Forces, Special Orders No. 144, December 3, 1862, Special Orders No. 14, January 8, 1863, RG 249, NA.

21. *OR*, 6:702, 806, 812.

22. Ibid., 5:194, 420.

23. Ibid., 4:727, 749, 771, 5:58–69, 348–49.

24. Ibid., 4:295, 359, 620, 5:124.

25. Ibid., 4:562, 638, 641, 5:86–87, 289, 699, 719.

26. Ibid., 5:175; the special orders regarding exchanges are in RG 393, NA.

27. Col. William Hoffman to Gen. James Cooper, December 29, 1862, Camp Chase, Letters Received, RG 249, NA; Headquarters, Paroled Prisoners, near Annapolis, Special Orders No. 41, April 6, 1863, RG 249, NA.

28. Gen. John S. Mason to Hoffman, September 22, 1863, Camp Chase, Telegrams Sent, RG 249, NA; *OR*, 5:516–17; Journal of Cost of Arrest and Transportation of Paroled Federal Prisoners of War, RG 249, NA.

29. *Morgan County Herald* (McConnelsville), March 13, 1863.

30. Ibid., March 13, April 3, May 8, June 5, 1863.

31. Benjamin Franklin Heuston to wife, March 15, 24, April 1, 1863, Benjamin Franklin Heuston Letters, Wisconsin Historical Society, La Crosse MSSJ.

32. Randolph C. Downes, ed., "The Civil War Diary of Fernando E. Pomeroy," *Northwest Ohio Quarterly* 19, no. 3 (1947): 129–42.

33. Entries for March 25–26, 1863, Charles Holbrook Prentiss Letters and Diaries, CWMC, USAMHI.

34. Entries for March 27–April 11, 1863, Prentiss Letters and Diaries, CWMC, USAMHI.

35. Entries for April 15–May 2, 1863, Prentiss to wife, May 5, 1863, Prentiss Letters and Diaries, CWMC, USAMHI.

36. Entries for May 3–7, 1863, Prentiss to wife, May 5, 1863, Prentiss Letters and Diaries, CWMC, USAMHI.

37. Prentiss to wife, May 10, 1863, Prentiss Letters and Diaries, CWMC, USAMHI.

38. Entries for May 13–June 12, 1863, Prentiss Letters and Diaries, CWMC, USAMHI.

39. Headquarters, U.S. Paroled Forces, Columbus, Special Orders No. 214, December 25, 1862, RG 249, NA; *OR,* 5:132.

40. Whitelaw Reid, *Ohio in the War: Her Statesmen, Her Generals, and Soldiers* (Cincinnati: Moore, Wilstach, & Baldwin, 1868), 2:757–58; August V. Kautz, Reminiscences of the Civil War, August V. Kautz Papers, CWMC, USAMHI.

41. Headquarters, Camp Chase, General Orders No. 2, January 10, 1863, General Orders No. 4, January 10, 1863, Headquarters, U.S. Paroled Forces, Camp Chase, Circular, January 21, 1863, RG 249, NA.

42. Entry for January 12, 1863, Kautz, Reminiscences of the Civil War, August V. Kautz Papers, CWMC, USAMHI.

43. Eugene H. Roseboom, "The Mobbing of the *Crisis,*" *Ohio State Archaeological and Historical Quarterly* 59, no. 1 (1950): 150–51.

44. James L. Burke, ed., "The Destruction of the *Crisis,*" *Civil War Times Illustrated* 9, no. 8 (1970): 40–43.

45. Roseboom, "Mobbing of the *Crisis,*" 151–52; entries for March 7–10, 1863, Kautz, Reminiscences of the Civil War, August V. Kautz Papers, CWMC, USAMHI.

46. Headquarters, U.S. Forces, Columbus, General Orders No. 16, March 6, 1863, RG 249, NA.

47. Headquarters, U.S. Forces, Columbus, General Orders No. 1, April 16, 1863, RG 249, NA; *OR,* 5:499.

48. Camp Chase, Monthly Returns, April, May, June, 1863, RG 248, microcopy 617, NA.

49. Hesseltine, *Civil War Prisons,* 70–71, 80, 93; *OR,* 6:523.

50. Camp Chase, Monthly Returns, April 1864, RG 249, microcopy 617, NA.

Chapter 4

1. *OR,* 3:433, 8:987–93; orders for transfers can be found among Camp Chase, Special Orders, RG 393, NA.

2. Entries for January 13–20, 1863, J. K. Ferguson Diary, Memphis.

3. Entries for January 18–20, 1863, Ferguson Diary, Memphis.

4. Entries for January 25–27, 1863, Ferguson Diary, Memphis.

5. Entry for January 31, 1863, Ferguson Diary, Memphis.

6. Entries for January 31, February 6–26, 1863, Ferguson Diary, Memphis.

7. Entry for March 4, 1863, Ferguson Diary, Memphis.

8. Entries for April 11–13, 1863, Ferguson Diary, Memphis.

9. Entries for April 11–12, 1863, Ferguson Diary, Memphis.

10. Entries for April 22–May 1, 1863, Ferguson Diary, Memphis.

11. Entries for May 4–19, 1863, Ferguson Diary, Memphis.

12. E. H. M., "Capture and Escape of a Confederate," *Southern Bivouac* 3, no. 4 (1884): 155–58.

13. Ibid., 158–59.

14. Ibid.

15. William H. Knauss, *The Story of Camp Chase* (1906; repr., Columbus: General's Books, 1994), 266–67.

16. Ibid., 267–268.

17. Ibid., 269.

18. *OR,* 4:321, 328, 547–48, 5:26.

19. Ibid., 5:593, 6:190, 943.

20. Register of Cases of Prisoners Who Were Tried by the Special Commissioner on the Charge of Having Been in the Confederate Service, RG 249, NA.

21. Ibid.

22. Ibid.

23. Ibid.; Correspondence between the Special Commissioner and Judge Advocate General relating to Release of Confederate Political Prisoners, RG 249, NA.

24. Hoffman to Capt. Edwin Webber, February 18, 1863, Letters from the Commissary General of Prisoners relating to Paroled Federal Prisoners and Confederate Prisoners of War, RG 249, NA; *OR,* 6:31.

25. *OR,* series 3, 3:791.

26. Richardson to Hoffman, August 6, 1864, Camp Chase, Telegrams Sent, John D. Hartz to Richardson, July 15 (two letters), 16, 1864, Camp Chase, Letters Received, RG 249, NA; *Delaware Gazette,* July 15, 1864.

27. *OR,* 8:986–1004.

28. Ibid.; Brig. Gen. Speed S. Fry to Brig. Gen. J. L. Boyle, November 3, 1863, Camp Chase, Letters Received, RG 249, NA; *Delaware Gazette,* October 23, 1863.

29. Entry for September 8, 1864, Thomas Sharpe Diary, MARBL.

30. R. M. Gray, Reminiscences, SHC, UNC.

31. Henry C. Mettam, "Civil War Memoirs: 1st Maryland Cavalry, C.S.A.," *Maryland Historical Magazine* 58, no. 2 (1963): 165.

32. Ibid.

33. Maj. J. Coleman Alderson, "Prison Life in Camp Chase," *Confederate Veteran* 20 (1912): 296.

34. James A. W. Wright, "War Prisons and War Poetry," *Southern Bivouac* 1, no. 7 (1885): 719–20.

35. George C. Osborn, ed., "A Confederate Prisoner at Camp Chase: Letters and

a Diary of Private James W. Anderson," *Ohio State Archaeological and Historical Quarterly* 59, no. 1 (1950): 48.

36. Gray, Reminiscences, SHC, UNC.

37. Ibid.

38. W. S. Whiteman to Mannie Whiteman Weekes, August 17, 1916, in *Confederate Reminiscences and Letters, 1861–1865,* (Atlanta: Georgia Division, United Daughters of the Confederacy, 1998), 7:226–27.

39. Richardson to Hoffman, June 3, 1864, Camp Chase, Telegrams Sent, RG 249, NA; *Delaware Gazette,* June 17, 1864.

40. R. H. Strother, "Attempt to Escape from Camp Chase," *Confederate Veteran* 4 (1901): 553–54.

41. Ibid.; *OR,* 7:474.

42. *OR,* 7:502.

43. James A. Ramage, *Rebel Raider: The Life of General John Hunt Morgan* (Lexington: University of Kentucky Press, 1986), 170–79; Eugene H. Roseboom, *The Civil War Era,* vol. 6 of Carl Wittke, ed., *The History of the State of Ohio* (Columbus: Ohio State Archaeological and Historical Society, 1944), 423–24.

44. Whitelaw Reid, *Ohio in the War: Her Statesmen, Her Generals, and Soldiers* (Cincinnati: Moore, Wilstach, & Baldwin, 1868), 1:139, 144; *OR,* 6:277.

45. *OR,* 6:153, 158, 235–36, 269–73; Ramage, *Rebel Raider,* 184, 189.

46. *OR,* 6:174, 420.

47. Nathaniel Merion to Mason, August 6, 1863, Merion to Robert Lamb, February 15, 1864, Camp Chase, Letters Received, RG 249, NA.

48. *OR,* 6:408–9, 495–96.

49. Webber to "Captain Green," August 13, 1863, Camp Chase, Letters Received, RG 249, NA.

50. Entries for August 29, 30, 1863, Thomas W. Bullitt Diary, SHC, UNC; *OR,* 6:240, 257.

51. *OR,* 6:670, 725; Ramage, *Rebel Raider,* 191.

52. *OR,* 6:665–66; Ramage, *Rebel Raider,* 191–94.

53. *OR,* 6:588–89, 606, 626, 632; William Wallace to Chiefs of Police, November 28, 1863, Camp Chase, Telegrams Sent, RG 249, NA.

54. *OR,* 6:649, 986, 1001, 1076; Lamb to Wallace, December 12, 1863, Hoffman to Carroll H. Potter, February 24, 1864, Camp Chase, Letters Received, RG 249, NA.

55. *OR,* 8:989–1001.

Chapter 5

1. *OR,* 8:991, 993, 997.

2. Mason to Rosecrans, June 3, 1863, Mason to Hoffman, November 23, 1863, Camp Chase, Telegrams Sent, RG 249, NA.

3. Headquarters, Northern Department, Columbus, Special Orders (unnumbered), February 10, 1864, RG 249, NA; Whitelaw Reid, *Ohio in the War: Her Statesmen, Her Generals, and Soldiers* (Cincinnati: Moore, Wilstach, & Baldwin, 1868), 1:945–46; *OR,* series 1, vol. 25, pt. 1, p. 638.

4. *Delaware Gazette,* June 17, 1864; Robert Earnest Miller, "War within Walls: Camp Chase and the Search for Administrative Reform," *Ohio History* 96, no. 1 (1987): 50–51; Maj. J. Coleman Alderson, "Prison Life in Camp Chase," *Confederate Veteran* 20 (1912): 295; John F. Hickey, "With Col. William S. Hawkins in Camp Chase," *Confederate Veteran* 11 (1903): 23–24.

5. Richardson to Hoffman, March 20, 1865, Camp Chase, Letters Sent, RG 393, NA; Stephen Sears, *Chancellorsville* (Boston and New York: Houghton Mifflin, 1996), 274.

6. Richardson to Col. James Hardie, May 18, 1864, Richardson to Rep. S. H. Boyd, November 20, 1864, Camp Chase, Letters Sent, RG 393, NA.

7. Reid, *Ohio in the War,* 2:492–93; *Delaware Gazette,* July 3, 1863.

8. *Delaware Gazette,* September 4, 1863.

9. Ibid., October 23, 1863, April 22, June 17, 1864.

10. W. C. Dodson, "Stories of Prison Life," *Confederate Veteran* 3 (1900): 121.

11. Ibid.

12. Col. George H. Moffett, "War Prison Experiences," *Confederate Veteran* 8 (1905): 105–6.

13. Entry for August 4, 1864, Thomas Sharpe Diary, MARBL; James A. W. Wright, "War Prisons and War Poetry," *Southern Bivouac* 1, no. 7 (1885): 719; Alderson, "Prison Life in Camp Chase," 296.

14. Alderson, "Prison Life in Camp Chase," 295.

15. Gray, Reminiscences, SHC, UNC; Wright, "War Prisons and War Poetry," 719; entry for February 9, 1864, James Taswell Mackey Diary, TSLA.

16. *OR,* 6:854–56.

17. Ibid., 6:868, 892–893.

18. Camp Chase, Monthly Returns, October–December, 1863, RG 249, microcopy 617, NA; Wallace to Col. James B. Long, December 11, 1863, Camp Chase, Telegrams Sent, RG 249, NA.

19. *OR,* 6:854, 1061.

20. Ibid., 6:1058–64.

21. Ibid. 6:1064–65.

22. Ibid., 6:1065–71.

23. Ibid., 6:1073, 7:1.

24. Ibid., 7:474–75; Alderson, "Prison Life in Camp Chase," 296.

25. *OR,* 7:475.

26. Ibid., 6:643; Lt. Col. Samuel W. Beall to Wallace, November 29, 1863, Headquarters, Department of the Ohio, Special Orders No. 454, December 9, 1863, RG 249, NA.

27. Camp Chase, Monthly Returns, December 1863–May 1864, September 1864–April 1865, RG 249, microcopy 617, NA; Lamb to Richardson, October 28, 1864, Alexander Sankey to W. A. McGrew, March 3, 1865, Camp Chase, Letters Received, RG 249, NA; Patricia L. Faust, ed., *Historical Times Illustrated Encyclopedia of the Civil War* (New York, Harper & Row, 1986), 321–22.

28. Entries for November 6, 8, 14, 1862, John D. Axline Diary, Duke.

29. *OR,* 7:529; U.S. Forces, Columbus, General Orders No. 2, April 17, 1863, RG 249, NA; *Delaware Gazette,* October 21, 1864.

30. *Delaware Gazette,* April 22, August 19, 1864.

31. Provost Marshall, Newark, Ohio, to Col. E. A. Parrott, September 1, 1863, John W. Skiles to Richardson, September 3, 6, October 21, November 19, 1864, Camp Chase, Letters Received, RG 249, NA.

32. Eugene H. Roseboom, *The Civil War Era,* vol. 6 of Carl Wittke, ed., *The History of the State of Ohio* (Columbus: Ohio State Archaeological and Historical Society, 1944), 428.

33. Gen. B. R. Cowen to Richardson, May 8, 17, 1864, Richardson to Cowen, May 15, 1864, reprinted in *Canton Repository,* June 1, 1864.

34. *Stark County Republican* (Canton), May 19, 26, 1864.

35. John Harrod to wife, May 15, 16, 1864, John Harrod Papers, USAMHI; *Stark County Republican* (Canton), June 2, 1864.

36. Moffet, "War Prison Experiences," 105.

Chapter 6

1. Moffett, "War Prison Experiences," (1905): 105.

2. George C. Osborn, ed., "A Confederate Prisoner at Camp Chase: Letters and a Diary of Private James W. Anderson," *Ohio State Archaeological and Historical Quarterly* 59, no. 1 (1950): 45; entry for January 18, 1864, James Taswell Mackey Diary, TSLA.

3. Osborn, "A Confederate Prisoner at Camp Chase," 46; James A. W. Wright, "War Prisons and War Poetry," *Southern Bivouac* 1, no. 7 (1885): 718.

4. *OR,* 7:382, 698, 1021; *Delaware Gazette,* June 17, 1864.

5. Entries for August 11, September 1, 1864, Sharpe Diary, MARBL; *OR,* 7:382; Hoffman to Richardson, November 7, 1864, Letters from the Commissary General of Prisoners relating to Paroled Federal Prisoners and Confederate Prisoners of War, RG 249, NA.

6. Osborn, "A Confederate Prisoner at Camp Chase," 55.

7. M. A. Ryan, Experiences of a Confederate Soldier in Camp and Prison in the Civil War, unpublished memoir, MDAH; Moffett, "War Prison Experiences," 105; Osborn, "A Confederate Prisoner at Camp Chase," 55.

8. Osborn, "A Confederate Prisoner at Camp Chase," 53; Moffett, "War Prison Experiences," 105; entry for January 19, 1864, Mackey Diary, TSLA; Joseph Mason Kern, Memoirs, SHC, UNC.

9. Wright, "War Prisons and War Poetry," 718; Kern, Memoirs, SHC, UNC; entry for January 20, 1864, Mackey Diary, TSLA; Henry C. Mettam, "Civil War Memoirs: 1st Maryland Cavalry, C.S.A.," *Maryland Historical Magazine* 58, no. 2 (1963): 164; Ryan, Memoirs, MDAH; Osborn, "A Confederate Prisoner at Camp Chase," 47; Moffett, "War Prison Experiences"; entry for August 29, 1864, Sharpe Diary, MARBL.

10. *Delaware Gazette,* June 17, 1864.

11. William Best Hesseltine, *Civil War Prisons: A Study in War Psychology* (1930; repr., Columbus: Ohio State University Press, 1998), 172–78, 195–96.

12. *OR*, 6:314–15.

13. Ibid., 6:446–47, 485–86, 524.

14. Ibid., 6:554–55, 602, 625, 628, 1014–15, 7:573–74.

15. Michael Horigan, *Elmira: Death Camp of the North* (Mechanicsburg, PA: Stackpole, 2002), 86; *OR*, 7:110, 113–14.

16. *OR*, 7:150–51, 183–84, 8:768.

17. Entries for August 25, October 13, 1864, Sharpe Diary, MARBL; Maj. J. Coleman Alderson, "Prison Life in Camp Chase," *Confederate Veteran* 20 (1912): 296; Osborn, "A Confederate Prisoner at Camp Chase," 50.

18. Entries for September 3, 9, 16, 22, 27, October 13, 14, 20, 22, 23, 1864, Sharpe Diary, MARBL; Alderson, "Prison Life in Camp Chase," 296; Mettam, "Civil War Memoirs," 164.

19. Gray, Reminiscences, SHC, UNC; Ryan, Memoirs, MDAH; Mettam, "Civil War Memoirs," 164–65; Alderson, "Prison Life in Camp Chase," 296.

20. Entry for October 10, 1864, Sharpe Diary, MARBL; William Cary Dodson, Unpublished Recollections, MARBL; Moffett, "War Prison Experiences," 106; Mettam, "Civil War Memoirs," 164.

21. Dodson, Unpublished Recollections, MARBL.

22. Wright, "War Prisons and Poetry," 719.

23. Horace Harmon Lurton to "My Dear Allen," January 19, 1863, February 5, 1864, Horace Harmon Lurton Letters, LC; undated entry, ca. July 1864, Sharpe Diary, MARBL.

24. Lurton to "My Dear friend Allen," December 7, 1864, Lurton Letters, LC; entry for September 14, 1864, Sharpe Diary, MARBL; George Washington Nelson, Unpublished Memoirs, VHS.

25. *OR*, 5:305–06, 317–18, 6:1036.

26. Entry for August 21, 1864, Sharpe Diary, MARBL; Camp Chase, Guard Report, November 18, 1864, RG 249, NA.

27. Tom Wallace to "Mary," September 19, 1863, Wallace Family Papers, Filson.

28. Osborn, "A Confederate Prisoner at Camp Chase," 46–47.

29. Wright, "War Prisons and Poetry," 718; Kern, Memoirs, SHC, UNC; entry for August 14, 1864, Sharpe Diary, MARBL.

30. George Levy, *To Die in Chicago: Confederate Prisoners at Camp Douglas, 1862–1865* (Gretna, LA: Pelican, 1999), 138, 148, 158, 161; *OR*, 6:315.

31. Charles W. Sanders Jr., *While in the Hands of the Enemy: Military Prisons of the Civil War* (Baton Rouge: Louisiana State University Press, 2005), 173–75.

32. Ibid., 173; Edwin W. Beitzell, "In Prison at Point Lookout," *Chronicles of St. Mary's* 11, no. 12 (1963): 4–6; Edwin W. Beitzell, "The Diary of Charles Warren Hutt," *Chronicles of St. Mary's* 18, no. 5 (1970): 1, 4, no. 6 (1970): 12.

33. Horigan, *Elmira*, 37–38, 66–67, 133–35.

34. Sanders, *While in the Hands of the Enemy*, 171–72; T. R. Walker, "Rock Island Prison Barracks," in William B. Hesseltine, ed., *Civil War Prisons* (Kent: Kent State University Press, 1962), 48–50.

35. Nancy Travis Keen, "Confederate Prisoners of War at Fort Delaware," *Dela-*

ware History 13 (1968): 1, 4–6; W. Emerson Wilson, *A Fort Delaware Journal: The Diary of a Yankee Private, A. J. Hamilton, 1862–1865* (Wilmington: Fort Delaware Historical Society, 1981), 29; *OR,* 6:277.

36. Wright, "War Prisons and War Poetry," p. 718; Kern, Memoirs, SHC, UNC; entry for July ?, 1864, Sharpe Diary, MARBL; Henry Massie Bullitt, Unpublished Reminiscences, Bullitt-Chenowith Family Papers, Filson.

37. Kern, Memoirs, SHC, UNC; Lurton to "My Dear Allen," July 18, 1863, Lurton Letters, LC; Gray, Reminiscences, SHC, UNC.

38. Kern, Memoirs, SHC, UNC; Wright, "War Prisons and War Poetry," 718; entry for February 13, 1864, Mackey Diary, TSLA; entry for July ?, 1864, Sharpe Diary, MARBL; George C. Osborn, "Writings of a Confederate Prisoner of War," *Tennessee Historical Quarterly* 10, no. 1 (1951): 164.

39. R. H. Strother, "Prison Life in Camp Chase," *Confederate Veteran* 8 (1900): 430–31; John Shields to sister, October 10, 1864, Shields Family Papers, TSLA.

40. Entries for September 11, 15, 1864, Sharpe Diary, MARBL; Lurton to "My Dear Allen," July 18, 1863, Lurton Letters, LC.

41. *Delaware Gazette,* October 23, 1863; entries for August 30, September 12, 1864, Sharpe Diary, MARBL.

42. Strother, "Prison Life in Camp Chase," 430; entries for March 9–11, 1864, Mackey Diary, TSLA.

43. Osborn, "Writings of a Confederate Prisoner," 168; Lurton to "My Dear Allen," July 18, 1863, Lurton Letters, LC; entries for September 11, 18, 1864, Sharpe Diary, MARBL.

44. Headquarters, Louisville, Kentucky, Special Orders No. 241, January 2, 1863, RG 249, NA; *OR,* 5:247, 295; John Moon to "Captain McMurray," April 15, 1863, Camp Chase, Letters Sent by the Prison Commander, RG 393, NA.

45. *OR,* 5:511, 514–15, 532–33.

46. Ibid., 5:943–44.

Chapter 7

1. Harrington to parents, February 2, 1862, Harrington Papers, Rutherford B. Hayes Presidential Center, Fremont, OH; entry for February 26, 1862, McNamara Diary, MDAH; Jill Knight Garrett, ed., *The Civil War Diary of Andrew Jackson Campbell* (Columbus, TN: privately printed, 1965), 27; entry for February 11, 1863, J. K. Ferguson Diary, Memphis; Harrod to wife, May 16, 1864, Harrod Papers, USAMHI.

2. Wright to Moody, March 22, 1863, Camp Chase, Letters Received, RG 249, NA; *OR,* 4:164, 250.

3. Dr. D. Stanton to Mason, August 3, 1863, Camp Chase, Letters Received, RG 249, NA; *OR,* 6:277.

4. *OR,* 4:199, 201, 5:133, 137, 210; Camp Chase, Special Orders No. 20, January 15, 1863, RG 393, NA.

5. Camp Chase, Special Orders No. 158, June 24, 1863, Special Orders No. 166, June 29, 1863, Special Orders No. 167, June 29, 1863, Special Orders No. 174, July 8, 1863, Special Orders No. 219, October 22, 1863, RG 393, NA; *OR,* 6:356, 389, 682.

6. *OR,* 7:51.

7. Ibid., 7:382, 698–99; George C. Osborn, ed., "A Confederate Prisoner at Camp Chase: Letters and a Diary of Private James W. Anderson," *Ohio State Archaeological and Historical Quarterly* 59, no. 1 (1950): 55.

8. Camp Chase, Special Orders No. 280, March 5, 1862, General Orders No. 48, February 1, 1862, RG 393, NA; L. C. Brown to Allison, July 2, 1862, Jonathan Morris to Allison, August 14, 1862, Alex McBinn to Allison, August 22, 1862, Camp Chase, Letters Received, RG 249, NA.

9. Camp Chase, Special Orders No. 280, March 5, 1862, Special Orders No. 309, April 1, 1862, RG 393, NA; *OR,* 3:359, 4:207.

10. Mack Curle, ed., "The Diary of John Henry Guy, Captain, Goochland Light Artillery," *Goochland County Historical Society Magazine* 33 (2001): 14.

11. Morris to Allison, August 14, 1862, McBinn to Allison, August 22, 27, 1862, Camp Chase, Letters Received, RG 249, NA.

12. *OR,* 4:389.

13. Ibid., 4:659, 5:135.

14. Brown to Allison, July 2, 1862, Camp Chase, Letters Received, RG 249, NA.

15. *OR,* 8:991–97; George C. Osborn, "Writings of a Confederate Prisoner of War," *Tennessee Historical Quarterly* 10, no. 1 (1951): 88; Maj. J. Coleman Alderson, "Prison Life in Camp Chase," *Confederate Veteran* 20 (1912): 294; entry for February 18, 1864, James Taswell Mackey Diary, TSLA.

16. *Delaware Gazette,* September 4, 1863.

17. *OR,* 6:480, 682, 819, 7:52, 581; Thomas McFadden to A. H. Loker, December 29, 1863, Dr. D. Stanton to Post Commander, February 6, 1864, Camp Chase, Letters Received, RG 249, NA; *Delaware Gazette,* March 18, 1864.

18. *OR,* 6:479, 662, 819, 7:581.

19. Ibid., 6:48, 7:581; John F. Hickey, "With Col. William S. Hawkins in Camp Chase," *Confederate Veteran* 11 (1903): 24; entries for July ?, August 27, 1864, Thomas Sharpe Diary, MARBL.

20. A. W. Clark to Commandant, Camp Chase, January 7, 1864, G. W. Brooke to Lt. Col. Bentley, January 8, 1864, Camp Chase, Letters Received, RG 249, NA.

21. Entries for January 29, February 20, 1864, Mackey Diary, TSLA; *Delaware Gazette,* February 12, 1864.

22. Entry for August 9, 1864, A. S. McNeil Diary, in William H. Knauss, *The Story of Camp Chase* (1906; repr., Columbus: General's Books, 1994), 257; entry for September 6, 1864, Sharpe Diary, MARBL; *Delaware Gazette,* October 21, 1864; *OR,* 7:972, 1069.

23. *OR,* 7:1161, 1189, 1236, 8:106; Osborn, "Writings of a Confederate Prisoner," 169; Alderson, "Prison Life in Camp Chase," 296.

24. *Delaware Gazette,* April 22, 1864.

25. Judge Advocate, Department of the Ohio, to Richardson, November 28, 1864, Camp Chase, Letters Received, RG 249, NA; *OR,* 7:1161.

26. *OR,* 8:999–1001.

27. *Delaware Gazette,* January 13, 1865; *OR,* 7:1282–83, 8:106; entries for March 12, 15, 1865, Samuel B. Boyd Diary, TSLA.

28. *Delaware News,* February 9, 1865; *OR,* 8:381, 1000–1; Camp Chase, Register of Deaths, RG 109, microcopy 598, NA.

29. Col. Charles Tripler to C. H. Potter, March 15, 1865, Camp Chase, Letters Received, RG 249, NA.

30. H. E. Warner to Col. Charles Tripler, April 1, 1865, Camp Chase, Letters Received, RG 249, NA.

31. Entries for December 23, 24, 26, 30, 31, January 3, 9, 11, 1865, Washington Pickens Nance Diary, ADAH.

32. Entries for January 12, 15, February 6, 11, 13, 1865, Nance Diary, ADAH.

33. Entries for February 13, 23, March 4, 1865, Nance Diary, ADAH.

34. Entry for March 18, 1865, Nance Diary, ADAH.

Chapter 8

1. William H. Young to family, March 18 1865, William H. Young Letters, Special Collections Department, Mitchell Memorial Library, Mississippi State University, Starkville.

2. Ibid.

3. Samuel Boyd to uncle, March 13, 1865, Boyd Diary, Samuel B. Boyd Papers, TSLA.

4. Ibid., entries for January 1–9, 1865, Boyd Diary, TSLA.

5. Entries for January 9–14, 1865, Boyd Diary, TSLA.

6. Entries for January 15, 16, February 18, 27, March 20, 1865, Boyd to uncle, March 13, 1865, Boyd Diary, TSLA.

7. *OR,* 7:1063, 1101, 1117.

8. Ibid., 7:1131, 1148–49, 1281, 1286, 1290, 8:14–15, 123.

9. Ibid., 7:1230, 1267, 1288–89.

10. Ibid., 8:241, 313–15; entries for March 7, 10, 12, 1865, Washington Pickens Nance Diary, ADAH.

11. *OR,* 8:241–42.

12. Ibid., 9:122–23, 170, 238.

13. Entries for January 24, 31, February 5, 1865, Boyd Diary, TSLA.

14. Entries for February 12, 17, 24, March 2, 4, 1865, Nance Diary, ADAH; *Delaware News,* March 9, 1865; entry for March 18, 1865, Boyd Diary, TSLA.

15. *Ohio State Journal* (Columbus) n.d., quoted in *Delaware Gazette,* February 10, 1865.

16. *OR,* 8:234.

17. Ibid., 8:239–40, 301.

18. Maj. Walter B. Scates to Richardson, March 13, 1865, Camp Chase, Letters Received, RG 249, NA; *Delaware News,* March 21, 1865.

19. Henry C. Mettam, "Civil War Memoirs: 1st Maryland Cavalry, C.S.A.," *Maryland Historical Magazine* 58, no. 2 (1963): 165–66; David Herbert Donald, *Lincoln* (New York, Simon & Schuster, 1995), 574.

20. Mettam, "Civil War Memoirs," 166–67.

21. Ibid., 167–69.

22. Richardson to B. R. Cowan, January 25, February 15, 1865, Richardson to C. H. Potter, February 23, 28, 1865, Camp Chase, Letters Sent, RG 393, NA.

23. *Delaware News,* March 9, 1865.

24. Richardson to C. H. Potter, February 28, 1865, Camp Chase Letters Sent, RG 393, NA; George Blagden to Richardson, April 8, 1865, Thomas A. Vincent to Adjutant General, State of Ohio, Camp Chase, Letters Received, RG 249, NA.

25. James F. Johnson to sister, March 6, 1865, Matoon Family Papers, OHS; *Delaware News,* March 9, 1865.

26. Richardson to Hoffman, May 3, 4, 1865, Camp Chase, Telegrams Sent, RG 249, NA.

27. Richardson to Lt. Col. L. H. Lathrop, April 5, 1865, Camp Chase, Telegrams Sent, O. H. Hart to Richardson, April 22, 1865, Camp Chase, Letters Received, RG 249, NA; entry for April 3, 1865, Boyd Diary, TSLA.

28. Richardson to Hoffman, April 26, May 17, 1865, Camp Chase, Telegrams Sent, Wilson T. Hartz to Richardson, May 8, 1865, Letters from the Commissary General of Prisoners Relating to Paroled Federal Prisoners and Confederate Prisoners of War, RG 249, NA.

29. *OR,* 8:641, 653, 656, 673, 691–92.

30. *Delaware News,* June 8, 1865; *OR,* 8:637–38.

31. *OR,* 8:673, 691–92, 700–1.

32. Alfred E. Lee, *History of the City of Columbus, Capital of Ohio* (New York and Chicago: Munsell, 1892), 2:157–60.

33. *Delaware News,* June 8, 1865; entries for June 10–11, 1865, Aaron S. Turner Diary, CWMC, USAMHI.

34. Col. James Wilcox to Richardson, May 13, 1865, Camp Chase, Letters Received, Richardson to Lt. Col. Samuel Buck, May 31, 1865, Richardson to Lt. Col. O. H. Hart, June 1, 1865, Camp Chase, Telegrams Sent, RG 249, NA.

35. Entry for June 14, 1865, Turner Diary, CWMC, USAMHI.

Afterword

1. Alfred E. Lee, *History of the City of Columbus, Capital of Ohio* (New York and Chicago: Munsell, 1892), 2:161; Richardson to Hoffman, July 25, 1865, Camp Chase, Telegrams Sent, RG 249, NA.

2. Lee, *History of Columbus,* 2:161; *Delaware Gazette,* September 8, 1865.

3. *Ohio State Journal* (Columbus), May 3, 1866.

4. William H. Knauss, *The Story of Camp Chase* (1906; repr., Columbus: General's Books, 1994), xii.

5. Ibid.; Paul Clay, Patti Ongaro, and Lois Neff, *The Men and Women of Camp Chase* (Columbus: Hilltop Historical Society, 2003), 26.

6. Knauss, *Story of Camp Chase,* xii–xiii.

7. *Confederate Veteran* 4 (1896): 248, 20 (1912): 297; Knauss, *Story of Camp Chase,* xiv, 1–2.

8. *Confederate Veteran* 4 (1896): 248, 6 (1898): 363; Knauss, *Story of Camp Chase*, xv, 92–93.

9. *Confederate Veteran* 6 (1898): 363–64.

10. Knauss, *Story of Camp Chase*, xviii, 64, 67.

11. *Confederate Veteran* 11 (1903): 313–14, 14 (1906): 328.

12. Clay, Ongaro, and Neff, *Men and Women of Camp Chase*, 27.

Bibliographical Essay

Virtually every writer researching the Civil War starts with U.S. War Department, *The War of the Rebellion: A Compilation of the Official Records of the Union and Confederate Armies,* 128 vols. (Washington, DC: Government Printing Office, 1880–1901). The eight volumes of series 2 deal with prisoners of war. They contain much correspondence and numerous inspection reports concerning Camp Chase as well as insights into the thinking of government and military officials.

Much, however, was left out of the *Official Records,* and the holdings of the National Archives in Washington, DC are essential for filling in the gaps. Those holdings are especially rich in papers relating to Camp Chase, particularly its role as a parole camp. Included in Record Group 249 are the categories Letters Sent, Letters Received, General Orders, Special Orders, and Monthly Returns. Record Group 393 also has information pertaining to Camp Chase as a parole camp and contains as well a number of items related to Camp Lew Wallace.

Manuscript collections relating to Camp Chase are numerous but scattered. Among the more useful ones are the Thomas Sharpe Diary, Manuscript, Archives, and Rare Book Library, Emory University, Atlanta; the Washington Pickens Nance Diary, Alabama Department of Archives and History, Montgomery; the Samuel B. Boyd Papers and the James Taswell Mackey Diary, Tennessee State Library and Archives, Nashville; the J. K. Ferguson Diary, University of Memphis, Special Collections Department; and the Camp Chase Letters, Virginia Historical Society, Richmond. For other collections providing helpful information in lesser quantities, the reader is referred to the endnotes.

A few Camp Chase diaries have been published. George C. Osborn edited the papers of James W. Anderson in "Writings of a Confederate Prisoner of War," *Tennessee Historical Quarterly* 10, no. 1 (1951) and "A Confederate Prisoner of War at Camp Chase: Letters and a Diary of Private James W. Anderson," *Ohio State Archaeological and Historical Quarterly* 59, no. 1 (1950). Another valuable diary is found in Mack Curle, ed., "The Diary of John Henry Guy, Captain, Goochland Light Artillery," *Goochland County Historical Society Magazine* 33 (2001). Published memoirs include Henry C. Mettam, "Civil War Memoirs: 1st Maryland Cavalry, C.S.A.," *Maryland Historical Magazine* 58, no. 2 (1963). Excerpts from diaries of Fort Donelson prisoners can be found in C. Wallace Cross, "The Incarceration of a Regiment," *Tennessee His-*

torical Quarterly 56, no. 2 (1997). Randolph C. Downes, ed., "The Civil War Diary of Fernando E. Pomeroy," *Northwest Ohio Quarterly* 19, no. 3 (1947), recounts the experiences of a paroled Union soldier.

Accounts of Camp Chase's role as a Union training camp can be found in numerous Ohio newspapers available at the Ohio Historical Society, Columbus. Published letters and diaries written by three prominent trainees are included in Charles Richard Williams, ed., *Diary and Letters of Rutherford Birchard Hayes, Nineteenth President of the United States*, 2 vols. (Columbus: Ohio State Archaeological and Historical Society, 1922); Frederick D. Williams, ed., *The Wild Life of the Army: Civil War Letters of James A. Garfield* (Lansing: Michigan State University Press, 1964,); and H. Wayne Morgan, ed., "A Civil War Diary of William McKinley," *Ohio Historical Quarterly* 69, no. 3 (1960). Also of interest for McKinley is William H. Armstrong, *Major McKinley: William McKinley and the Civil War* (Kent: Kent State University Press, 2000).

Postwar published memoirs are dubious at best as sources, and they were generally avoided in this work. Exceptions were made for a number of articles appearing in *Confederate Veteran*, a journal consisting largely of soldier reminiscences published from 1893 to 1932. Some of its accounts add details to events that can be found in manuscript sources. They were used primarily when the basic facts were corroborated elsewhere.

Secondary accounts of Camp Chase are rare. The only book devoted to the facility is William H. Knauss, *The Story of Camp Chase* (Nashville and Dallas: Publishing House of the Methodist Episcopal Church, South, 1906). Based largely on the reminiscences of former prisoners, it can be consulted as a primary source if approached with caution. An updated edition, published in 1994 by the General's Books of Columbus, contains useful supplemental information. Paul Clay, Patti Ongaro, and Lois Neff, *The Men and Women of Camp Chase* (Columbus: Hilltop Historical Society, 2003) blends primary and secondary sources in a brief history.

Robert Earnest Miller, "War within Walls: Camp Chase and the Search for Administrative Reform," *Ohio History* 96, no. 1 (1987) credits Col. William Richardson with bringing much-needed administrative stability to the camp. Miller also praises Richardson for his efforts to improve the living conditions of the prisoners.

Eugene H. Roseboom provides a lively account of the attack by members of the Second Ohio Volunteer Cavalry on the *Columbus Crisis* newspaper office in "The Mobbing of the *Crisis*," *Ohio State Archaeological and Historical Quarterly* 59, no. 1 (1950). A firsthand account, written by a member of the unit, can be found in James L. Burke, ed., "The Destruction of the *Crisis*," *Civil War Times Illustrated* 9, no. 8 (1970).

Alfred E. Lee, *History of the City of Columbus, Capital of Ohio* (New York and Chicago: Munsell, 1892) provides a wealth of information about the city during the Civil War years, much of it gleaned from local newspapers.

Recent years have witnessed the publication of a number of books about Civil War prisons, including several excellent studies of individual camps. Among them are George Levy, *To Die in Chicago: Confederate Prisoners at Camp Douglas, 1862–1865*

(Gretna, LA: Pelican, 1999); Michael P. Gray, *The Business of Captivity: Elmira and Its Civil War Prison* (Kent: Kent State University Press, 2001); Michael Horigan, *Elmira: Death Camp of the North* (Mechanicsburg, PA: Stackpole, 2002); and Benton McAdams, *Rebels at Rock Island: The Story of a Civil War Prison* (DeKalb: Northern Illinois University Press, 2000).

Originally published in 1930, William Best Hesseltine's *Civil War Prisons: A Study in War Psychology* remains a useful starting point for study of the topic. A 1998 reprint, published by Ohio State University Press, includes an excellent historiographical foreword by William Blair. *Civil War Prisons*, edited by Professor Hesseltine (Kent: Kent State University Press, 1962), contains eight essays that first appeared in the journal *Civil War History*.

Lonnie R. Speer, *Portals to Hell: Military Prisons of the Civil War* (Mechanicsburg, PA: Stackpole, 1997) provides an excellent account of the who, what, and where of the many facilities. Unfortunately, it relies heavily upon dubious postwar published accounts in relating the conditions in those prisons. Charles W. Sanders Jr., *While in the Hands of the Enemy: Military Prisons of the Civil War* (Baton Rouge: Louisiana State University Press, 2005) cites the papers of high-ranking military and political officials to assert that both the Union and the Confederacy pursued intentional policies of prisoner abuse.

Index